ACTION LIKELY
IN PACIFIC

'A young Korean American would often drop into my office. He was in touch with the anti-Japanese underground in Korea. Pearl Harbor, he would tell me, before Christmas. He could get no audience at the State Department.'

Eric Sevareid, CBS News

ACTION LIKELY IN PACIFIC

SECRET AGENT KILSOO HAAN, PEARL HARBOR AND THE CREATION OF NORTH KOREA

JOHN KOSTER

AMBERLEY

First published 2019
This edition published 2022

Amberley Publishing
The Hill, Stroud
Gloucestershire, GL5 4EP

www.amberley-books.com

Copyright © John Koster, 2019, 2022

The right of John Koster to be identified as
the Author of this work has been asserted in
accordance with the Copyrights, Designs and
Patents Act 1988.

ISBN 978 1 3981 1247 6 (paperback)
ISBN 978 1 4456 9252 4 (ebook)

All rights reserved. No part of this book may
be reprinted or reproduced or utilised in any
form or by any electronic, mechanical or other
means, now known or hereafter invented,
including photocopying and recording, or in any
information storage or retrieval system, without
the permission in writing from the Publishers.

British Library Cataloguing in Publication Data.
A catalogue record for this book is available
from the British Library.

Typesetting by Aura Technology and Software
Services, India.
Printed in India.

CONTENTS

'Surprise, when it happens to a government, is likely to be a complicated, diffuse, bureaucratic thing. It includes neglect of responsibility but also responsibility so poorly defined or so ambiguously delegated that action gets lost. It includes gaps in intelligence, but also intelligence that, like a string of pearls too precious to wear, is too sensitive to give to those who need it. It includes the alarm that fails to work, but also the alarm that has gone off so often it has been disconnected... It includes, in addition, the inability of individual human beings to rise to the occasion until they are sure it is the occasion – which is usually too late.'

From Thomas C. Schelling's foreword to Roberta Wohlstetter's *Pearl Harbor: Warning and Decision*, Stanford University Press, 1962. Schelling's foreword was quoted at the beginning of the report of the National Commission on Terrorism to Congress, June 2000, 'Countering the Changing Threat of International Terrorism'.

ACKNOWLEDGEMENTS
AND SOURCES

The single most important source for this book is the Kilsoo Haan File from the American Heritage Center of the University of Wyoming at Laramie. Alongside this are the autobiography of Dean Rusk and the biographies of Dean Acheson, Stanley Hornbeck and Owen Lattimore written by their admirers. Admiral James Otto Richard's account of the lead-up to Pearl Harbor and Admiral Husband Kimmel's account of the months before the attack were important sources of contemporary communications.

I thank Shizuko Koster – Shizuko Masuda, Countess Obo, a child survivor of several iron-bomb air raids on Tokyo – who located a number of vintage Japanese newspaper articles with the help of her brother, *kamikaze* trainee Takeo Obo, who was at home during the Tokyo Fire Raid. Shizuko also translated several Japanese books for a complete picture of a number of events not well covered in the Anglo-Saxon history books. A large amount of the information provided in American books of this era is biased, so I tried to stay as close to first-hand sources as possible. Shizuko's mother, the late Toyoko Obo, was a neighbour of the Tojo family and sometimes shopped for vegetables with Tojo's wife or listened through the window to his children's piano lessons.

Thanks to Jessica Mok who translated the DoSan books, known to all Koreans and almost no Anglo-Saxons or Japanese, which offer a patriotic narrative of Korean history, checked as far possible against outside sources. They are not found anywhere in English or in Japanese. Jessica also translated the Korean portions of the 2001 Korean Broadcasting System documentary about Kilsoo Haan, which contained an interview with Stan Haan, Kilsoo Haan's son. She provided a detailed analysis of the 2004 South Korean feature film about Kilsoo Haan. I interviewed the late Togo Tanaka, who offered his own perspective for additional balance.

I provided my own translations concerning three tangential figures: the biographical notes on Gerardus Johannes Berenschot from the original Dutch and the biographical sketches for Klemens Jacob Meckel and Alexander von Falkenhausen from the original German. As far as I know, not much information about these three is available in English.

Thanks also to Paul J. Duggan and John LaFianza, who provided computer arts services and back-up.

I

DOWN TO THE WIRE

'On the night of December 3, 1941, I could not fall asleep,' Kilsoo Haan remembered a few weeks after the Pearl Harbor attack. 'I went to the Chinese Chop Suey House, the Chinese Lantern, and ordered a bowl of Chinese soup called Won-ton. It was 11:45 pm when I got there.'[1] Next to my table, a Japanese was trying to sell a Chinese a second-hand automobile. After the Japanese left, the Chinese said to me, "You like to buy cheap automobile?" After a pause he said, "This Japanese is selling four automobiles owned by the Japanese Embassy workers because they are going to Japan pretty soon." When I asked the Chinese what price he wants, he replied, "Oh so cheap." Examples were, $1,000 for a 1941 Buick Town Sedan, $750 for a 1940 Buick Coupe, $300 for a 1938 Chrysler Sedan, and $850 for a 1941 Buick Two Door.'

Kilsoo Haan shifted into high gear in a last desperate attempt to get the executive branch of the United States government to act on his warnings during the first week of December, after five months of trying to warn of a Pearl Harbor attack he now believed would take place in a matter of a few days. This last-minute effort sounds as if it came from an old Hollywood movie about Charlie Chan or Mister Moto, but Kilsoo Haan was frantic to save as many American lives as possible – now that the war between Japan and the United States that he saw as a chance to liberate Korea from Japan was about to break out.

Kilsoo Haan, in fact, had been was so astounded by the Japanese Embassy bargain sale and what it seemed to predict, and possibly so exhausted and giddy because of the constant stress of trying to warn the US State Department of what he saw coming, that he went home from the Chinese Lantern and wrote a letter on his official stationery to Japan's Ambassador Kichisaburo Nomura.

Dec. 3, 1941

Your Excellency:

I note that the embassy staff members are trying to sell their automobiles. May I make the following offer:

Offer
I hereby submit $10.00 as an offer for the automobiles you have for sale. I am sure this offer is a justified one in the moral sense; since you have witnessed the International gangsterism in China and Korea which succeeded in looting millions of dollars worth of properties from Koreans and the Chinese, you would not miss it very much if you would accept our offer. If and when you do let me have them for $10.00 I would have them auctioned for the benefit of the refugees, the victims of Japanese aggression in China and Korea. At least, you would be thankful that I would be in a position to do this much for those helpless men and women and particularly the relatives of the Korean who threw the bomb in Shanghai which resulted in the loss of your eye.

Very sincerely yours,
Kilsoo K. Haan[2]

Nomura's response is not recorded, but like everyone else in Washington, he had a lot to think about the next morning. On 4 December 1941 the *Washington Times-Herald*, the largest newspaper in the nation's capital, ran a story with the headline, 'FDR'S WAR PLANS!' The story was based on a verbatim copy of Rainbow Five, the joint Army-Navy plan to draft a ten-million-strong army and to invade Nazi-occupied Europe with five million men in 1943. This plan had been drawn up under orders from President Franklin D. Roosevelt, whose most famous election quote had been delivered at the Boston Garden on 29 October 1940, a few days before he was elected to his third term as President: 'While I am talking to you mothers and fathers, I give you one more assurance. I have said this before but I shall say it again and again and again: Your boys are not going to be sent into any foreign wars.'

The Rainbow Five plan was nevertheless now before the American public. Newspaper headlines around the country ran front-page banner headlines like that of the *St Paul Pioneer Press* of 5 December 1941: 'JAPS ANSWER TODAY: BREAK NEAR.' Secondary front-page stories covered the investigation of the Rainbow Five leak.[3]

Kilsoo Haan made a last-ditch effort to warn the US State Department that the war the newspapers across the country were predicting would start at Pearl Harbor in the next few days. On 5 December, Haan telephoned Maxwell Hamilton of the State Department and said he had been warned by the Korean Underground that the Japanese would attack Pearl Harbor that weekend.

> Pursuant to our telephone conversations regarding our agents' apprehensions that Japan may suddenly move against Hawaii 'this coming weekend,' may I call your attention to the following relevant and pertinent information.
>
> One: The publication of US Army Air Corps maneuvers throughout the Hawaiian Island by the Japanese daily *Nippu Jiji*, Nov. 22, 1941. This timetable of air maneuvers is from November through Dec. 31, 1941, 'every day except Sundays and holidays.' Two: The Italian magazine *Oggi* of Oct. 24, 1941, published an article in Rome forecasting war between Japan and America. The article forecast war between Japan and America by air and naval attack of the Hawaiian Islands and eventually attacking Alaska, California and the Panama Canal ... It is our considered observation and sincere belief, December is the month of the Japanese attack and the SURPRISE FLEET is aimed at Hawaii, perhaps the

first Sunday of December ... No matter how you feel toward
our work, will you please convey our apprehension and this
information to the President and to the military and naval
commanders in Hawaii.[4]

The last-minute warning followed a number of others to US
officials:

August 29, 1941
President Franklin D. Roosevelt
White House
Washington, D.C.

Dear Mr. President Roosevelt:

As one who represents the Korean Underground in America; as
the one who on January 8, 1940 wrote you from Los Angeles,
California the information contained in Japan's war plan
book, Three Power Alliance and the US-Japanese War, that at
the opening of the US-Japanese War, Japan will call for peace
negotiations and during these peace talks, Japan is to carry-out
the surprise attack upon Pearl Harbor, Hawaii, may I sincerely
appeal to you not to trust the Japanese Ambassador Nomura?
I have learned that in July your excellency, Mr. President
had proposed to Nomura that America and England will
supply Japan's need of oil, gasoline, scrap irons and essential
food supplies if Japan get out of French Indo China and
acknowledge the neutrality of French Indo China. As long ago
as April 1933 I informed Secretary of War Dern, the US-Japan
War is inevitable, hence the July proposal by Mr. President to
Ambassador Nomura is of no use to America, whereas it will
encourage the Japanese Emperor and his military advisors to
implement Japan's war plan, the surprise attack on Hawaii.
Please cease fooling yourself and be-prepared for war.

Respectfully,
Kilsoo Haan[5]

Kilsoo Haan was a man who loved two countries, the United
States and Korea, and hated two other countries – Japan and

Russia, now the Soviet Union but seen since Tsarist times as the leading menace to North Asia. Through the autumn of 1941, Kilsoo Haan had attempted at least eight times to warn the US of an impending Japanese attack on Pearl Harbor. There were many indications that a war with Japan was about to break out, but Kilsoo Haan consistently predicted a surprise attack on Hawaii on the first weekend of December for at least four months before the bombs actually fell.

Oct. 28, 1941
Hon. Henry L. Stimson
Secretary of War Information

I am at the request of my agent submitting this information sent to me from the Orient, dated Aug. 26, 1941. A copy will be sent to the State Department, Cordell Hull.

Information: Hirota, former foreign minister, now the 'big stick' of the Black Dragon Society, in their Aug. 26 meeting, told of the news that war minister Tojo has ordered a total war preparation to meet the armed forces of the United States in this Pacific emergency. Tojo is said to have told him of the Navy's full support of his policy against America. He also spoke of Tojo giving orders to complete the mounting of guns and rush supplies of munitions to the Marshall and Caroline group (mandated islands) by November 1941. Hirota and others present in the meeting freely discussed and expressed opinions as to the advantages and consequences of a war with America. Many expressed the most suitable time to wage war with America is Dec. 1941 or Feb. 1942. Many said: 'Tojo (now Premier) will start the war with America and after 60 days Tojo will reshuffle the cabinet and become virtually a great dictator.'

Note: based on this information dated Aug. 26, 1941, Japan's recent and sudden change of cabinet is a planned one, stalling for time for closer collaboration and more effective cooperation in the interest of the Axis Powers. Mounting of guns and rushing of munition supplies to the Mandated

Islands is a significant sign. Our men requested not to give out a press release as I have done in the past without your consent. Kindly inform me of your decision. I honestly believe in informing the American public of what the Japanese militarists are doing against America – in the belief [that] once the Americans know these facts they will give full cooperation in the preparation for National Defense.

In the interest of America's security in the Pacific, I am

Very sincerely yours,

Kilsoo K. Haan[6]

Kilsoo Haan's attempts were directly rebuffed in some cases and apparently ignored in others. Eric Sevareid, a newsman for CBS who had covered the fall of France to Nazi Germany in 1940, a man of immense integrity and also an ardent interventionist, recalled many years later that Kilsoo Haan had offered detailed evidence to the State Department that Japan was planning a surprise attack and that Pearl Harbor would be the target. 'One piece of evidence in the jigsaw was that a Korean working in the Japanese consulate in Honolulu had seen full blueprints of our above-water and underwater naval installations – spread out on the consul's desk.' Kilsoo Haan told Sevareid that White House Secretary Steven Early told him that the State Department considered the Sino-Korean leagues reports were the product of Haan's imagination – anti Japanese propaganda. 'He always ended up seeing very minor officials who took a very minor view of his warning,' Sevareid remembered years afterwards.[7]

In October, Haan had urged a Japanese-American editor who had opposed his Korean underground reports, Togo Tanaka, to expose what Haan said was a Japanese Consulate attempt to conscript Nisei, born in the United States to Japanese parents, to serve Japan. Kilsoo Haan had learned of this from several Japanese-Americans who were loyal to the US and resented what they said was an attempt to coerce them into acting on Japan's behalf.

'I have been told by the State Department that you are imagining the worst of Japan and the Japanese-American dual citizens,' Togo Tanaka wrote to Kilsoo Haan. 'I am not aware of the conscription of Nisei, dual citizen, by the Japanese Consulates. The so-called Japan's war plan book and the surprise attack on Hawaii, in fact is Japanese propaganda fiction to scare boys like you. So don't be alarmed and be afraid. The State Department considers you and your anti-Japan group "troublemakers" and war mongers.'[8] Since Togo Tanaka was 26 at the time and Kilsoo Haan was 41, Tanaka's description of Kilsoo Haan as a 'boy' was a studied insult.

The next partisan to enter the controversy over Kilsoo Haan's credibility was Senator Guy Gillette, who was a non-interventionist Democrat but a supporter of Korean Independence and a friend of Kilsoo Haan's from as early as 1937.[9] Gillette, who had served as a sergeant in the Spanish-American War and a major in World War I, contacted Colonel Rufus S. Bratton, the Chief of the Far Eastern Section of US Army intelligence to ask if the Japanese-American editor Kilsoo Haan had accused of complicity, Togo Tanaka, was in fact employed as an adviser to US Army intelligence.

November 21, 1941

Dear Senator Gillette,

I have your letter of November 19, 1941, in which you say that various newspaper stories have appeared recently reporting that I have made arrangements to utilize the services of Mr. Togo Tanaka, English Editor of *Rafu Shinto*, as adviser in my work as Chief of the Section of the Intelligence service of the Army in work connected with my investigation of facts pertaining to the Far Eastern Situation. In reply to your query as to the truth of this report I have been authorized by the Assistant Chief of Staff, G-2 to inform you that the report is false and without any foundation in fact.

Sincerely yours,
R.S. Brattion, Colonel, G. S. C.
Chief, Far Eastern Section[10]

The fact that Kilsoo Haan's war warnings were received by government officials is a matter of record because some of the officials he contacted responded on official stationery. He donated copies of the files to the University of Southern California and to the American Heritage Center at the University of Wyoming.

April 26, 1941

My dear Mr. Haan:

Your letter of April 15, 1941 and its very interesting enclosure are much appreciated. Some of your facts and predictions have indeed been borne out by the passage of time and I assure you that the information that you have given us has always been highly appreciated.

> Very sincerely yours,
> Frank Knox,
> The Secretary of the Navy[11]

Kilsoo Haan received another acknowledgement of his Pearl Harbor warnings the day after the attack, the worst disaster in the history of the US Navy. He received a telephone call from Maxwell Hamilton of the US State Department who reportedly demanded that Haan never release information about his numerous Pearl Harbor warnings to the press: 'If you do, I can have you put away for the duration,' Hamilton reportedly said.[12]

In the context of the times, this was a potential death sentence. Emotionally, Kilsoo Haan was a Korean patriot. Politically, as a Korean, he was an unwilling Japanese citizen. Korea had been annexed by Japan in 1910 with the tacit approval of Theodore Roosevelt. Koreans had been horrified by the Japanese annexation, which fostered the resistance movement Kilsoo Haan worked for. Most Japanese-Americans in 1941 were shocked and outraged by the Pearl Harbor attack, but a hard core of ultra-nationalists – Togo Tanaka estimated the pro-Japanese nationalist numbers at about 2.5 per cent, with another 2.5 per cent estimated as 'Reds' – who would have killed for Japan. If Kilsoo Haan went into the same detention camp as the Japanese extremists whose arrests were already in progress, he might not have come out alive.

In a story layered with irony. Kilsoo Haan may have owed his freedom to speak without being strangled to Drew Pearson, the most liberal of American's newspaper columnists. On 15 December 1941, Pearson's nationally syndicated column, 'Washington Daily Merry-Go-Round', revealed that some State Department officials – he named names – wanted to go over Maxwell Hamilton's head because they did not trust Japan, given the credit freeze and the oil embargo imposed by the United States earlier that year. Pearson – something of a sensationalist – reported that Hamilton had forced Cabot Colville to resign, but that Assistant Secretary of State Adolph Berle refused to accept Colville's resignation and sent him to the Philippines instead. Frank Schuler was sent to the British Virgin Islands, a diplomatic backwater. Then Drew Pearson took up the case of Kilsoo Haan.

About this time Secretary Hull was receiving letters from Koreans in the United States, warning that Japan was preparing to attack the United States. Koreans, being a subject race, hate their Japanese conquerors. Frequently operating as servants, they have maintained an amazing underground intelligence system in Japan.

On October 23, 1941, Kilsoo K. Haan, a Korean who had been a member of the Japanese consular service, wrote Mr Hull, reporting a meeting of the Black Dragon Society (secret Fascist order of the Japanese military) on 29 August, in which Foreign Minister [Koki] Hirota revealed 'a total war preparation to meet the armed forces of the United States.'

He (Hirota) also spoke of Premier Tojo giving orders to complete the mounting of guns and rush supplies to the Marshall and Caroline group by November 1941. Hirota and others in the meeting freely expressed the view that the most suitable time to wage war with America was December 1941 or February 1942.

Mr Haan was introduced to Secretary Hull by Senator Guy Gillette of Iowa, so his letter did not come from an unknown crackpot. In fact, Gillette thought so highly of the Korean's information that he proposed a Senate investigation of Japanese activities, but was discouraged by the State Department.[13]

Drew Pearson was a clever enough diplomat to make Cordell Hull the good guy who acted responsibly and to depict Hull's expendable underling, Maxwell Hamilton, as the malicious villain of the piece. Pearson's influential syndicated column, read by millions of readers in the US, gave Kilsoo Haan a reprieve. Locking up Kilsoo Haan for the duration as a security risk because he tolled the bell in the market square to warn of Pearl Harbor and got it incredibly right was no longer politically acceptable. Kilsoo Haan was now officially known to have warned the United States that a devastating Japanese sneak attack was about to take place. He was, at least for the moment, an American hero.

2

THE TWO HERMIT KINGDOMS

KIlsoo Haan was born in Chang Dan, Korea, on 31 May 1900. Korea was still an independent country threatened both by Russia and by Japan at the time he was born The Japanese military seized control of the peninsula during the Russo-Japanese War of 1904-1905 with the diplomatic support of Britain and the sympathetic support of United States. Kilsoo Haan's parents emigrated to Hawaii in 1905, possibly due to national pride, possibly due to economic need. He was shortly working as a child sugar cane laborer for the Oahu Sugar Company while he attended bilingual Korean school up to the 8th Grade. What he learned at the school, from his parents, and from outside reading of Asian history, set him on his future course while he was still a teenager.[1]

Three events began to form the future of Korea, Japan, and America half a century before Kilsoo Haan was born. In the United States, Commodore Matthew Perry left on a mission in 1852 to force the isolated kingdom of Japan to permit foreigners to land on its shores and to establish diplomatic relations with America. Japan and Korea, friends in the remote past, had each chosen an extreme form of isolation after a disastrous war which ended in the 1590s. A Japanese attempt to invade Korea by the Shogun Hideyoshi had been thwarted by the Korean invention of history's first armored ship, 'the tortoise boat,' which could reverse directions without turning. The 'tortoise boat' was armed with cannon that fired exploding shells, and with caltrops (spikes) on the armored carapace to cripple death-defying *samurai* who attempted to board. The Japanese had held the Koreans to a stalemate on land. But the tortoise boat, a stunning innovation in naval warfare, sank so many of the Japanese ships that the Japanese evacuated Korea.

The Japanese isolated themselves from the outside world after a subsequent internal rebellion by Japanese Catholics against the national government. The isolation was not a reaction to the success of the Koreans but to the depredations of western nations such as Spain and Portugal, which were rapidly conquering most of the world outside Europe. Japan and Korea, acting separately, both excluded Catholics because they feared that power of the Spanish conquistadors. Korea martyred thousands of converts and missionaries. The Catholic Church today commemorates 103 Korean martyr saints, some of them missionaries from France but most of them men and women of Korea. In Japan, which had once been about 20 per cent Catholic through voluntary conversion, there were 30,000 Christian martyrs. Many of the martyrs brought the wood for their own crosses when they were told to give up their Catholic faith or face crucifixion.

The Japanese survivors went underground as *nam-ban* Christians, developing a faith based on their own understanding of Christianity. *Nam-ban* means 'southern barbarian,' because the Spanish had arrived in Japan from the south, after conquering most of the Philippines. The *nam-ban* were always cautious but never barbaric. Japanese officials of the shogunate had no trouble singling out the *nam-ban* villages; they were the only villages in the Japanese countryside with no brothels and no money-lenders. Since the *nam-ban* Christians were pacifists, the officials usually left them alone.

During their last war on the mainland in the 1590s, the Japanese had devastated the Koreans, who fought with bows and spears, while the Japanese used matchlock muskets copied from an original by a Portuguese gun-maker. The Japanese made thousands of heavy muskets. Once the Japanese closed their country, the muskets were seen as a destabilizing influence on the samurai, the professional warrior caste who served the Japanese as soldiers and policemen and were the only Japanese permitted to wear the two swords: the *katana*, used for fighting, and the *tanto*, used for ritual suicide in disgrace, *seppuku*, commonly called *hara kiri*, belly cutting. The Japanese stopped making guns and put their matchlock muskets away in armories.

When Commodore Perry's 'black ships' – so called because two of them were steamers that belched black smoke – arrived in 1853, the Japanese were thrown into a panic, especially when they realized that the 8-inch guns on the American ships were several centuries ahead of their own archaic artillery. The Japanese reluctantly signed treaties and began to open their doors to the West. They began a frantic effort to copy American technology.

Commodore Perry saw the Japanese as a pawn in the real political game between the European powers. After his epoch-making voyage to Japan, he said: 'If Russia possessed Japan, she would have an abundance of harbors, unrivaled in the world for excellency, and with her resources would control the commerce of the Pacific. It is not, therefore, in the interest of any part of the commercial world that Russia should ever own Japan.'

Before Perry set foot on Japan, two births had taken place in 1852 that would mean drastic changes in the future of Asia.

In Japan, a son named Mutsuhito was born to the emperor Komei. Mutsuhito would be the emperor Meiji, the first modern Japanese emperor. Emperor Meiji's Japan startled the world with the speed of its modernization even more than the elegance of its arts. The French Impressionists and Post-Impressionists were influenced by Japanese painting, just as the Japanese were influenced by Western science and technology, especially railroads, steamships, telegraphs – and weapons. The Japanese Arisaka infantry rifle, copied from the German Mauser, had the strongest bolt of any bolt-action rifle.

In Korea, a son was born to the hereditary king, Yi He-eung, a monarch who ruled at the end of the once-brilliant Yi Dynasty. Sejong, a king at the beginning of the Yi Dynasty, had introduced the *hangul* phonetic alphabet, over the opposition of scholars who argued that the common people didn't need to read: Chinese characters were the only authentic writing, the alphabet of Confucius. The *hangul* alphabet fitted the Altaic speech of the Koreans, the Manchus, and the Mongols so perfectly that even the Japanese seriously considered using *hangul* during their frantic campaigns to promote mass literacy in their Asian colonies. Koreans of the remote past had also invented the navigator's compass, the astrolabe, movable type for printing, and *ongul* central heating to circulate warmed air under floorboards during the icy Korean winters. The ancient Koreans loved tinkering, and like the Americans of the 19th century, they tinkered to good effect.

Their social system, however, was adopted from China. Korea followed the teachings of Confucius: society was a family, with authority flowing down and loyalty flowing up. During the 250 years of isolation, Korea had become static rather that dynamic, with the power in the hands of the *yangban*, a caste of scholar-landlords who maintained their positions by having their sons educated by private tutors so they could pass strenuous examinations in Chinese writing and literature – and would never care to learn anything else, or need to. According to lower-class Koreans, who had no outlets for their skills or intelligence, the *yangban* stole other people's women and taxed the poor ever deeper into poverty.

In Japan, the samurai were often respected, sometimes hated – but always feared. The samurai alone possessed 'the right of killing and going away' – a license to kill if the victim were a commoner or a rival samurai. In Korea, the *yangban* were despised by the more than 90 per cent of the population who didn't qualify. Yi He-eung, the last strong king of the Yi Dynasty, kept afloat by the *yangban* system, was now the father of a son who would be remembered as Kojong, the tragic last king of independent Korea.

Meiji in Japan and Kojong in Korea, both born in 1852, each inherited a world where drastic change was forced on them, but they reacted in different ways. Meiji lost his father in 1868, according to official sources from smallpox introduced by sailors from the West, possibly followed by pneumonia. He is said to have advocated an immediate attack on the interfering Westerners before his untimely death.

His son Mutsohito's early reign was turbulent beyond belief: Rebellions against the shogun, the nominal governor who had ruled in the emperor's name, broke out all over the country after the Americans forced a landing. Townsend Harris, the first

American emissary, demanded a young *geisha* named O-Kichi as his concubine, told her he loved her, and abandoned her. Townsend Harris also demanded an ox and had it slaughtered so he could eat beef. The Japanese were horrified that anyone would murder an ox, and the tree where the unfortunate ox was tethered before it was slaughtered became a shrine.

Yet the American technology – primarily, their firepower and steam engines – were seen as vital to Japan. Yoshida Shoin, a young Japanese who had begged Commodore Perry to take him to the West so he could acquire learning, had been confined in an iron cage, like a stray *gai-jin* foreign sailor. He was released. He founded a school. Then he was executed.

Of the three elder statesmen who frantically reformed and modernized Japan in Mutsuhito's name, and won the future Meiji Era tangential credit, two died violently. Takamori Saigo – 'the last *samurai*' –committed hara kiri after losing a rebellion. Toshimichi Okubo, who had betrayed Saigo, was hacked to pieces by six vengeful *samurai* a year later. Only Takayoshi Kido, a legal advisor, died in bed. Gentlemen settled their differences with swordplay and assassination and nobody above the rank of peasant went to bed sober if he could avoid it. If women cheated, their husbands were encouraged to kill them. Meiji, a nervous child who saw ghosts, got through all this terror and turmoil with a phenomenal capacity for liquor, five wives, and a harem of 300, later dismissed because they meddled in politics. The five wives stayed, including the Empress Haruko, two years older than he was, Meiji's favorite wife. She never produced an heir, or even a daughter, but Haruko was kept in place because he loved her and respected her intelligence, and because her family had influence. Meiji probably died, probably from complications of alcoholism, at 56 in 1912– the official cause was stomach cancer – but he held together well enough and adapted well enough so that his able advisors, in one generation, were able to turn Japan from a farmer-and-fisherman land of exquisite oriental elegance to a first-rate world power with a modern army and navy, massive heavy and light industry, and commercial outlets to China and the West.

Kojong succeeded to the throne of Korea in 1863 because his father Yi He-eung, now known as the Tae Won Gun, felt that he would rather rule as regent for his son. Even before he became king of Korea, Kojong had been married to Min Chii Rok, known to history as Queen Min, at his mother's insistence. He was eleven and Min was fourteen. She was an orphan raised by the Min family, who regarded her as an uncommonly beautiful and forceful child-woman. Caught between his beautiful 'older' wife and a father who soon came to envy her influence, Kojong emerged as a well-meaning but timid man, reasonably intelligent but lacking in force. Min became bitter and suspicious, especially after her first child died in 1871 and another consort produced an heir apparent – who then also died. The heir Min ultimately produced, to be known as Sojong, was either mildly mentally handicapped or seriously repressed. By 1873, Queen Min had used her power over the king and court to deprive the Tae Won Gun, her father-in-law, of his power over the throne.

Members of the Min family assumed many important positions. The Korean court was all-powerful in a society where there were no manufacturers or merchants of any importance and the aristocrats were not warlords but bureaucrats subject to royal approval. The government locked into a lurid feud between the Yi family and Min's adoptive family. Queen Min favored friendly relations with foreign nations – ironically, with Japan in particular. But her father-in-law the Tae Won Gun, head of the Yi faction, struck back in revenge for his loss of power. He sent a beautiful lacquer box to Queen Min's family. The box blew up and killed her step-father and a number of other relatives. When the Tae Won Gun attempted to use the royal entrance to the palace, reserved for the actual king, he found the gateway decorated with the severed heads of twenty of his own Yi supporters.

Court warfare between the Queen and the Tae Won Gun claimed thousands of Korean lives – almost 3,000 according to one Korean courtier who hated the Queen. The Queen and the Tae Won Gun pursued totally independent foreign policies depending on which of them had access to King Kojong at any moment. Queen Min, clever enough to realize that Korea was too backward and much too small to stand up to Russia or China, tried to use the rising power of Japan and the friendship of the United States to keep the Russians and the Chinese in counterpoise and retain Korean independence. The Tae Won Gun wanted to exclude all foreigners from Korea at any cost.[2]

In 1875, a Korean fort fired on a Japanese ship. The Japanese, who with French advisors had already begun to modernize their army, debated how to react to this challenge. Takamori Saigo argued that a war against Korea would unify feuding clan factions in Japan. Meiji and his European-influenced advisors disagreed. The emperor's faction felt that the pretext was inadequate to justify an aggressive war and that the armed forces weren't ready in any case. Saigo, a giant of a man – 6 feet tall and 240 pounds – was defeated leading his sword-wielding *samurai* warriors against Meiji's French-trained army and modern artillery. One bridge into the *samurai* country was defended by *samurai* women – *bushi-jo* or soldier girls – armed with *narinaga* halberds, the favored weapon of *samurai* wives and daughters. The *bushi-jo* put up a memorable fight but were largely deleted from official Japanese history because girl soldiers might have encouraged defiance on the part of less warlike women. Wounded, Takamori Saigo requested pardon for his followers and committed *hara kiri*. Pardon was granted and in death Saigo became a hero.

The government that had defeated his followers commissioned a statue that depicted the hefty giant Saigo in his Japanese rabbit-hunting costume with his little dog at his side. His wife hated it. She preferred the statue that showed him in his German-style military uniform. The Western-style painting said to depict him is actually a painting of his lookalike younger brother, who later served the Emperor. Six of Takemori Saigo's admirers murdered Toshimichi Okubo, whom they felt had betrayed him at court, by hacking him to pieces with *samurai* swords.

Possibly aware of these events in Japan, Queen Min was able to influence a Treaty of Amity between Korea and the US in 1882. Like the more astute Japanese statesman of her time, she recognized that 19th-century America was more honorable or perhaps simply less predatory than the European powers. She also befriended Yoshimoto Hanabusa, the Japanese ambassador who delighted her with a toy telephone and other marvels imported to Japan from the US.

Queen Min had, however, reckoned without her vengeful father-in-law. The Tae Won Gun used the new treaty with the United States, the presence of the Japanese – still resented after

250 years – and the arrival of a swaggering German adventurer name named P.G. von Moellendorf who represented China, to stir up the common people of Seoul against the evil foreigners – and against his daughter-in-law.

The Korean people were told that the drought that had caused the bad rice harvest was caused by the disruptive influence of the European whites and the Japanese on Korea's cosmology. Rice riots broke out in late July of 1882. The Japanese ambassador, Hanabusa, received a note from Queen Min:

> In great hurry, cannot write long. A band of riotous people with soldiers on their side seems to be intending attack on your legation. Be prepared for defense, and should they come to actual attack, will it not be better for you to get out of danger even by the use of arms?

Ambassador Hanabusa gathered his forces at the Japanese legation. When the Korean mob arrived, clearly bent on murder, the Japanese shot their way out with rifles and pistols and ran for Chemulpo, modern Inchon. The Japanese diplomatic personnel at Chemulpo barricaded themselves with their backs to the sea, reinforced by Japanese officers and 'students' – all of whom seemed to be familiar with firearms as well as swords. A Japanese fishing boat arrived and Hanabusa escaped to Nagasaki.

Back in Seoul, a Korean mob arrived with matchlocks and spears and stormed the palace. They found Queen Min lying in state in her royal robes, dead. The mob killed four of the King's council. When the formal execution of a courtier was decreed, the courtiers' whole family also perished. The fathers of the family and their grown sons were beheaded. Wives and daughters were sequestered in back rooms and poisoned with the juice of boiled centipedes, which induced agonizing convulsions before death. The rioting in Seoul led to the execution of 300 Korean supporters of modernization, and large numbers of their wives and children. Two of the king's diplomats asked China for help. The Chinese arrived at Chemulpo with six gunboats, seized the Tae Won Gun, and proclaimed Korea a vassal state of China – which violated understandings with both Japan and the United States.

Ambassador Hanabusa, back from his narrow escape from the rice riot, arrived at Chemulpo with 2,000 Japanese troops and a cruiser commanded by Heihachiro Togo.

Queen Min also returned from the dead. The body found in her bed had been that of a serving girl whose remarkable resemblance to the Queen had given her a soft job as a double or decoy – until the fatal moment when the rioters broke down the palace gates. The obedient girl, one of three expendable decoys, had dressed in the Queen's robes and taken a cup of poison. The beautiful decoy was found lying dead in the Queen's robes while Queen Min hid until the satisfied rioters wandered off in search of souvenirs.

Since the Chinese were now holding her hated father-in-law as a state hostage, Queen Min turned on the Japanese – which turned out to be a serious mistake. The Russians and the Chinese began to establish ever-increasing powers in Korea while the unhappy Japanese watched the power slip through their fingers. Abruptly, the French showed up and in retaliation for China's opposition to their control of Viet Nam blew up and sank the entire Chinese fleet. The Japanese barely tried to conceal their delight. Tacitly supported by the British and Americans, who saw Japan as a counterweight to the ponderous and obnoxious Russians, the Japanese demanded powers in Korea equal to those of China. Many Koreans in positions of influence supported them, possibly because the Japanese seemed the least exotic and preposterous of all the violent foreigners now trampling on Korean rights.

The Japanese also began to organize an army with the advice of Major Klemens Jacob Meckel, a Rhinelander from Cologne trained in Prussian military academies and decorated during Prussia's victorious war with France. Meckel, a Catholic in largely Protestant Prussia, was not a member of the aristocracy: his father was a notary and his mother the daughter of a respected tailor. But he became the mentor of a whole generation of Japanese officers from 1885. Meckel is also said to have invented the phrase: 'Korea is a dagger pointed at the belly of Japan.'[3]

New fighting shortly broke out based on a plot no one to-date has completely unraveled. When a fire broke out at a palace in Seoul, a mixed mob of Korean progressives and Japanese agents assassinated a number of Korean statesmen known to favor

China over Japan. The king was kept under Japanese 'protection.' Korea now declared its independence from China, with the Korean king's endorsement and British and American approval.

China struck back. Chinese and Korean troops attacked the Japanese, the Korean progressives and the foreign legations and the streets of Seoul ran red with the blood of men, women, and children, families implicated in a plot approved by their own king. Once again, the Japanese shot their way out of Seoul and headed for Chemulpo, and once again they barely made it out alive. The Korean women of the Japanese who couldn't escape were slaughtered and their bodies were thrown into the harbor to float past the Japanese warship. The Japanese wept and raged – and swore revenge.

China and Japan negotiated. A few more Koreans, this time men from the anti-Japanese faction, were beheaded as a concession to Japan's hurt feelings. Then both sides stood down and glowered at one another. Korea still maintained a shaky independence with the proviso that either Japan or China could interfere in Korean affairs at any time, provided that they kept one another informed. The Korean conservatives, now back in power in Seoul, demanded that those Korean progressives who had fled with the posse of Japanese soldiers and 'students' be handed over for the traditional mass butchery – women and children included. The Japanese public, sentimental where children were concerned, supported the Japanese government wholeheartedly when Japan's statesmen refused to hand over their few surviving Korean friends. The Korean government then dispatched assassins to Japan to eliminate at least the men of the Korean progressive families. Some of the assassins were caught by the Japanese police. Stories appeared in the Japanese newspapers.

Beyond the Korean conservatives were the Korean ultra-conservatives – the *Tong Haks*, a peasant group akin to the Boxers in Manchu China who hated all foreigners, white or Japanese, and who believed that the foreign presence was messing up Korea's meteorological metabolism. If it rained too much in Korea, or not at all, the Europeans and the Japanese were somehow to blame. The *Tong Haks* also preached a religion in which all men and women were equal, which meant that they were as much of a threat to the *yangban* scholar landowners as they were to the Japanese or the Europeans. The *Tong Haks* believed that getting rid of the Japanese and especially of the strange-looking whites would restore Korea's atmospheric health and usher in a new age of prosperity. They also believed that whites ate Korean children and cut the breasts off Korean women to get milk which they drank. The *Tong Haks* attacked the forces of the Korean government. Government troops first lost and then gained ground in a war with the peasant rebels. King Kojong, however, called for help from China. The Chinese sent troops to put down the *Tong Haks*, the Japanese sent troops to oppose China, and the first Sino-Japanese War broke out.

The Sino-Japanese War was a massacre in which both sides had modern weapons and one side knew how to use them. Heihachiro Togo, who had seen the once-friendly Koreans floating in Chemulpo harbor, started the fighting when he destroyed one Chinese battleship and damaged a second with more than 400 shell hits off the coast of Korea. While the Chinese battleship was burning, Togo stopped a Chinese troopship and ordered the ship to surrender. The Chinese first surrendered, then tried to escape. Togo blazed away at the troopship with every gun on his cruiser, sank it, and stood by as his sailors used the bobbing Chinese heads in the water for rifle practice. The British seamen who had been part of the crew were allowed to row away in the Chinese ship's two lifeboats. Every Chinese was shot or drowned.

The British press exploded with indignation, but British politicians smoothed things over because they needed Japan to counter Russian ambitions in the Pacific. Emperor Meiji quietly told Togo that he had done the right thing. The Chinese admiral committed suicide, the Chinese prime minister was shot in the face by an assassin, and the Japanese won the war with 800 dead and 1,600 wounded – fewer than the Chinese had lost to Togo in one day. The Japanese took Formosa, today's Taiwan, as the spoils of war. General Nogi, who had fought against the redoubtable Takamori Saigo as a young officer, said that the Sino-Japanese War had been about as tough as twisting a baby's arm. It was a vivid metaphor. Jacob Merkel had returned to Germany by this time but he left behind the best-trained army in Asia.

Queen Min, once Japan's friend and admirer, refused to withdraw her support for China, whose power was clearly waning – or perhaps refused to give up on the notion that China could be used to retain a measure of Korean sovereignty and her own family's power. She alone had the stubborn courage to stand up to the increasingly drastic changes the Japanese were demanding of indignant Koreans – the clipping of the men's topknots, a symbol of virility and adult status, the abolition of harems in favor of nominal monogamy, and the disruption of the opulent pomp and circumstance of the Korean court.

Abruptly, the Tae Won Gun emerged from his hostage status in China, perhaps realizing before Queen Min did that Imperial China was played out and Japan was now holding all the cards. Hating his daughter-in-law even more than he had once hated the Japanese, the Tae Won Gun conspired for her removal with Goro Miura, a Japanese general sent to represent Japan in Seoul. Queen Min's case was assigned the code name *kitsune* – 'fox' – the wicked enchantress in Japanese or Korean folklore. Gangsters from the Tokyo slums were borrowed from Mitsuro Toyama, the dread lord of the Black Dragon Society, or *kokuryukai*, an anti-colonial group based in Japan but open to all non-whites who wanted to keep Europeans at a safe distance east of the Amur River – 'Black Dragon river' in both Chinese and Japanese. Recruited according to their own romantic legends from *samurai* who had become *ronin*, or wanderers, when their feudal lords lost power, the Black Dragons were more identifiably composed of gamblers, extortionists, pimps, and hired killers as well as from upper-class Japanese who liked to live dangerously after dark. Mitsuro Toyama, a pauper child who once peddled Asian sweet potatoes as fast food, now lived as an elder prince through a mixture of crime and influence. Toyama became Japan's Al Capone, and the villain of several World War II propaganda movies. He was mixed up in everything – including Japanese politics and Korean politics. His Black Dragon Society henchmen were dispatched to Korea because some of Japan's Imperial German-trained officers might balk at killing a woman.[4]

On the night of 8 October 1895, a mixed mob of Japanese and Koreans broke into the palace in Seoul, guarded only by Japanese troops, and pursued Queen Min through the corridors. A heroic courtier who tried to throw his body between hers and the assassins had both his hands cut off and stumbled away, bleeding, to die at King Kojong's feet. Queen Min, cornered, called out her son's name three times, and was cut down by the swords of her pursuers. The three ladies-in-waiting who identified her body were also murdered to prevent them from identifying the individual killers – and to make sure none of them was actually the Queen in disguise. Queen Min's body was wrapped in a blanket and carried to a pine grove not far from the palace, where she and her ladies-in-waiting were burned with repeated doses of kerosene imported from Japan. King Kojong, protected by his father, the Tae Won Gun, was not touched. He issued a proclamation reducing the dead Queen Min to the rank of common prostitute – the lowest social caste in Korea, along with butchers.

'We knew the extreme of her wickedness, but we were helpless and full of fear of her party. We are convinced that she was not only unfitted and unworthy to be the Queen, but also that her guilt is excessive and overflowing... So we hereby depose her from the rank of Queen and reduce her to the lowest of the low class.'

King Kojong and his son Prince Sojong then fled to the Russian embassy disguised as women with the help of the surviving ladies-in-waiting. They left the Japanese to explain the royal murder to a world that revered royalty. The Japanese government subjected the Japanese suspects to a farcical trial where everybody was guilty and nobody was convicted. The official Japanese verdict was that while the accused had certainly plotted to kill Queen Min, there was 'insufficient evidence to prove that any of the accused actually committed the crime originally meditated by them.' In the words of the Japanese historian Kentaro Yamabe, the trial was 'a deliberate miscarriage of justice, designed to protect the culprits.' The Korean Supreme Court then tried thirteen Koreans who were part of the murder gang, and these culprits also got off. Goro Miura, the prime instigator among the Japanese, retired as an honored elder statesman. Mitsuro Toyama, who loaned the Japanese some of the probable killers, became an underground national hero.[5] The Tae Won Gun's role in Queen Min's murder and that fact that some of the killers were Korean was largely excised from Korean patriotic history.

Safe under Russian custody, King Kojong asked the Tsar's government for $3 million so he could build a proper tomb for Queen Min without taking money from the Japanese who murdered her – overlooking his own father's complicity. The Russians happily donated the money. They also maintained a strong and growing presence in Korea.

The queen was dead, but she would not die unavenged. And her avenger would play a role in the turbulent relations of Korea and Japan that would contribute to Japan's national instability at the worst possible time.

Kim Chang-an was the son of a *yangban* family, born in 1876 when Korea was still entirely independent. He was a headstrong, mischievous boy with a strong sense of right and wrong. Stories from his village told of how, when he was beaten up by bullies, he went looking for them with a meat cleaver. He was five years old. As a *yangban*'s son, he was supposed to study for the test in Chinese classics, but he once was seen using the precious ink for experiments in how colors change when inks are mixed, and how beautiful the colors looked when they drifted down the village stream. In 1894, he failed to pass his examination – according to his admirers, he was repelled by the whole examination process because of the amount of bribery involved and refused to have any part of it. His detractors say that, while highly intelligent, he had problems concentrating because his father was a drunkard and his mother, a child bride, was silly and irresponsible. He also disliked his own appearance – he was a big, bearish youth with a lumpy head and prominent teeth like a beaver. He resolved on a program of self-improvement: 'How handsome you are is nothing compared to how healthy you are, and how healthy you are is nothing compared to how healthy your mind is.' Kim, disgruntled with the *yangban* system of old Korea, joined the *Tong Haks*, attracted by their belief in social equality and their slogan: 'Let's save our country from the Westerners and the Japanese.' Chaos broke out as some *Tong Haks* fought the national troops of Korea in 1894 – patriotic propaganda describes them as 'the Japanese' – while others preferred to loot the countryside. Kim was organizing his own honest faction of *Tong Haks* for an attack on the rogue *Tong Hak* brigands when the national troops saved him the trouble and wiped them out.

At a loose end once the rebellion ended, Kim was staying at a country inn when the people received the news of Queen Min's murder. Mulling over this insult, he noted a stranger in the inn. They nodded to one another politely, but when Kim tried to speak to the stranger, the stranger said 'I'm from Chang Hwang He-Do' – in the wrong regional accent. Kim looked the stranger over carefully and saw to his shock that the stranger was wearing a Japanese sword concealed under the fold of his robe. Kim decided that the man must be one of the Japanese gangsters who had murdered the queen – but he had to be sure. As the stranger left the inn, Kim followed him down the steps, and shouted: '*Inu*!'

Hearing himself called a dog – in Japanese – the stranger whirled in rage. Kim knew his man. He kicked the stranger in the chest, knocked him down the stairs, and ran him through with the Japanese sword he plucked from the fold in the stranger's robe. Kim fumbled around for papers inside the man's robe and found that the stranger's name had been Tsuchida – a Japanese – and that he was carrying 800 yen, a sizable amount of money for a casual tourist. Kim tossed the money to the country folk at the inn and left a note pinned on the dead Tsuchida's body: 'To revenge my country, I killed this man.' He was now 19 years old, and the course of his life was firmly set.

Three months later, Kim Chang-an was arrested and sent to Chemulpo Prison by the Korean authorities. His feet were clapped into stocks and twisted, causing agonizing pain, and the filthy cell or the frequent beatings gave him a dose of jaundice that left him nauseous and unable to eat for twelve days and almost killed him. Hauled before three Korean judges and a Japanese observer, Kim Chang-an was charged with the murder of Tsuchida – whose presence in the back country of Korea was never explained.

'I did kill one Japanese for the sake of my country, not for his fortune,' Kim told the judges. Then he turned to the Japanese observer. 'Why did you kill our queen? As long as I'm alive, and even if I have to come back as a ghost, I'll kill your royalty so your royal blood will end!'

The three Korean judges, impressed by his courage, gave him a cleaner cell. They had no choice but to sentence him to death. The sentence was to be carried out on 26 August 1897. Kim read books about the West while he calmly awaited execution. He also taught his jailers how to read. At the last minute, King Kojong – perhaps remorseful over Queen Min's death and post mortem degradation – granted a stay of execution and quietly cancelled the death sentence. The king intimated that he would have pardoned Kim Chang-an outright had it not been for his fear of the Japanese. Instead, he urged the jailers to show him every kindness. They did. On 9 March 1898, Kim escaped from prison. He spent the next six years exploring the world.

While Kim was exploring, the West was exploiting. On 30 January 1902, Great Britain signed a treaty with Japan. Each country pledged to remain neutral if the other went to war with a single party. Each country pledged its help if the other went to war with two countries at the same time. The British were concerned with the possibility that either the French in Indo China, the Germans who now controlled Shantung or, by far the most menacing – the Russians – would seize Korea and threaten British influence in China. Having seen how the Japanese did most of the actual fighting during the Boxer Rebellion of 1900, and knowing that Japan also felt menaced by Russia, the British, in effect, backed Japan against 'the Russian bear' for control of the Pacific Rim.

In 1904, as both Russia and Japan had one eye on the total control of Korea and the other on the incredible resources of Manchuria just to the north, Russia and Japan went to war. The war with Russia was no walkover, like Japan's war with China. The Japanese lost 100,000 soldiers in battles to capture Port Arthur – the first war in which both sides had machine guns, and the first war in history when an Asian people defeated a major European power with home-made battleships. Tsarist Russia's coarse oppression of Polish Catholics and the recent murders of scores of Russian Jews by anti-Semitic mobs had made Russia many enemies. One of them was President Theodore Roosevelt. Shocked by the Russian government's failure to prevent the oppression of Catholics and the mass slaughter of Jews, Roosevelt told Germany and France not to support Russia against Japan, with the subtle threat that if they did, the US would support Japan. 'I thoroughly admire and believe in the Japanese,' Roosevelt said.

'No human beings, black, yellow, or white could be quite so untruthful, as insincere, as arrogant – in short, as untrustworthy in every way – as the Russians under the present system.'

For the Russians, the Russo-Japanese war was just another colonial escapade. For the Japanese, it was a war of survival, and keeping the Russians out of Korea, 'a dagger pointed at the belly of Japan,' was the key to that survival. During the war, and immediately afterwards, the Japanese took over Korea in fact if not in name, a strategic necessity which the Americans and the British regarded as understandable in the context of a war between two modern powers. The world was stunned – and in many cases delighted – when the 'gallant little Japs' triumphed over the Russians with the financial and political help of Jewish and Polish dissidents who resented Tsarist oppression. When the war ended, the Japanese were stockpiling Browning automatic pistols in a London bookstore in case Polish and Finnish patriots and Jewish avengers had to be sent in to assassinate Russian officials. A large part of the world – Germany and France excepted – was delighted when Japan won the Russo-Japanese War. The British were exultant that they had backed a winner and had kept Russia substantially out of the Pacific. The Poles, the Finns, and the Jews – all victims of Tsarist oppression – were especially delighted. But the story of what happened to Korea was largely ignored in the victory celebration.

3

DEATH OF AN AMERICAN DICTATOR

Durham White Stevens was described in the *New York Times* of Tuesday 24 March 1908 as holding 'a post of such importance that he became known as the American dictator of the Hermit Kingdom.' His death at the hands of a Korean assassin touched off a near-lynching in San Francisco and continued to raise questions about exactly what was going on in Korea with the knowledge of the US in the first decade of the new century.

Stevens had come to San Francisco in the spring of 1908 and been quoted in an article in the San Francisco newspapers on 21 March, which described the Japanese protectorate of Korea in terms that the Korean immigrants in San Francisco found unacceptable. 'Japan is doing in Korea and for the Koreans what the United States is doing in the Philippines for the Filipinos, modifying its methods only to suit the somewhat different conditions with which it has to deal,' Stevens said. He declared that the Korean Council of State was a real governing body, composed entirely of Koreans, though he was the advisor. Stevens denied that the Japanese were exploiting Korea for profit or that the its revenues were being used to support an army of Japanese office holders. The salaries of Korean officials and the many extensive improvements going on in Korea were being paid for by the Japanese, he said, and the future of the great mass of Korean people, formerly without hope, was beginning to look bright:

> When the Japanese assumed charge of Korea, the Koreans were spending annually 3,000,000 yen for the support of 20,000 woefully inefficient soldiers, and 60,000 yen a year on education. The army is no longer necessary and Prince Ito is carrying out an extensive and skilled campaign of education. There are certain classes in Korea that never will be reconciled to the new order but the mass of the people – the real backbone of the country – are already beginning to regard the Japanese as good friends.

While their good friends the Japanese were wiping out what was left of Korea's woefully inefficient soldiers, two Korean groups in America, the *Kongip Hyop Hoe* (Mutual Assistance Association) and the *Taedong Pogukhoe* (Great Eastern Protection Association) convened a meeting to protest Stevens' article and to try to refute his argument that the Japanese protectorate of Korea was actually beneficial to most Koreans and was well received by the peasants. Two representatives of each group were sent to the Fairmont hotel to confront Stevens. On 22 March Earl Lee – actually Il Lee, a Korean newsman run out of Korea by Japanese influence – served as the spokesman for the four Koreans. Lee asked Stevens if he had made the statements attributed to him in the press. Stevens said that he had.

'Aren't the Japanese killing off the Koreans?' Lee asked.

'No.' Stevens said.

'Haven't all the Korean officials been eliminated?' Lee asked.

'No.' Stevens said. 'You've been probably away from your country too long to know the exact condition of the government.'

The four Koreans suddenly snatched up rattan chairs from the hotel lobby and began to beat Stevens with them. The big American fell and his head struck the marble floor but he jumped up with his face bleeding, grabbed a chair and stood against the wall battling all four Koreans with his own chair. The Americans at the hotel subdued the four angry Koreans and threw them out of the lobby.

'We are all very sorry that we did not do more to him,' Lee said, as he was being shoved out of the hotel. He said that if the Koreans had actually expected to be able to talk to Stevens they would have found something harder than rattan chairs to hit him with.[1]

The next day Chang In Hwan and Chun Myung Un went to the train station to ambush Stevens and to silence what they saw as a Japanese propaganda campaign with an American mouthpiece. Stevens didn't show up at the station so the two Koreans decided to wait by the ferry landing instead. Stevens was leaving the Fairmont hotel omnibus with the Japanese Consul General, Chozo Koike, who actually carried his luggage – rather unthinkable for a consul – when the two Koreans walked up and one of them said something to him. Chang In Hwan had a pistol in his hand, concealed in a handkerchief. Chang pointed the pistol at Stevens, who looked aghast, but the pistol jammed. The handkerchief had caught in the trigger. Chang kept trying to pull the jammed trigger. The pistol wouldn't go off. Finally he struck Stevens in the face with the gun. Stevens, 56, was 'a man of fine physique and in splendid health.' The big American ran after Chang to avenge his bleeding face. Chun stepped in behind Stevens, leveled his own gun at Stevens and hit Chang square in the chest when Chang turned around to see if Stevens was gaining on him. Chun's next two shots hit Stevens twice in the back. Stevens stumbled and fell. A crowd came to his rescue and grabbed the two Koreans, shouting 'Lynch the Japs!'

Chang and Chun fully expected to be lynched until an American lawyer in the crowd stepped out and urged the other Americans not to do anything violent until they heard both sides of the question.

Stevens was seriously hurt but he was in good enough shape to make a statement to the police, 'As I got out of the Fairmont hotel omnibus, several Koreans approached me. One of them struck me in the face, lacerating my cheek. As I started to pursue him, another Korean began to shoot at me. The first shot missed me and struck the Korean I was pursuing. The next two shots took their effect in my back. This evidently is the work of small group of student agitators in and about San Francisco, who resent the fact that the Japanese have a protectorate over Korea and believe that I am to some extent responsible for this condition of affairs in their country.'

One bullet had penetrated Stevens' right lung and the other lodged in his groin. Chang was also seriously wounded. The Koreans received no sympathy for an attack on an American in San Francisco. While no one lynched them they got a bad press. 'The Korean Chang who shot Mr Stevens to-day is about as large as a twelve-year-old boy, but he says he is thirty years old and that he has been in this country for two years, coming from Hawaii,' the *New York Times* reported, confusing Chang, the first assailant, with Chun, the actual assassin.

'Yes, me shoot him,' the shooter said to a reporter, as quoted in *The Times*. 'Me sorry? No. Him no good. Him help Japan. Bye and bye Korea all the same Japan.'

Stevens was taken to the San Francisco harbor emergency hospital, where he was described by the newspapers as 'the coolest man in the place.' 'I don't feel any pain,' he said as he lay on the operating table. 'Is that a bad sign?'

When Stevens didn't get an answer, he lapsed into silence. Koike, the Japanese consult general, stared at the Korean being treated in a nearby bed. Then he noticed Stevens' huge diamond stickpin lying with his rumpled, bloody clothes.

'What shall I do with this?' Koike asked the nurse. 'It looks rather valuable and should not be left lying around.'

'You had better wear it yourself until you have an opportunity of turning it over to the other party,' the nurse told him. Koike put the diamond stickpin in his pocket and sadly gathered up Stevens' clothes and luggage.

The two Korean assailants didn't receive much support from the American public, but two Korean organizations in San Francisco and one in Hawaii raised money for their legal expenses.

Stevens was reported doing well the next day and Chang, the Korean hit by mistake, was also reported recovering. Chun, the Korean who did the actually shooting, wrote out a neatly lettered statement in *hangul*. The *San Francisco Call*, less committed to the little yellow devil image than the *New York Times*, translated his message.

This day I shot Stevens. I shot him because he was the main factor in the Japanese reign of bloodshed and oppression in

Korea and because he, as the head advisor of the regime, was responsible for the deaths of our fathers, mothers and brothers in Korea.

Stevens is the advisor of the Korean government, paid by the Korean government, but who is working for the interests of Japan and against those of the nation who looked to him as an American for justice and good rule. He has endeavored to make the people of the United States of America believe that Japanese protection for Korea is the best thing for the nation in the present and would be in the future. He lied when he said that the Korean people were happy under Japanese rule. So, for his falsehoods, I shot Stevens. I shot the man as an expression of the sentiment of the Korean race and its hatred of Japanese government. I knew I would die when I shot him, but so angered was I at his falsehoods and the misuse of his power that, with the knowledge of my own death, I shot him. What is life without liberty?

How can I be calm, knowing our fathers, mothers and brothers in Korea are being murdered by agents of the Japanese government? A man in whose breast there is not a love for his country greater than all else and who can remain passive, knowing that the fathers, mothers and brothers of his country are being murdered has no right to live.

Stevens was the man who forced the Korean emperor to sign a treaty giving away the independence of his country into the keeping of Japan. Stevens is an enemy of the world and a disturber of the peace. Therefore I shot Stevens. If I kill him and I die it will be a warning for others who take his place to rule justly and to deal with the people in his care with kindness and humanity. I will make no complaint for the punishment that is meted out to me, and should my act aid my country in struggles for freedom, I will die nobly and well. I shot Stevens and I wish to die.

The Koreans explained their actions to their own community in a flyer distributed immediately after Stevens was shot.

To all Koreans in all parts of the world.

Loyalty to his nation and fealty to his parents is the primal law of man's nature. The right to live and the right to die for duty is also the rule of nature.

But, alas! Grievous times have come upon Korea, our compatriots. We who have been educated by our 500-year-old dynasty and raised up by our 4,000-year-old ancestry have come under the domination of the barbarous, savage islanders – the Japanese. They have swooped upon our country and are indulging their barbarous appetites with a cruel heart. It is so much we could not say it with our tongues, nor could we write it with our pens.

The Japanese have abdicated our Emperor, destroyed our villages, killed our brethren, robbed our land, seized our benefits and are the enemy not only of Korea, but of all the world – for they have violated the peace of humanity.

Compatriots, we must unite and consecrate ourselves to our land and restore our independence. We are sure our God will help us. We must all do our best to kill all Japanese, their spies, allies, and barbarous soldiers.

The Japanese may compare the rising of our righteous army to the attempt of an insect to move a big tree but right is on our side, and we are confident that in the end we shall be victorious, opposing their treachery with the justice of our cause. We sacrifice our lives to their guns and swords and as the front men fall the men behind them will take their places. Defeated to-day, we will again attack on the morrow until our vow to exterminate the Japanese or die has been accomplished.

> E. Yie Lin Yung
> General, Korean Righteous Army

Stevens died late on the night of March 25, after an operation disclosed that he had been more seriously injured than the surgeons first believed. Chun, the assassin, was said to have received the news of Stevens' death with 'manifest delight.' At Stevens' bedside was the Japanese Consul, General Chozo Koike.

'This is most unfortunate, a great loss to Japan, Korea, and this country.' Koike said. A few days later, the Korean cabinet voted 50,000 yen to Stevens' two sisters, who lived in Asbury Park, New Jersey, and the Japanese later voted 100,000 yen.

Who was Durham White Stevens? Stevens had graduated from Oberlin College in 1871, the second generation of his family to graduate from Oberlin Prep and from the college itself. Stevens' father, Ezra, was a resident of Washington DC and worked for the Indian Department, where he was remembered for originating the policy of Indian schools from the 1870s to his death in 1890. The Indian Department – later the Bureau of Indian Affairs – was a magnet for grafters and swindlers of all stripes, especially in the 1870s. The Indian schools may have been a model in Stevens' mind for what the Japanese would have to do to Korea. The US Indian Schools may have even made Japan's policy at the turn of the century seem comparatively lenient. Koreans in Japanese schools were allowed to study their own history and literature in Korean. All other subjects were in Japanese.

Stevens entered the United States diplomatic corps in 1873 with an appointment from President Ulysses S. Grant, an early advocate of responsible treatment for the Indians and also for the Chinese and the Japanese, two nations Grant felt has been much abused by Europeans. While Stevens was working in Japan for the US as secretary of the American legation in Tokyo, Grant visited Japan on the last leg of his world tour while working with Stevens and expressed his admiration for the Japanese to Adam Badeau, one of his last remaining friends.

My visit to Japan has been the most pleasant of all my travels. The country is beautifully cultivated, the scenery is grand, and the people, from the highest to the lowest, the most kindly and the most cleanly in the world... The progress they have made in the last twelve years is almost incredible. They now have Military and Naval Academies, Colleges, Engineering schools, schools of science and free schools, for male and female, as thoroughly organized, and on as high a basis of instruction, as any country in the world. Travel in the interior is as safe for an unarmed, unprotected foreigner as it is in the New England

States. Much safer from extortion. This is marvelous when the treatment their people – and all eastern people – receive at the hands of the average foreigner residing among them is considered. I have never been so struck with the heartlessness of Nations as well as individuals as since coming to the East. But the day of retribution is sure to come.[2]

Stevens worked as Secretary of the legation until 1883, when he rather surprisingly resigned to enter the Japanese diplomatic corps, as Secretary to the Japanese legation in Washington. In the following year Stevens was back in Japan. He accompanied Japan's Count Kaoru Inoue to Korea when Korea was still an independent monarchy. The Koreans at this time were better disposed toward Americans than other Westerners, because the Americans the Koreans knew best – Protestant missionaries and their families – were kindly, upright people who respected the Koreans' penchant for hard work, personal cleanliness, scholarship and good manners.

Stevens was officially representing Japan at the time the first Sino- Japanese War broke out in 1894. His contributions as a publicist were recorded in an issue of *North American Review* in which the causes of the war were discussed by three notable Americans: Augustine Heard, former United States minister to Korea, Howard Martin, ex-secretary of the United States legation at Peking, and Durham White Stevens, counselor of the Japanese legation at Washington. The series of articles is a study in overt or concealed bias. Augustine Heard, supposedly representing the interests of the US in Korea and of the Korean people themselves, was the nephew and heir of the New England merchant Augustine Heard, who made his fortune in the China trade in the 19th century and had later represented the interests of the Chinese empire in several European capitals. Heard's article was consistently pro-Chinese rather than pro-Korean and he saw Japan as having intrigued to stir up the *Tong Haks*. This scenario is very improbable, since, like most Koreans, the *Tong Haks* regarded Japan as the ultimate enemy and disliked and distrusted the Japanese as much as they scorned Europeans.

Howard Martin, supposedly representing China to the American reader, portrayed the Chinese army as a pathetic collection of buffoons armed with bows and arrows and matchlock muskets, building ships made out of bamboo and silk to bamboozle gullible westerners, and trying to talk their way out of a fight whenever possible.

Durham White Stevens was utterly consistent. He worked for the Japanese and he put their case on the table in no uncertain terms. 'Korea is a natural bulwark to Japan. Its state of complete isolation at that time invited aggression and possible conquest. The French and American expeditions only a few years before had shown that China was either unwilling or unable to defend the integrity of the peninsular kingdom. Other nations might not have been so lenient as France and the United States had been, and the occupation of Korea by a strong foreign power, or a partition of the country between several such powers, constituted a grave menace to Japan. Other so-called tributary states of China had been thus absorbed; and there could not have been a stronger augury of a similar fate for Korea than China's own actions had furnished.'

Stevens went on to report how the Japanese had attempted to avoid trespassing on Korean rights and to develop Korea financially and strengthen the country against Western aggression. Meanwhile, Stevens said the traditional Korean *yangban* administration was so corrupt that Japanese financial initiatives failed, He said that *yangban* graft and extortion kept the country backwards and poor.

Corruption extends throughout every branch of the public service. Offices are bought and sold, and the revenues are farmed out to the highest bidder. Officials swarm over the land, and the people are ground down by their exactions. A few powerful families divide the spoils, and at times plunge the kingdom into disorder by their factional quarrels. At other times the peasantry revolt and attempt to throw off their burdens. The present sovereign, however well meaning he may be, is powerless to carry out his good intentions. The fault is in the system; the system is borrowed from China, and China seems determined to perpetuate it at all hazards. In all of Korea's domestic dissensions the hand of China can be traced. Her influence is secret, but none the less potent. She shirks responsibility to other nations, but hesitates at no means – cajolery, bribery, menace – to dominate Korea. Whatever object her policy may have, its plain result has been to paralyze progress, and to leave the country weak and defenseless, a ready victim for foreign aggression.[3]

All three American commentators predicted that Japan would win the war with China, and they were right. The handful of Westerners who saw the Japanese war against China were favorably impressed with the discipline of Japanese troops in dealing with Asian civilians, if not with their quality of mercy on their Chinese adversaries. Durham White Stevens had accurately predicted Japan's victory and his career benefited from his work on behalf of Japan.

Stevens was not the first American to become a Japanese diplomat involved in Korean politics. On 1 September 1899, the world little noted nor long remembered the death of Charles William LeGendre, who died in Seoul due to apoplexy or stroke – Westerners involved in Japanese or Korean politics seem to be extremely susceptible to stroke. LeGendre, born in France in 1830, a Franco-American with an American wife, had been a colonel and brevet general during the American Civil War before he suffered two horrendous wounds that destroyed his face. At New Bern, in North Carolina, in 1862 he was hit in the lower jaw by a large-bore rifle ball and lost nine teeth and part of his jawbone. In the wilderness in Virginia in 1864, he was hit in the face and lost his left eye and the bridge of his nose.[4] He joined the American diplomatic service, and when the Polynesian aborigines of the mountains in the center of Taiwan slaughtered fourteen American merchant sailors from the American bark, *Rover*, LeGendre joined the punitive expedition, which turned into something of a disaster. The aborigines routed the Americans and the Chinese authorities said they couldn't do much about it. In 1871, the same aborigines killed and possibly ate fifty-four Japanese fishermen from the Ryukyu Islands (Okinawa) and the Japanese home government tapped LeGendre's expertise to cow the aborigines. The American colonel and brevet Civil War general organized a Japanese punitive expedition to Taiwan in which 3,000 Japanese soldiers forced the aborigines to behave themselves. LeGendre – born in France – became the first foreigner to receive the Order of the Rising Sun, and the first person of any race to receive the second and higher degree. In 1890, after two decades as a Japanese diplomat, he was dispatched to Korea to help the Japanese get on top of whatever was going on there. The Japanese continue to honor him. When LeGendre died near the end of 1899, Durham White Stevens was getting ready to take over.

'Because of his ability and knowledge of affairs in the Orient, he was in 1904, appointed by the Japanese government to be foreign adviser to the Emperor of Korea, a post of such importance that he became known as the American dictator of the Hermit Kingdom,' the *New York Times* reported shortly after Stevens was shot. While he was still alive, Japan had given him a grant of $10,000 and an annuity of $540. He also received two important Japanese decorations, the Order of the Rising Sun and the Order of the Sacred Treasure.

The conflict over control of Korea and Manchuria, the Texas-sized province of Imperial China, led to a showdown between Japan and its remaining rival, Imperial Russia. As previously mentioned, American and British hostility to the Russian presence in the Pacific Ocean led both Anglo-Saxon powers to remain neutral but tacitly to support Japan. The Japanese went to war with Russia – by way of a naval surprise attack at Port Arthur in Manchuria –with a treaty of alliance with Great Britain in their national breast pocket, right over the heart. Britain in 1902 had pledged to remain neutral if Japan went to war with a single power, and to intervene on Japan's behalf if Japan went to war with two major powers. France, a major colonial power in Asia, and Germany, whose eccentric Kaiser Wilhelm II was the dear cousin of the Tsar and constantly fulminated about 'The Yellow Peril' taking over the world, both supported Russia – from the sidelines, without entering into the fighting. The world got to see what the Japanese soldier was made of – sometimes through the eyes of best-selling author Jack London, reporting for the *San Francisco Examiner*, though he kept getting arrested. London wrote from the front in 1904:

The Japanese are so made that nothing short of annihilation can stop them, Patriotism is their religion and they die for their country as the martyrs of other peoples die for their gods ... the Japanese are Asiatics, and the Asiatic does not value life as we do... The prestige Japan has appreciated all over the world is because of the remarkable success of her navy at Port Arthur, and yet the world wagged its head dubiously and said: 'Wait till we see what Japan does on land.' Perhaps it was to settle this doubt and to gain from the outset land-prestige equal to its sea-prestige that prompted Japan to make a frontal attack across the naked sands of the Yalu. It certainly demonstrated that its soldiers have dash and go, and it took four hundred Russian prisoners, twenty-eight guns, and some baggage...

At the headquarters at Antung a Japanese in civilian clothes addressed me in English. He did all the talking, and he talked of the victory. He was beaming. Not a hint of the thoughts in his own mind had I breathed to him, and yet he said at parting 'Your people did not think we could beat the white. We have now beaten the white.'[5]

The Japanese had done their own fighting, but the diplomacy and finance behind their victory over Tsarist Russia was another story. Angered by the latest Tsarist *pogroms* that murdered about 100 Jews in Russia – Japanese propaganda claimed 17,000 – the German-Jewish American banker Jacob Schiff helped finance Japan for a war against Russia by way of revenge for the murdered Jews, and the Tsarist government's failure to punish the murderers. First on his own, then in cooperation with two other Jewish bankers, Sir Ernest Cassel in England and M. Warburg in Hamburg, Schiff floated $180,000,000 in loans to Japan and also financed revolutionary propaganda among Russian prisoners-of-war held by the Japanese. (A quarter-century later, the Japanese rescued tens of thousands of German Jews from Nazi persecution and settled them in Shanghai or Manchuria by way of gratitude to Schiff and his colleagues who financed Russia's catastrophic defeat.) Schiff's popularity as the secret sponsor of Japan's 1905 victory enabled him to escape most of the blame for a less successful escapade, the attempt to buy up the South Manchurian Railroad, Japan's most valuable piece of booty in a war that cost the Japanese 100,000 dead and 110,000 injured, but failed to gain Korea.

Theodore Roosevelt won the Nobel Peace Prize for the Treaty of Portsmouth, which ended the war between Russia and Japan but left Korea nominally independent and let the Russians retain nominal control of Manchuria. The treaty, applauded by Americans, touched off rioting in Tokyo. Outraged mobs burned thirteen Christian churches and every police station in the city and tipped over the beloved Tokyo trolley cars in a blind fury.

Japanese sources claimed that Stevens compounded the bad relations after the Portsmouth Treaty when he tried to broker a deal in which the US would buy control of the South Manchuria Railway, post-war. 'Thanks to the good offices of Stevens, advisor to the Japanese Government, and the United States Minister in Tokyo ... an interview resulted in a secret contract between them for the purchase of the South Manchuria Railway by the United States,' the Japanese propagandist Matsuo Kinoaki wrote long after the fact. 'According to this contract, arrangements were made to bring into being a United States-Japanese syndicate (supervised by American railroad tycoon Edmund Harriman) as a preliminary for the purchase by the United States of the Railway and its subsidiaries from Japan. The contract stipulated that the syndicate should be organized in accordance with Japanese law and put under Japanese control, but that finally, the organization should be altered in such a way that the rights of both sides would be equal.' Harriman a few years before had led and sponsored a celebrated expedition include John Muir to Pacific maritime Canada and coastal Alaska and studied flora, fauna – and transportation routes.

Unfortunately for the United States railroad industry – dubbed 'The Octopus' by muck-raking American novelist Frank Norris – the Japanese delegates from the Portsmouth Conference got back to Tokyo, having been fleeced as they saw it by Theodore Roosevelt, before the railroad treaty got back to the United States.

'From the legation standpoint, the transfer of the South Manchuria Railway and its subsidiaries and properties should, first of all, be approved by the Chinese Government,' Marquis Jutaro Komura, Japan's chief delegate to Portsmouth, reported to his prime minister, Taro Katsura. 'And from the political standpoint, Japan has just acquired the South Manchuria

Railway by sacrificing 210,000 casualties and 2,500,000,000 yen; therefore, it is absolutely impossible for Japan to trade the Railway for the benefit of American capitalists. More than that, if this contract is disclosed and reaches the ears of the nation, which is not satisfied with the Portsmouth Treaty, nobody knows what serious incidents would happen in Tokyo, not to mention the destruction of street cars and police boxes in the city.'

The Japanese spiked the treaty, which made some American businessmen so angry that they began to agitate for a war of revenge with Japan. Instead, President Roosevelt sent the Great White Fleet on a cruise to show Japan America's new battleships. This blustering public relations stunt turned out, in fact, to foster amity rather than hostility. Japanese and Americans who encountered one another got on well, and Japan and America remained wary friends.

Durham White Stevens' own role in the South Manchuria Railway fiasco remains unclear. The Japanese may have foisted him off on Korea because the railroad deal was so obviously to America's benefit and Japan's detriment. On the other hand, Stevens may have won their undying loyalty by convincing the Japanese that they could renege on the tentative treaty without touching off a war. Stevens' career in Korea also benefited from the fact that he was an American. Apart from the missionaries, highly moral people who actually appeared to love Koreans and treated them with respect – which the Koreans reciprocated – other Americans had arrived to install telegraphs, telephones and trolley cars in Seoul, and these harmless and constructive innovations were cheerfully accepted.

While Stevens was making his transition between working for the Japanese and supposedly working for the Korean government of King Kojong, and after the Russo-Japanese War had broken out, the secret Taft-Katsura agreement was signed on 29 July 1904 between William Howard Taft, a justice of the Supreme Court and later President of the United States, and Taro Katsura, later prime minister of Japan under Emperor Meiji. Japan agreed to accept the US presence in Hawaii, where there were a large number of Japanese settlers and where a plebiscite might have handed the Hawaiian Islands to the Japanese Empire.

Nobody appears to have consulted the Hawaiians, who ducked one takeover bid in 1893 because President Grover Cleveland knew it was unfair and refused to approve it, only to lose their independence in 1898, during the Spanish-American War. The Japanese also agreed to accept the US presence in the Philippines, where a protracted and very dirty war was going on between US troops and Filipino resistance fighters who had never accepted the American takeover after the Spanish-American war as being permanent. In return for uncontested ownership of Hawaii and the Philippines, the US agreed to quietly nullify the Chemulpo Treaty of 1882 that had bound the United States to protect Korea from foreign domination, and to give Japan a free hand in Korea.

> ...In regard to the Korean Question, Count Katsura observed that Korea being the direct cause of our war with Russia, it is a matter of absolute importance to Japan that a complete solution of the peninsula question should be made as a logical consequence of the war. If left to herself after the war, Korea will certainly draw back to her habit of improvidently entering into any agreements or treaties with other powers, thus resuscitating the same international complications as existed before the war.
>
> In view of the foregoing circumstances, Japan feels absolutely constrained to take some definite step with a view to precluding the possibility of Korea falling into her former condition and of placing us again under the necessity of entering upon another foreign war.

Theodore Roosevelt was very much of the same opinion. In 1905, While helping to negotiate the peace treaty that ended the Russo-Japanese War and winning the Nobel Peace Prize for it, at the same time – to console Japan for getting less than they felt they deserved – he also approved the top-secret Taft-Katsura Agreement. Japan was to have a free hand in Korea and the United States was to have a free hand in the Philippines.[6]

William Howard Taft, once US Commissioner to the Philippines and Roosevelt's successor in the White House, was a prisoner of policy – and also, of the belief that the Japanese with their frantic emulation of the West were the only hope for good government in Asia. His administration of the Philippines had become mired in a war of ambush and massacre, where US Army firing squads cut down 20,000 Filipino prisoners-of-war, some of them young female warriors, even 10-year-old boys. The death toll from battle was said to be 200,000 – and from disease, as many as two million.

'It's peaceful on Luzon now,' an American officer observed the year of the Taft-Katsura Treaty. 'The people are all dead.'

Taft is said to have concurred with the justice of Count Katsura's observation, but the treaty itself remained secret as far as Americans were concerned until 1922 – by which time nobody cared. The Japanese however, knew all about the treaty. In 1907, the year before Stevens was assassinated in San Francisco, a Japanese publicist named Kinosuke Adache told the *New York Times*:

> We shall be frank about it. We shall say that we are carrying things with a high hand in Korea. We have gone into the back yard of our neighbor and are telling him to kindly move on simply because we need his home. We are doing just as the Americans have done with the Indians, the rightful owners of America; just as the British have done with the Hindus; just as the Russians have done with the Tatars; as Germany did in South [West] Africa, and France in Cochin China. Nippon has joined the house of the great powers. She has become civilized.

Durham White Stevens remains one of history's enigmas. He obviously wasn't serving Korea, but whether he was representing the US or Japan or both at the same time when he influenced the agreement that ended Korean sovereignty is not clear. Elihu Root, America's Secretary of War, was one of the pallbearers at White's funeral. Most Americans forgot about him after his sisters in Asbury Park received their condolences and the Japanese pension. But in the curious half-life of Hollywood, he returned in the person of the sinister Dr. Lorenz in *Across the Pacific*, with Humphrey Bogart, Mary Astor and Sen Yung. Lorenz, played by Sydney Greenstreet, holds a chair in sociology in 'the Philippines', a stand-in for Korea since in 1942 all Americans were aware of the Philippines: Few Americans knew anything about Korea.

The film, directed by John Huston, was originally pegged on Japanese plans for an attack of Pearl Harbor – such an obvious target that Huston and his writers seized on it even though the film was started several months *before* the actually attack on 7 December 1941. Once fiction became fact, the cinematic Japanese target was switched to the Panama Canal. Professor Lorenz's first comments on the Japanese are pure condescension: 'Japanese make wonderful servants ... wonderful little people, wonderful. Completely misunderstood. To know them, that is, to really know them is to feel a really deep affection for them.' Bogart saves him from an assassination by a 'Filipino' (read here Korean) patriot who for some reason wants him dead. The patriot gunman is deftly despatched by the Japanese ship's crew in a New York City alley and Lorenz is gradually revealed as a full-fledged traitor more despicable than the Japanese he serves because they at least have the class to get killed by Bogart. Lorenz attempts *hara kiri* and can't bring himself to do it.

Mention of the Philippines conjures up Charles Arthur Conant, an American who advised the Philippines very much as Durham White Stevens advised Japan, and later Korea, at about the same time. Born in 1861 of old Puritan stock – one of his ancestors had served as acting government of Massachusetts Bay Colony in 1632 – Conant, a journalist and banker, was selected by Secretary of War Elihu Root and appointed by President William McKinley to investigate and reform the currency system of the Philippines. Conant did so to such effect that the new silver pesos were called 'Conants' and his vignette appeared on the paper money. He also served on the Board of Directors of the Manila Railway. In 1911, Conant was criticized by the Washington *Evening Post* for having written articles in 1896 explaining the economic improvements the Spanish government had carried out in Cuba – the scene of a Cuban insurrection against Spain which led, two years later, to the Spanish-American War and the annexation of the Philippines. Conant indignantly refuted the charge that there was anything suspect or shady about a loyal American taking money from a foreign government.

'...the late Durham W. Stevens, who was killed on his return from Korea, was regularly employed by the Government of Japan, and was very active in presenting the views of Japan on the tariff and other matters pending in this country, without impairing in any degree the respect in which he was held by all who knew him,' Conant wrote of Stevens in 1911.

The film makers may have been right after all. On the other hand, it's always possible that Durham Stevens was not serving Japan alone in his dealings with Korea.

4

MURDER MOST FOOLISH?

Ahn Jong Gun was a man on a mission. A handsome young man with regular features, a plausible moustache and a dapper grey Western suit, he could have easily passed for a Japanese businessman as he walked through the crowds at the Russian-controlled railroad station in Harbin, Manchuria, a nominal part of China under Russian control. He kept one hand tucked in his sleeve and wrapped in a white cloth.

Earlier, he had severed the tip of one of his own fingers – in Japanese and Korean culture the ultimate pledge, other than suicide, of loyalty to a cause or a gang. Suicide was the next step.

Actually, Ahn Jong Gun was one of four men on a mission that morning of 26 October 1909. A guide who kept out of sight showed him the way through the confusing Chinese streets of Harbin to the railroad station. Two other Korean patriots had also volunteered to take part in Ahn Jong Gun's personal attempt to avenge Korea. But at the last minute the Korean-born innkeeper who had sheltered them overnight had locked the two young men in their room and wouldn't let them out. Perhaps the old man sensed that something lethal was about to take place. Whether the kindly old innkeeper wanted to protect the two young men or himself, he effectively scrubbed their part in what was to follow.

Russian troops had occupied Manchuria at the end of the Russo-Japanese War four years before under an agreement that the Japanese felt was a betrayal engineered by Theodore Roosevelt, the same fair-weather friend who had secretly handed Korea to Japan on a silver platter with the Taft-Katsura Agreement in return for a free hand in the restive Philippines. At the time of the Portsmouth Treaty, Japanese newspapers had suggested the diplomats who represented Japan at the negotiations might like to commit suicide, and Japanese mobs went on the rampage.

The Russian troops in Manchuria were lined up for an official reception of Hirobumi Ito, former prime minister of Japan and former resident-general of Korea under the Japanese protectorate. Ito had come to Manchuria to resolve some sort of border dispute with the Russians.

As the chubby five-foot-three Ito, in a snug derby and grey topcoat, nodded with satisfaction after inspecting the guard of honor, Ahn Jong Gun stepped out of the crowd and pulled his bandaged hand out of his other cuff. He stuck out a Browning automatic pistol. Ahn Jong Gun shot Ito three times from 6 feet away, twice in the chest and once in the belly. Swinging the pistol, Ahn shot four other Japanese, once each, without hitting a single Russian or Manchurian and without wasting a single bullet. Then he hauled a Korean flag out of his vest. Instead of running away he stood fearlessly on the railroad platform shouting '*Kara ure!*' – Korean victory!

'I've been shot, I think three times,' Ito gagged. 'Who did it? Did they get Mori?' Then his chubby face turned blue-green and he lost the power of speech.

Those Japanese who hadn't been hit picked him up and carried him back into the railroad car. Mori, his assistant, had also been hit, in the right lung, but he later pulled through. Ito was unconscious within a few seconds and lived for another twenty minutes. None of the other Japanese died, but all four were seriously injured.[1]

Ahn was interrogated by the Russian authorities who were deeply embarrassed by their failure to protect the man sometimes known as the Bismarck of Japan. 'The Minister (Russian finance minister, Kokovsoff) points out that no blame is to be attached to the railroad police, who had been specially requested to admit all Japanese to the station,' the *New York Times* said. 'The murderer stood with other foreigners until Ito and Kokovsoff approached each other, when he rushed through the crowd and forced his way a few feet in front of the Prince. He then discharged an automatic pistol seven times. He made no attempt to escape, and with three others was arrested and delivered to the Japanese authorities for trial, the Koreans coming under the jurisdiction of the Japanese courts.'

Under his initial Russian interrogation, Ahn had explained that his killing of Hirobumi Ito showed the world that there was a Korean resistance. 'He is a great enemy of our country. Ito Hirobumi invaded our country and killed many of our country's citizens. Ito said this was for the peace of Asia but on the other hand he actually ruined it.'

Once under Japanese jurisdiction, Ahn Jong Gun was subjected to routine questioning: which Koreans sources say consisted of being put on a rack upside down and beaten so as to cause substantial bleeding but no broken bones. As he described his motivation, without fear or repentance, he actually won a considerable measure of respect from the Japanese, whose own culture tended to glorify assassins who throw away their lives out of loyalty to a country or a clan. The 32-year-old Korean described his resentment over the eclipse of Korean culture under Japanese influence and his intense anger at the loss of Korean autonomy through the actions of Hirobumi Ito. He had dreamed of revitalizing his country through education. As a convert to Catholicism he had asked the advice of his priest about founding a school to combine Western and Asian learning, and had been told that this was a wonderful idea. Ahn began to collect money to build his school and offer both Western and traditional Korean knowledge to peasant children – who were more than 90 per cent illiterate at this time. Unfortunately, the priest heard from the Bishop, a European, who felt that an independent school might take away some of his own influence over Korean Catholics. Ahn was forced to drop his plans to restore the country through Western and traditional education. He then fell back on the traditional Asian method to engender political change. At his trial, the three Japanese judges nodded with understanding as Ahn explained his motivation. 'I am not a sinner, I only did this deed for our country... I was caught killing my enemy doing my mission and I don't have anything else to say.'

The judges rose and bowed to show their deep respect for his courage and idealism. Then they passed the death sentence.

Ahn was allowed extended visits from his weeping parents and from his wife, his brothers and sisters before he was executed. Oddly enough, the court was extremely lenient with the three conspirators who hadn't actually pulled a trigger in the Ito assassination. The guide who took Ahn through the unfamiliar streets of Harbin got off with three years in prison and the two young men who were locked up by the innkeeper got a year and a half each. Considering that the US had hanged John Wilkes Booth's landlady after Abraham Lincoln's assassination, the Japanese judicial system seemed positively benign. The Japanese allowed Ahn's mother to make traditional clothing for his execution. His last words were memorable: 'When I die put my corpse in a place in Harbin because I don't want to see the Japanese attack Korea.' And he shouted 'Korean Victory' just before he was shot.

Ito's assassination served as the perfect pretext to abolish the Japanese protectorate over Korea and annex Korea directly – the very move that Ito himself had argued against until just before his death.

Hirobumi Ito was a sort of metaphor for the dynamic explosion of Japanese modernization and its expansion into Korea and Taiwan. Born Hirobumi Hayashi, he was a peasant child whose father scratched a living out of three acres of rocky hillside in northern Honshu, Japan's largest and central island. Hirobumi was born in 1841. He was twelve when the Americans arrived with their 'black ships.' As a teenager he was conscripted into the *samurai* armies of the Chosu Clan, which dominated his part of Japan. Foreign policy toward the Japanese had resolved itself into a predictable pattern: some foreign group, usually English, would forget they were still in a sovereign country and commit some breach of etiquette. *Samurai* warriors loyal to one of the clans would then kill or mutilate the foreigners. The naval ships of whatever European nations were in the area would then bombard the fort the *samurai* were presumed to have come from. The bombardments killed a number of Japanese and humiliated the survivors, who didn't have large enough cannon to retaliate.

Hirobumi Hayashi's first battle was a rescue mission after one of these bombardments. Carrying a bow and arrows in case his two-hundred-year old matchlock musket refused to discharge, he helped *samurai* and other warriors put out a fire started in this case by a French bombardment. The French had landed marines and left two Japanese stripped and displayed in an iron cage like monkeys. Things like this were part of his Hayashi's formative experience.

Hayashi impressed a *samurai* family and was adopted under the name of Hirobumi Ito. He distinguished himself in opposing foreigners and foreign sympathizers in the days when the Japanese were still worried about being turned into a European colony like the Philippines. Ito was a suspect in at least one murder. In one exploit, he fled after an attack on a rival group and ducked into a house where he asked the housemaid to hide him. She tucked him into the toilet and calmly concealed his whereabouts by sitting on it. After climbing out, he assuaged her embarrassment by asking her to marry him. She did, and finished her life as Princess Ito with an estate and servants of her own.

In another exploit, Ito and some friends set fire to the British legation. He followed up on this outrage by putting on Western sailor clothing and somehow escaping to England. Under the sponsorship of the Prince of Chosu he completed an education in which he became fluent in English, French, and German. Ito also impressed English observers with his intense thirst for claret and his determined and sometimes successful pursuit of white women.

'What do you think we need to change in Japan?' the Prince of Chosu asked when Hirobumi Ito returned to Japan.

'Everything,' Ito replied.

Hirobumi Ito had returned from England with his *samurai* friend Karuo Inoue just in time to try to head off the next big Western assault on Japanese sovereignty and self-respect. His own Chosu clan had been firing warning shots at European and American ships in the Shimonseki Straits between Honshu and Kyushu, hoping to close the straits to foreign ships and demonstrate Chosu primacy. The firing had approval from the Tokugawa shogun and from Komei, the emperor, who hated the foreigners and wanted them out of Japan. The Shimonoseki Straits separate Honshu, home of the Chosu clan, from Kyushu, the hothouse of Japanese culture and home of the Satsuma clan, Chosu's greatest rival for influence with the Shogun and the Emperor.

The foreigners, and the British in particular, wanted the firing stopped. A year before, on 16 July, the USS *Wyoming*, a screw sloop –a sailing ship with a propeller – had shot it out with two smaller Japanese warships in the Shimonoseki Straits, bursting one American-made Japanese ship's boiler with an 11-inch projectile and scalding a large number of the Japanese crew to death. Five Americans also died and eleven were wounded. Both Japanese ships were sunk. The Japanese negotiators, realizing that they were completely out-gunned, were stalling for time and trying to save face when Ito arrived to help them temporise.

Unfortunately for everyone involved, time ran out and no face was saved. On 5 September 1864, seventeen Western steam warships – nine British, three French, four Dutch, and one American – cruised past the Chosu forts at the Shimonoseki Straits blasting away with every gun on their port sides. The Japanese tried to shoot back with their archaic undersized cannons until they were overwhelmed by the sheer firepower of the aggressors. The Japanese were so badly battered that the Western fleet was actually able to land sailors and marines and finish smashing the Chosu forts with axes and crowbars. The Americans, leerily stepping around the dead Japanese and wondering if they had done the right thing, helped the Japanese survivors put out some of the fires. The Westerners then demanded that the Japanese pay $3,000,000 to defray the cost of the bombardment. They also imposed 'extraterritoriality' on Japan – Americans accused of defrauding Japanese merchants or assaulting Japanese girls could not be tried in Japanese courts. Special American courts would be convened for the purpose of generally acquitting the American offenders.

Suppressing a volcanic inner rage, the Japanese smiled, paid the $3,000,000 in six installments, and began working frantically to build up a modern army and navy. The Chosu clan founded a modern Japanese army of mixed peasant conscripts and *samurai* warriors, advised first by the French and, after the Franco-Prussian War, by Klemens Jacob Meckel. The Satsuma clan hired British advisors to build a modern Japanese fleet, to be manned by their own fisherman and the latest generation of pirates.

Through a long career as a Japanese government official, Hirobumi Ito remained committed to hostility to any influence of Western powers over Japanese or other Asians – while at the same time urging the use of Western technology to defend Japan. His dislike of European dominance, which started in his teens, was reinforced by the Shimonoseki Straits incident that took place when he was in his early 20s.

Japan and Korea were still civil if not exactly friendly in 1864, and word of what had happened at Shimonoseki reached Korea in a matter of weeks. Two years later, the Koreans received a home demonstration in their own 'hermit kingdom' after acting with forbearance and dignity until push came to shove.

Early in the year 1866, the American merchant ship *Surprise* was wrecked off the coast of Korea. The Koreans – now confirmed in their absolute isolationism by what they'd seen the Westerners doing to China and to Japan – rounded up the shipwrecked Americans, fed them, told them firmly never to come back to Korea, and sent them to the Chinese Treaty Ports mounted on shaggy little Asian ponies, alive and unmolested.

A few months later, another American merchant ship, the *General Sherman*, steamed up the Taedong River, then at high tide, and demanded to trade with Korea – despite signs posted along the river in Chinese telling them to go away. The *General Sherman*, designed as a warship during the US Civil War, was studded with cannon and manned by a crew of four Americans including the owner, W. B. Preston, and by an Englishman, thirteen Chinese and three Malays.

The Korean dignitaries came on board to tell the Americans to leave. A Korean official was captured at gunpoint. At this point, the tide receded and the ship was stuck in the mud of the Taedong River. Fighting broke out and for the next four days the terrified crew of the *General Sherman* with its modern cannon stood off the Koreans who attempted to attack with archaic cannons and bows and arrows. Thousands of spectators lined the Korean shores to cheer for their side, and a shell from the American ship struck the crowd, killing thirteen Korean civilians and wounded many others. The Koreans tried to improve a 'tortoise boat' by covering a scow with cowhides and shields, but the *General Sherman*'s guns sank her. Finally, the Koreans sent rafts loaded with burning wood and hay down the Taedong and the *General Sherman* caught fire.

The American survivors jumped off the blazing ship and swam for shore. The Koreans massacred them all. One missionary handed a Korean warrior his Bible and told him that this would save him. The puzzled Korean wrapped the Bible up to keep it safe and clean. Then he cut off the American's head. The Koreans recovered their hostage from the ship, and they purposefully forgot the whole incident.

In October of 1866, a few months after the *General Sherman* had disappeared up the Taedong, a French squadron arrived off Chemulpo (modern Inchon) and attacked Kang-wha Island with 160 marines and sailors. The Koreans, aroused to the Western menace by the *General Sherman*, met the French force with 5,000 warriors armed with spears, swords, and bows and arrows. These were the famous 'tiger hunters,' each man pledged to face a tiger in single combat. The French lost half their men the first day and fled back to their ships. Korea remained independent.

In 1871, US Navy Commander John Febiger arrived in Korea and tried to find out what had happened to the *General Sherman*. Angry at the American intrusion, the Koreans first stalled and then fired on the American ship. The Americans came back with reinforcements, blasted Korea's stone forts at Kang-Wha Island as the Western fleet had blasted Shimonoseki, and then landed 105 US Marines and 645 armed sailors for a showdown on land. The Marines had a howitzer and seven-shot Spencer repeating rifles. The Koreans had matchlock muskets, swords, bows and arrows and the trident spears of the 'tiger hunters.'

'The fighting inside the fort was desperate,' Rear Admiral John Rodgers wrote in his official report. 'The resolution of the Coreans [sic] was unyielding; they apparently expected no quarter, and probably would have given none. They fought to the death, and only when the last man fell did the conflict cease... Two hundred and forty-three dead Coreans were counted in the works. Few prisoners were taken, not above 20, and some of these were wounded.'

The United States lost eleven men. The Korean casualties numbered about 350. Korea, like Japan, had now learned to respect the US as they respected the Europeans. The Japanese took note. Hirobumi Ito continued to study the European nations with an eye toward protecting the Japanese from further encroachment by emulation rather than isolation.

Hirobumi Ito was the father of Japan's constitution. Familiar with Europe by 1882, he dismissed Britain, France, and the United States as possible models for Japan. Ito concentrated on Prussia, the central state which had re-unified Germany, and on Austria-Hungary, an absolute monarchy he studied and then discounted as too fusty and reactionary. The Japanese understood the Prussians best of all, perhaps because the Prussians were still serious about swordsmanship. Students at Heidelberg and other universities fought duels with the express idea of testing one another's courage, and scarifying one another's faces to prove it. The Japanese admired that custom. The Prussian constitution also had two features that Ito liked: the ruling monarch appointed the prime minister, and the ruling monarchy appointed the war minister. Male citizens got to vote for the Diet, a legislature with some – but not all – of the powers the United States Congress or British Parliament. But the Prussian throne retained a greater measure of power than in a republic or many constitutional monarchies.

Hirobumi Ito also invented State Shinto. Most Japanese of his time were Buddhists and Shinto at the same time, and many were attracted to Christianity. Ito was not himself a religious person – he once said he had only prayed on three occasions – but in devising State Shinto he formulated a belief that had huge political implications. Traditional Shinto is a nature religion with overtones of spiritualism, very similar to beliefs in Korea and in China, and among some Native American tribes. In State Shinto, life after death is taken for granted – many Japanese and Koreans, even today, can 'see' ghosts and accept them as a part of the landscape. Magazines regularly offer 'ghost maps' of all the best sightings. Ito took this evidence and ran with it. In State Shinto, the soul lives on, but all rewards and punishments take place on earth, not in the afterlife. Good and evil are repaid only on Earth, while the dead continue to exist in the same state whether they were saints or sinners. Westerners find this difficult to accept, but most Japanese have no fear of death, and regard people who do fear death as degenerate weaklings. Eliminating fear of punishment in the afterlife turned a naturally courageous people into an utterly remorseless one. State Shinto – an invention of the late 19th century, rather than of traditional Japan – facilitated a

Japanese tendency to obey blindly and to serve the interests of the state without too much consideration of the individual conscience.

Ito's big moment in terms of Korean history came in the autumn of 1905, shortly after the conclusion of the Russo-Japanese War. The Japanese had been traumatized by 100,000 dead in the war with Russia, even as the rest of the world was shaken by the spectacle of an Asian power defeating Europeans with home-built battleships. Ito arrived in Seoul to make sure that Korea, which the Japanese had expected as a prize of the war, did not fall into the hands of Russia or China during the disappointing peace that followed.

Ito sought an interview with the King of Korea, Kojong, while Japanese soldiers conducted drills and artillery practice outside the city walls. The King refused to see him so Ito pushed his way past the retainers and politely demanded that the King sign a treaty granting the Japanese a protectorate over Korea. King Kojong was terrified but brave enough to refuse to sign.

'Please go away – I have a sore throat,' the king said.

Ito then went looking for Han Kyu Sul, the King's prime minister. The secretary of the Japanese legation had already located Han and pushed the prime minister into a closet and was holding him at pistol point.

Ito told Han Kyu Sul to sign the treaty on behalf of the King. Han Kyu Sul spat at him and refused to sign, even with a gun pointed at his head. Ito nodded brusquely and smiled with respect for the man's courage. He left him covered in the closet and found a group of older courtiers who were more easily frightened. By the next morning, after a night of shouting, screaming, and waving *samurai* swords, Ito and his aides had convinced five of the terrified old scholars that they would be massacred if they failed to sign the treaty that made Korea a Japanese protectorate. Shaken as they were, the old men insisted on adding a clause that Korean independence would be returned as soon as the country was financially and politically able to run its own affairs. The other Koreans still held out despite plausible threats of death, and Han was still being sequestered in the closet with a gun trained on him, but the Japanese found the Korean royal seal and put it on the treaty. Korea was now a Japanese protectorate.[2]

Prince Min Young Whan, King Kojong's military advisor, committed suicide. 'A bamboo shoot grew up through the floor of the room in which he died, and all during the generation of Japanese rule of Korea, a favorite subject of Korean art was a spray of bamboo leaves – a memorial which the Japanese never found an effective means to prevent,' wrote the American author Robert Tarbell Oliver.

Back at Japanese headquarters, Hirobumi Ito was enjoying *sake, sushi*, and calligraphic Chinese poetry with Yi Wan Yong, the Korean prime minister who had agreed to replace the stubbornly courageous Han, and with General Masatake Terauchi, Ito's military commander. Their poems in Chinese characters – their common language – praised 'sweet spring rain,' 'new beginnings,' and 'two peoples under one roof.'

King Kojong, however, shortly repudiated the treaty: 'I declare that the so-called treaty of protectorate recently concluded between Korea and Japan was extorted at the point of the sword and under duress and is therefore null and void,' King Kojong said in a telegram to the US State Department. 'I never consented to it and I never will.' The State Department diplomatically refused to receive the telegram.

King Kojong then sent three emissaries to the Second Hague Peace Conference in 1907 to urge the world to restore Korean independence in the face of Japanese determination and American indifference. The Korean envoys were Yi Chun, prosecutor of the Korean Supreme Court and Yi San Sol, a former cabinet officer, both in Western suits and with Western haircuts. Homer Hulbert, an American missionary trusted by the king, was the third envoy.

The Hague Peace Conference refused to admit the envoys, and Yi Chun committed suicide in protest. A dozen other scholar-aristocrats committed suicide as well – in noble protest against oppression, in despair that their world had ended, and perhaps in shame for their own neglect of the common people of Korea, a neglect which had left the country a patspaw among the rival powers of China, Russia, and Japan.

Menaced by this passive resistance despite the rebuffs at the US State Department and at The Hague, the Japanese decided to squash any possibility of active resistance. A faction of the Korean cabinet, headed by Song Pyong Jun, who was pro-Japanese, told Kojong that it was time to abdicate. The weary king resisted a few days, then gave in, and his timid, supposedly mentally handicapped son Sojong became king of Korea. Song Pyong Jun was placed in charge of the bureau that controlled the Korean National Police – with a Japanese in control of the actual police force.

Hirobumi Ito declared that the Korean army was no longer necessary, and in August of 1907 the Japanese put 9,000 Korean soldiers they themselves had trained out of work. The Japanese-trained commander of the First Infantry Guards, Pak Song Hwan, committed suicide in outrage and his loyal troops took up their rifles and shot their way out of Seoul, joined by many troops of the Second Guards Infantry Regiment, with the Japanese in hot pursuit. Those Korean soldiers who survived the running gun battle through the streets against Meiji's Japanese troops and German-trained officers joined peasants and bandits in the countryside and fought on for years. A few months after the escape, a force of 10,000 disbanded soldiers, students and peasants tried to recapture Seoul, and were not turned back by the Japanese until they were 8 miles from the capital. By 1908, the Japanese stated that 69,832 Koreans had taken up arms against Japan and 1,500 clashes had taken place. These figures explain the rage the Koreans in San Francisco felt against Durham White Stevens for pontificating about how well the Korean peasants loved the Japanese.

For Hirobumi Ito this violence was needless – and pointless. He knew that the Koreans had no chance of overwhelming the Japanese by armed rebellion, and in this he was right. When the fighting finally ended in 1912, after his own death and the death of the Emperor Meiji, the Japanese estimated that 141,815 Koreans had fought against Japan – this out of a population of about 20 million – and that 17,697 had been killed and 3,706 wounded. The fighting in Korea cost the Japanese 136 dead and 2,777 wounded.

Most Japanese were unrepentant about the violence in Korea, even though some Americans had begun to question why so much fighting was going on in a country where the Japanese were supposed to be loved and befriended.

'That country had become a nest of intrigue against us,' Baron Togoro Takahira, the Japanese minister in Washington, told the *New York Times* in March of 1908.

An impotent dynasty was totally unable to administer any sort of government; the rights and privileges of Japanese resident or doing business there were constantly violated; order was not kept; it was plain that the greatest danger to the peace of the world and the independence of Japan existed; the Emperor [*Kojong*] was incompetent to keep his own people or foreigners in order, and at any moment, foreign embroilments that must have ended with the conquest of Korea might break out. The events of last summer, after the dispatch by the Emperor of Korea of emissaries to the Hague Conference, will give you a full explanation of our assumption of the administration in the interest of civilization. You have done the same in the Philippines and, as I understand, you accept the [Monroe] doctrine that the countries to the south of the United States must maintain efficient governments, keep order, and observe their foreign obligations. In our place, you would have done precisely as we did. And, like us, you would then have been accused of harboring deep-seated ambitions, of planning for the domination of the earth.

The American response was double-edged: Theodore Roosevelt sent the US battleships of the Great White Fleet – a nominative warning if ever there was one – on a round-the-world cruise that stopped off at Japan to display some gun power, as Perry had in 1853. But in secret, he approved the top-secret Root-Takahitra Agreement which recognized Japanese ascendancy in Manchuria in return for Japanese acceptance of the Open Door policy of no new colonies in mainland China. Roosevelt warned Taft that a war to defend the Open Door Policy in China 'would require a fleet as good as that of England plus an army as good was that of Germany.'[3] Letting Japan control Korea and develop Manchuria while keeping an eye on China – still an uneasy Manchu Dynasty empire – was cheaper both in American money and in American lives.

Hirobumi Ito served as resident general of Korea for several years, in a Japanese building set down on top of what was once a Korean royal place, consoled by four Japanese geisha and Korean singers and dancers who came and went. Older Koreans were scandalised.

The Japanese also imposed extraterritoriality on Korea, just as the Americans had on Japan before the Japanese stirred themselves and defeated China in 1894 and Russia in 1905. Japanese accused of crimes by Koreans could only be tried before Japanese judges. The likelihood of guilty verdicts in Korea was what it had been when Americans were tried before Americans in Japan, before the extraterritorial courts were discontinued in 1899.

Ito spent much time seeking out Koreans who were willing to trade a measure of sovereignty for popular education and progress in Western technology. One of the Koreans he attempted to befriend was a reformer named Ahn Chang Ho, called Dosan as an honorific, who wanted Koreans to work for their own autonomy through industry and education. Ito met with Dosan in November of 1907, two years after the gunpoint protectorate treaty. After the customary pleasantries, Ito asked Dosan calmly about the speeches he had been making all over Korea advocating a national resurgence.

'I am trying to do what you did for Japan for the last 50 years,' the Korean patriot told Ito. Ito shook hands with him and said, 'The strength of Japan alone cannot defend us from Western attacks. Why don't we participate together in the operation of developing power of China and Korea for everlasting peace in the eastern world?' Dosan refused to agree with Ito on the best way to establish the peace of Asia.

Japanese made Japan prosper so Korea should be reformed by hands of Koreans. If Americans came over to your country for your Meiji Restoration, would you just have watched them? Moreover, the reform movement would not have been successful. Unfortunately, Japan lost generosity toward Korea and China. This is a tragedy not only for Japan but for all three countries. This will be a source for attracting the Western power and cause the attacks which you are fervently trying to stop. Koreans under Japanese oppression will seek assistance from Russia and America. Nations that do not want Japan to grow stronger will listen to Koreans' request. But I am afraid that Japan might be an enemy to stronger nations in the world and eastern countries. If you came to our country as a friendly guest, I would have visited you every day to have you serve as my master and teacher. However, since you came to our country to rule Korea, I neither wish to visit you nor to be friends with you.[4]

Many less scrupulous Koreans were less reluctant to work with Ito and a number of them began to take a role in the protectorate. The Japanese also began to recruit Koreans for the Korean National police, which throughout its history included 40 to 50 per cent of Koreans among its ranks.

Dosan moved to the United States where his first-born son, future Hollywood actor Philip Ahn, became the first official Korean-American by birth. Like his father, Philip Ahn worked for Korean independence by portraying the Japanese as villains – in Philip's case, in Hollywood war movies. Ito's world view – that all Asians were brothers who should unite against the avaricious and imperialistic whites – may not have played well with the patriotic faction in Korea, but the Japanese had an easy time convincing many other Asians, including some Koreans, that the Russians and the Americans were racist brutes. Jack London had noted in 1904 that the Korean common people he saw, humble villagers cheated by their own *yangban*, didn't fear the Japanese much and actually enjoyed doing business with them. London, who often described himself as a conscious racist, wrote of the Japanese troops in Korea:

I doubt if there be more peaceable, orderly soldiers in the world than the Japanese, Our own soldiers, long ere this, would have painted Seoul red with their skylarking and good-natured boisterousness, but the Japanese are not boisterous. They are deadly serious. None of the civilian population is afraid of them. The women are safe; the money is safe; the goods are safe. The Japanese established a reputation in 1894 for paying for whatever they took and are living up to that reputation. 'But if they were the Russians' – say the Koreans, and the European and American residents ominously shake their heads. I have yet to see one drunken Japanese soldier. Not one disorderly nor even boisterous one have I seen – and they are soldiers.[5]

Zealous in building Japan's reputation among the Europeans, and smoothing the way for a peaceful absorption of Korea, the Japanese from the Emperor Meiji down had ordered the Japanese soldiers to behave: 'He who affects to be a warrior and behaves like a beast will be despised,' Meiji said. Japanese soldiers who roughed up Koreans or stole from them were brought up short by their own officers. Russian prisoners sometimes had their excellent boots stolen – most Japanese soldiers of this era grew up wearing sandals or going barefoot. But once the Russians were rounded up, they received food, medical treatment, shelter, and even entertainment. The Russian General Stoessel was so impressed by Japanese chivalry that he gave the Japanese General Maresuke Nogi his own horse as a token of esteem. The Russian officers in the Russo-Japanese War, on the other hand, were so eager to get out of Port Arthur after the armistice that they left the soldiers' wives and children on the railroad platform as they made their escape with courtesans imported from all over Europe.

'This is incredible,' a Japanese officer gasped. 'They treat their women worse than we treat ours.' The Japanese put the Russian women and children on the next train, unmolested and fed, and took the thoroughbred back to Tokyo where he became a treasured mascot.

A year after the defeat of the odious Russians in 1905, the Americans gave Ito a chance to cite the need for Asian brotherhood. When the San Francisco earthquake of 1906 devastated the West Coast's greatest seaport, former Mayor James Duval Phelan led some of the town fathers in an attempt to eliminate Chinatown and force the Chinese to remove to Hunter's Point instead of concentrating in the heart of the city. Phelan's bid failed because some of his colleagues were the landlords of profitable Chinese brothels. Thwarted, Phelan recommended that all Chinese, Japanese, and Korean children – who had previously attended public schools near their homes – be segregated in one Asians-only school. The Asians, and the Japanese in particular, were indignant. The order was rescinded, mostly due to protests from Japan, but Phelan was unrepentant.[6] Himself the son of Irish immigrants James Phelan Duval – the Duval appears to have been appropriated in a reach for some Gallic elegance – an honest man when it came to administering relief for the earthquake victims so long as they were white, was also honest about his feelings about the Japanese. Phelan told the Boston Herald in an article published on 16 June 1907:

> The Japanese question with us today is not a race question, but a labor question. The Chinese question has been solved by the restriction of these coolies and the Chinese now are never molested... As soon as Japanese coolies are kept out of the country, there will be no danger of irritating these sensitive and aggressive people. They must be excluded because they are non-assimilable; they are a permanently foreign element; they do not bring up families; they do not support churches, schools, or theatres; in time of trial they will not fight for Uncle Sam, but betray him to the enemy.
>
> They now occupy valleys in California by lease or purchase of land to the exclusion of not only whites but Chinese, and if this silent invasion is permitted by the federal government, they would, at the rate that they are coming, a thousand a month, soon convert the fairest state in the union into a Japanese colony. If they are naturalized, they will outvote us.
>
> But California is a white man's country, and the two races cannot live side by side in peace, and inasmuch as we discovered the country first and occupied it, we propose to hold it against either a peaceful or a warlike invasion.[7]

Smoothing ruffled feathers in Japan, Theodore Roosevelt ended school segregation in San Francisco – but also promulgated the 'Gentleman's Agreement.' America would not forbid Japanese immigration if the Japanese stopped sending immigrants who intended to become permanent residents. The drastic reduction from a flow of a thousand Japanese a month to about 300 a year temporarily soothed white working-class fear of 'cheap Oriental labor' but it put pressure on nations closer to Japan: a few years after the Gentleman's Agreement, about 10 per cent of Korea's population was Japanese. Contact with kindly missionaries rather than the drunken sailors and California politicians the Japanese knew best led to diametrically opposed views of America: the Koreans saw most Americans as decent people, while those Japanese who had never visited America, and some who had, saw most Americans as ignorant racist bullies. Japan felt menaced by Russia and America. Korea felt menaced by Russia and Japan.

Ito resigned as resident-general of Korea in June of 1909, unable to convey to the Koreans the threat he saw after the sail-by shootings and Japanese in iron cages he had seen as a young *bushi*, or soldier, and aspiring *samurai*.

The Japanese believed they had found a friend in Bismarck's Germany, but when the insecure, posturing Wilhelm II pushed Bismarck aside in 1890, the friendship soured. In 1897, after the murder of some German Catholic missionaries in China, Wilhelm began to talk about the perceived threat that Asians, led by Japan, would soon dominate the entire Eurasian Continent: 'The Yellow Peril ... the greatest peril menacing Christendom and European civilization...' The Kaiser said in 1905, 'If the Russians go on giving ground, the yellow race would, in twenty years' time, be in Moscow and Posen.'[8] Jack London agreed with him, even though Jack and his wife Charmian habitually relied on their Korean houseboy Yung-yi Man and then their Japanese houseboy Paul Nagata to keep their dissolute lives on track.

Ito also knew England, France, and Germany inside out and realized that every white man wasn't a Christian missionary or a short-term hired engineer. King Kojong's attempt to repudiate the protectorate at the Second Hague Conference and the fighting that followed in Korea had put Ito into an impossible situation as far as his fellow Japanese were concerned. He had argued with them that the Koreans could be received not as slaves or serfs but as junior partners in a Japanese attempt to fortify northern Asia against the sort of European colonialism he had feared and hated since he was a teenager. The fighting had alienated the Koreans from Japan and had dissuaded the Japanese from trying to treat the Koreans as equals or near-equals. The text of Ito's last speech, on 22 October 1909, advocated cooperation between the Japanese, the Koreans, the Chinese and the Russians to develop the vast resources of Manchuria, on Korea's northern frontier, to foster prosperity and peace. He also said that he'd rather be assassinated than die of old age – the dream of many a *samurai*. Ito's assassination at the age of 69 shocked the Japanese and put the final seal of approval on plans to annex Korea that had been pending before his death. For good measure, Ito's Korean friend Yi Won Yong was stabbed by a young Korean that December and seriously wounded, relieving the Japanese of the necessity of removing Korea's pro-Japanese prime minister. The third man at the *sake* and *sushi* party, General Masatake Terauchi, arrived to take over Korea as a military governor-general, not as a political advisor. 'It was as though a chill had passed over the city,' one Korean wrote. The chill would last for 35 years. Korea was now annexed.

The terrifying Terauchi, 10 years younger than Ito, whom he saw as a revered older brother, paraphrased the Old Testament Book of Kings in a tacit comparison between his friend Ito as the tolerant King Solomon and himself as the harsh King Rehoboam: 'I shall scourge you with scorpions.' He did. The Righteous Army of Korean soldiers and peasants was pulverized. About a dozen Korean courtiers committed suicide in despair. Ahn Chung Ho, called Dosan, left for China in voluntary exile. Thousands of other Koreans joined him. With Hirobumi Ito murdered and Yi Won Yong severely wounded, the vengeful samurai General Terauchi was in no mood for *sake* and *sushi,* let alone Chinese poetry.

Born into the lowest level of *samurai* in the Chosu clan, Terauchi was elevated when a higher-ranking *samurai* who had no son of his own adopted him, just as Ito himself had been elevated one class, from peasant to *samurai*, before he started to battle his own way to the top. Terauchi had lost his right hand in Japanese feudal wars against Takamori Saigo in 1877, and later served as a brigade commander in the Sino- Japanese War of 1894. People who met him described Terauchi as a metaphor for late Meiji Japan, half European and half Asian. 'Short but powerfully built, his massive head set tightly on broad shoulders, the lower half of his face seemed European, the determined line of his mouth and jaw accentuated by an iron gray moustache and close-cropped goatee, but in the upper part of his face, small slit-like eyes and diagonal eyebrows stood out against a broad, bald forehead,' James William Morley wrote. This was a man who understood the power of intimidation. But he also understood the power of titles and honorifics. Terauchi held out the olive branch to those upper-class Koreans not dead or fled. He offered 75 senior Korean courtiers and diplomats cognomens of Japanese nobility, in ranks ranging from baron to marquis – all titles imported from Europe and often given to lower-class Japanese who had earned them. Eight Korean traditionalists stood on their own honor and refused the Japanese titles. The other 67 tripped over themselves accepting them – in part because Japanese titles were hereditary and didn't require a *yangban* examination for their sons.

Terauchi then eliminated some of the worst detritus of the *yangban* era Jack London has so despised. He had Japanese and Korean scholars conduct a shared research program and gave outright grants of farmland to many Korean peasants who could show they had once had title to them. Some of the land where the titles weren't clear were bought up by Japanese investors, which led cynical Koreans to see the whole program as a self-serving Japanese land-grab. But those Koreans who owned their own farms after a hiatus of generations were pleased and grateful. Terauchi also gave out cash awards to Koreans for traditional behaviour: 9,811 awards to Confucian scholars alone, with others to such categories as 'virtuous wives' and 'filial sons.' Cynical Koreans asked one another how Korea ever produced virtuous wives or filial sons without the help of the Japanese...

Kim Chang-an, the Korean who had killed the mysterious Tsuchida to avenge Queen Min, had quietly returned to Korea in 1905 and was running a school in the western part of Korea to teach young Koreans patriotic values and Western technology. The Japanese picked him up in a round-up of suspects shortly after the annexation of Korea and hung him upside down and beat him to find out if he had played any role in Hirobumi Ito's assassination. They appear to have confused Ahn Chang Ho, the philosopher known as Dosan, with Ahn Jong Gun, the assassin at the Harbin railroad station. Kim didn't confess – possibly because he wasn't guilty and didn't know who was – but the night-long beating made an impression on him all the same. 'If they can stay awake all night beating me to make their country strong, I can stay awake all night to make *our* country strong.'

Kim wasn't charged with Ito's murder due to a complete lack of evidence, but as an escaped convict he was sent back to the prison at Chemulpo, where he worked as a janitor. Disgusted with the fact that so many of his own *yangban* class had denied 90 per cent of Koreans an education, or even basic literacy, Kim was also appalled that so many educated Koreans collaborated with the Japanese. Durham White Stevens had told the truth standing on its head in San Francisco: many upper-class Koreans actually admired the Japanese skills of organization, or at least feared any social disruption that threatened their own role as a privileged elite; most Korean peasants held the Japanese in absolute dread. To Korean peasants the Japanese were goblin monsters – they looked something like Koreans, acted like the worst of Westerners, and spoke a language no one could understand. They were a threat to everything Koreans were accustomed to. They were weird. Kim agreed with the peasants. He discarded his *yangban* name and heritage and took the name 'Ku Kim,' a name suitable to a peasant rather than a scholar-landowner. He would soon also have an honorific name – 'The Assassin.'

The assassination of Hirobumi Ito also turned the Americans around. Ito had been extremely popular in the US and had presented Japan's progressive policies to appreciative audiences. He was a lot of fun at parties, singing poems he had composed on the spur of the moment, and giving the Princeton Tiger cheer as appropriate. Americans who had been moved to sympathy by Korean eloquence after Durham White Stevens' assassination began to ask how many more cute people would have to be murdered to appease the hurt feelings of glum people who had shown they couldn't run a government.[9]

Terauchi was also considered cute, at least in Japan, especially after he came prime minister – his bald head and mischievous eyes reminded Japanese of the Billiken doll, invented in the United States in 1908 by Florence Pretz in St Louis, Missouri, and popular in Japan ever after. The resemblance, while accidental, was rather remarkable. Terauchi's legacy in Korea was mixed – vast improvements in the Korean school system, some improvements of land tenure; an obvious desire to turn Korea into the land-locked fifth island of Japan left most Koreans more prosperous than they had been under the disintegrating Yi Dynasty, but also suspicious of Japanese cultural arrogance. Japanese skeptics also asked themselves some questions about Ito's assassination.

'It is suspected that the assassin is a hired killer,' one Japanese newspaper wrote just after the murder. The Japanese asked where an unsophisticated young Korean got his hands on a Browning automatic pistol, which was considered the world's premium handgun, the professional assassin's weapon of choice. The Japanese had purchased 200 Brownings during the Russo-Japanese War a few years before Ito's murder and stockpiled them in the basement of a London bookstore for distribution to Russian revolutionaries if the war continued.[10]

The security of the Harbin railroad station and the fact that Ahn knew just when to meet the train were also questioned. In fact, Ito's visit to Harbin had been anounced three months before in Japanese newspapers, and it wouldn't have been hard for Ahn to spot. But some Japanese who had joined Ito in opposing an outright takeover of Korea wondered if his murder hadn't been a great political convenience for those forces in Japan who were more interested in exploiting Korea economically than in protecting both Korea and Japan from Western encroachment.

5

PACIFIC PARADISE

Kilsoo Haan was one of the first Korean-Americans in history. On 3 January 1903, the SS *Gaelic* arrived in Honolulu Harbor carrying Korean immigrants, the first to land in United States territory. The SS *Gaelic* carried 56 Korean men, 21 women, and 25 children – including Kilsoo Haan. He was two years old when he first set foot in Hawaii, a child of Korean peasants caught up in a less than noble experiment on the part of the sugar companies that ran the Hawaiian Islands as their private fiefdoms.

The sugar companies needed cheap Oriental labor, and they were having a hard time finding it. The Chinese, the first Asians to reach American shores, came over before the US existed. Spanish and Mexican authorities reported that more than 200 wrecked Chinese or Japanese boats had been found on the coast of Mexico or of California in the days when Spain or Mexico still owned the Pacific Coast. Some of the crews may have escaped shipwreck and joined Native Americans, who abounded in the region as hunter-gatherer tribes before the Gold Rush. During the Gold Rush itself, the first recognized Chinese began to arrive. Driven from their gold claims by Americans, Australians or Chileans with guns, the Chinese had become cooks, laundrymen, tailors, undertakers, and contract laborers. The Indians, if they showed fight, were simply exterminated by the prospectors. Those who survived murderous one-sided warfare were debauched by coercive prostitution and alcohol, and finally eliminated almost entirely by contagious disease. Some whites shot the surviving fugitives for sport. The fate of the California Indians is one of history's least known genocides. But the Japanese knew about it.

After years of agitation white labor interests pushed Congress to adopt the Chinese Exclusion Act of 1882, forbidding Chinese from immigrating to the US. For years afterwards, union organizers and Socialists advocated deporting those Chinese who were already residents. Hard work in America paid off – unless you were Chinese.

Unable to import plantation workers from China after 1882, the sugar planters who owned a large portion of the Hawaiian Islands began to import laborers from Japan. Few Japanese left their countries to work for whites if they had a choice – the memory of gunboat diplomacy and Shimonoseki was too strong. Those who left for Hawaii were sometimes referred to as 'water-drinking peasants' by the other Japanese because they didn't have the money to buy tea. Even these Japanese, however, had a powerful sense of pride – or arrogance, according to the planters and their foremen. The word went out among the planters, 'Don't hire Japs – when you hit them, they hit back.' The Chinese Immigration Act left the planters no choice: by 1900, there were more than 60,000 Japanese living in the Hawaiian Islands.

The first Koreans on the SS *Gaelic* were very much a test case. American planters wanted to see if they worked hard without protesting abusive treatment. The first shipload passed the test. An article in the *Honolulu Evening Bulletin* reported: 'They appear to be hard workers, yet they are paid the least ... would work ten hours from dawn to sunset for 69 cents a day.' Since most other workers expected a dollar or more, the Korean experiment was a success. Between 1903 and 1905, 7,843 Korean laborers were imported to Hawaii – 6,701 men, 677 women, and 465 children. The Korean experiment was encouraged by favorable evaluations from missionaries who knew the common people of Korea and liked them.

'To the writer it seems that there is a close parallel between the Irishman and the Korean,' Mrs Lillian Underwood wrote in her book *Fifteen Years among The Top-Knots*, published in 1904:

> Both are happy-go-lucky, improvident, impulsive, warm-hearted, hospitable, generous. Take either in the midst of his native bogs, untutored, without incentive ... he has apparently little ambition for anything better. But give him a chance to make a good living, and a certainty that he may keep his own earnings, and you will not find a better citizen, a more brilliant scholar... They are not, perhaps, *par excellence* fighters like the Japanese or merchants like the Chinese ... they have not the volatility and headstrong earnestness of the one or the stolid conservatism of the other, but they are the equals if not the superiors of either.

Hiram Bingham King, an agricultural writer who had invented the circular silo to avoid wasting hay in corners, wrote about the same time in *Farmers of Forty Centuries* that the hard-working Koreans were the great tinkerers and practical inventors of North Asia: Their white billowing costumes enabled them to deal with extreme heart and extreme cold and their *ondul* floors with hot air circulating made them comfortable in the most bitter cold.

The planters also liked the Koreans, because they didn't want rival businessmen and they definitely didn't want fighters. Horace Allen, an American missionary-doctor and businessman, told Sanford E. Dole, governor of Hawaii, that Koreans were '...a patient, hard-working, docile race, easy to control from their long habit of obedience.' Shortly, Koreans were being divided into work gangs, assigned numbers rather than names, and slapped or even flogged when their white supervisors felt they weren't working fast enough under the Hawaiian sun.

In 1907 as we have seen, responding to more protests and pressure from organized labor on the mainland, President Roosevelt endorsed the so-called 'Gentlemen's Agreement': the United States wouldn't forbid immigration from Japan if Japan would agree to curtail it. Hawaii, however, continued to admit Japanese and Koreans, including women. These were the so-called 'picture brides.' Girls whose families couldn't provide for them in Japan or in Korea got in touch with single men in Hawaii and exchanged pictures and letters. If the men agreed – the women usually had no choice – the brides were shipped off to their new husbands in a new country. Korea accounted for 951 'picture brides' and the larger Japanese population of Hawaii accounted for several thousand more. In Japan and in Korea, wives often married men they had never met through family arrangements or match-makers, and of course many American settlers of the previous generation had married 'mail-order brides.'

Most of the Korean immigrants to Hawaii had little or no formal education, but all of them had grown up in a culture where education was valued perhaps more highly than in any other. The scholar was to Korea what the *samurai* was to Japan. The husbands and wives worked grueling hours but wanted their children to have an education, both in Korean and in English. Through churches – many Koreans were Christians before they came to America, and many others converted shortly after they arrived – schools were organized to offer it.

The Korean Compound School in Honolulu enrolled Korean boys from first through sixth grades, with classes conducted partly in English and partly in Korean. The mornings were devoted to Western instruction and to the Korean language, and the afternoons to the Chinese classics, the hallmark of a traditional Korean education at that time. The school was subsidized by the Methodist Church, but the parents or children were expected to pay at least part of the cost.

Kilsoo Haan's parents enrolled him in the Korean Compound School with bright hopes for his future. Young Kilsoo himself tried to work part-time while he was still in school to cover the cost of his own education, taking some of the burden off his parents. Like many children of immigrants who came to the US as toddlers, he picked up English quickly and became the family translator. In the best Horatio Alger tradition of working-class America, he got himself a paper round. Some upper-class people of the era considered being a newsboy a form of begging. Others liked 'newsies' and believed that newsboys learned business initiative and social skills.

The older Koreans took the dimmer view. Kilsoo Haan's career as a newsboy was frowned upon by the leaders of the Korean Compound School.

'He was told by the elders of the Compound that they didn't want you to leave the Compound to sell papers,' his son Stan Haan remembered. 'But he told them he had to sell papers to pay for the school. So one night when he got back to the school all his belongings were out on the sidewalk and the door was locked.'¹

The director of the school who ousted Kilsoo Haan was Syngman Rhee – the man who to Americans symbolized the Korean independence movement. Rhee, son of a *yangban* family, had been imprisoned by the Korean government in 1897 for activities deemed subversive to the antic government of King Kojong after the murder of Queen Min. Tortured and held in custody for seven years by his own government even before the Japanese takeover, Rhee had become a Christian and had also developed a belief in his own personal destiny to liberate Korea from all enemies. This dream sustained him through his harrowing youth. A gifted scholar, once released from prison as part of an amnesty program, Syngman Rhee attended Princeton University, He was sometimes a guest in the home of Woodrow Wilson, then the president of Princeton. He also took courses at Harvard, though whether or not he graduated became a matter of some controversy between his admirers and his detractors.²

In his role as an educator in Hawaii, Syngman Rhee had opposed assimilation. Rhee believed that Koreans should marry only Koreans, though he once rescued some Korean girls who were about to be coerced into unwanted marriages. He found shelter for them with white missionaries. He believed that Koreans should speak and write Korean and Chinese, though he supported the necessity of English as a stop-gap. Above all, he believed that the goal of the entire Korean community should be a return to Korea, to oppose the Japanese who by 1910 had annexed the country outright and had started their own bilingual schools to teach young Koreans how to function as young Japanese.

Rhee's hatred of Japan was almost monomaniacal, so much so that some of his American supporters believed that as a young man he had been tortured by the Japanese, rather than by Koreans. In fact, like many other progressive Koreans of the 1890s, he had rubbed shoulders with Japanese agents who also urged modernization of Kojong's decrepit tyranny. He later disavowed these conversations and told gullible Americans that he had been privy from his teens to Japan's sinister plans to take over the world even before the annexation of Korea – plans that the Japanese had dryly predicted they would be accused of by anyone to resented their resistance to white colonialism.

Syngman Rhee had temporarily spiked Kilsoo Haan by leaving his belongings on the curb. Kilsoo Haan's future wife, Stella Yoon, also had had problems with Syngman Rhee's arbitrary management of the Compound School. Brought to Hawaii from Korea as a child, as Kilsoo Haan had been, Stella Yoon told of crying with home-sickness until she was eight years old. A pretty child who grew up to become a beautiful and quietly forceful woman, she had disliked the Compound School and left to pay for her own high school and college education as a nanny to an Australian couple while her parents worked on the sugar cane plantations. She eventually graduated from college with excellent grades and became a teacher in the Honolulu school system.

Shortly after Kilsoo Haan's departure from the Compound School, Hawaii almost spiked Syngman Rhee. In 1916, having split with the Methodist Church, which favored amalgamation of the various Asian groups in Hawaii, and having left the Korean Compound School, Rhee opened his own school, openly dedicated to preserving Korean culture in America and preparing for a showdown with Japan. The school had 140 students by 1920, at which time the Hawaiian Department of Public Education began to require an examination for admission to public high schools that put Korean-language schools at a serious disadvantage. Rhee was able to save his school by emphasizing Korean patriotism and resistance to Japan rather than education for American citizenship.

Syngman Rhee, the former houseguest of Woodrow Wilson and the former headmaster of Kilsoo Haan's school days, then miscalculated his influence with Wilson in a way that was to have tragic consequences. Wilson – according to Rhee – had once introduced Rhee to some Americans as 'the future redeemer of Korean independence.' Wilson was probably joking, but Rhee took him very seriously.

During World War I, there had been three major Korean independence groups: all three had backed Germany – Japan's enemy and since 1893 the resented owner of Shantung, the Chinese peninsula south of Korea. The Japanese, honoring their 1902 treaty with Britain, and following their own common sense, had backed England, France and Italy, and ultimately became allies of the United States. The Japanese escorted Australian and New Zealand troops to Gallipoli on the Turkish coast, sent a flotilla of destroyers to the Mediterranean, where they hunted German and Austrian U-Boats, and rescued some Greek and Armenian fugitives from the massacres that took place when the Turkish Empire imploded. The Greeks and the Armenians still remember this random act of kindness, which has otherwise disappeared from Western history.

More to the point from the British perspective, the Japanese threw their shipyards open to replace British freighters being sunk in the Atlantic, building 123 merchant ship for Britain in yards that no U-Boat could reach. The Japanese public, scarred by the Russo-Japanese War, protested vociferously at the idea that Japanese soldiers might be sent to the wasteful carnage of the Western Front – and none were. Instead, the Japanese gladly rounded up the stranded Germans in Germany's Pacific and Chinese colonies and sent them back to Europe with a minimum of bloodshed – while keeping the colonies for Japan. No nation did better from World War I than Japan: at a cost of 300 dead, mostly sailors washed overboard or influenza victims, the Japanese gained German's colony of Shantung in China, Saipan and Tinian in the Marianas in the Pacific,, the good will of the Allied victors, and the grudging good will of the Germans, whose surrenders had been handled with dignity and decorum. The single greatest loss was of 77 Japanese sailors who were blown up or drowned when their frigate was torpedoed by a German U-Boat escorting a convoy in the Mediterranean. They were buried on Malta with full military honors.

In Korea, things were looking up. Herbert Hoover – who tended to favor China over Japan, which he called 'a nation of 70 million egotists' – also noted that the Japanese administration of Korea had led to vast material and economic improvements and improved sanitation and health. Before the Japanese annexation, education in Korea, except through Christian missionaries, had been restricted to the sons of the rich, who hired personal or group tutors. Poor children sometimes picked up reading *hangul* by osmosis, but most Koreans were illiterate. By 1919, under Japanese rule, Korea had 482 elementary schools, five middle schools – comparable to high schools for boys – and two girls' high schools. The principal language for mathematics, science, and written exercises was Japanese, but Korean language and literature courses were offered in the Korean language. The Japanese maintained a separate school system for those Japanese who lived in Korea – about 12 per cent of the population.

This educational advance was disrupted by an absurd incident called the 'Christian Conspiracy Case,' in which 135 Korean clergymen were arrested on charges of plotting to assassinate the Japanese governor-general. Three of these hapless men had died in prison, reportedly under torture, certainly under duress, nine were exiled, and 106 were given prison sentences of five to 10 years, on charges that no one in America found plausible. 'The standing of Japan among Western nations would be improved by judicious modification of her preliminary proceedings against alleged criminals,' Dr. Charles W. Eliot, president of Harvard, concluded after investigating the case, meaning that torturing the accused was not acceptable.

The Japanese, however, often got people into Harvard, including the future Admiral Isoroku Yamamoto, who went twice, and they were sensitive to this kind of moral suasion. They stood down on the torture and concentrated on progress and prosperity. Syngman Rhee himself couldn't deny that in material terms, the first years of the Japanese occupation after the rout of the Korean Righteous Army had been astounding: 'Within the space of three years Korea has been transformed from a slow-going country where tradition reigned into a live, bustling center of industrialism,' he said through Robert Tarbell Oliver. 'Seoul can hardly be told nowadays from Cincinnati except for the complexion of its inhabitants.'

Harmony seemed the norm – until Woodrow Wilson announced his 14 Points in 1918, including the self-determination of all nations. A number of the Koreans, urged on by Syngman Rhee, took the 14 Points seriously. A more cynical view was that the

14 Points had been a ploy to urge Poles in the German Army and Czechs in the Austro-Hungarian Army to slack off while serving their German-speaking masters in the hope of receiving their long-awaited independence when the Germans and Austrians lost the war. The ploy was demographically useful: one Prussian soldier out of five was Polish, and while the Poles of this era didn't hate the Germans as much as they hated the Russians, they had a long history of agitating for independence. Polish agents and defectors had done a tremendous number on Tsarist Russia during the Russo-Japanese War. The Czechs, who were master organizers and master publicists, had their own Czech Legion of defectors from the Austrian Army, a factor in the Russian Revolution, now spreading to Siberia, just north of Korea. The Eastern world was becoming a powder keg while the Western world concentrated on Paris, where the Treaty of Versailles was being negotiated. The Germans signed an armistice expecting the 14 Points and lost six million citizen who were neither Polish nor French. In New York the Palmer Raids were rounding up foreign-born radicals and sending them to Russia. In 1919, something was about to break out in Korea as well.

On 20 January, King Kojong died. The Japanese, who released the news of his death on 22 January, gave the cause of death as apoplexy – in other words, stroke. Skeptics said that King Kojong had been suffering from low blood pressure for years and was an unlikely stroke victim. Korean rumors began that he had taken poison, or that poison had been administered, because he opposed the marriage of his son Eumin, also known as Prince Yi, to the Japanese Princess Masako Nashimoto. The marriage, ironically in terms of what transpired for both countries, turned out quite well. Eumin was an intelligent man who shared Princess Nashimoto's love of flowers and horticulture, and they attracted many upper-class Japanese to the greenhouse where they raised rare orchids. Princess Nashimoto became a force in the Japanese Girl Scouts, and Eumin and Yi Bangja, as Princess Nashimoto was re-named, founded an asylum and school for Japanese-Korean orphans and cast-off children. Princess Nashimoto remains an anomaly – a Japanese heroine acceptable to even the most patriotic Koreans, if only under her Korean name.[3]

The Koreans of 1919, despite having suffered under Kojong's vacillating rule, asked for a period of mourning. The Japanese, strongly committed to the special status of royals of all sorts, gave permission. But the Korean patriotic groups secretly decided to turn the mourning for King Kojong into a huge passive demonstration to ask the world to recognize their independence. Their leaders drew up a manifesto, signed by 33 prominent Koreans, both Christian and Buddhist, which was both a request for independence and an indictment of Japanese control.

We herewith proclaim the independence of Korea and the liberty of the Korean people. We tell it to the world in witness of the equality of all nations, and we pass it on to our posterity as their inherent right...

We have no desire to accuse Japan of breaking many solemn treaties since 1876, nor to single out specially the teachers in the schools or the government officials who treat the heritage of our ancestors as a colony of their own, and our people and our civilization as a nation of savages, and who delight only in beating us down and bringing us under their heel...

To bind by force twenty millions of resentful Koreans will mean not only loss of peace forever for this part of the Far East, but also will increase the ever-growing suspicions of four hundred millions of Chinese – upon whom depends the safety of the Far East – besides strengthening the hatred of Japan... Today Korean independence will mean not only life and happiness for us, but also Japan's departure from an evil path, and her exaltation to the place of true protector of the East, so that China too would put all fear of Japan aside. This thought comes from no minor resentment, but from a large hope for the future welfare and blessings of mankind.

As word of the demonstration traveled around the country, a brief instruction was issued to the hundreds of thousands of Koreans who wanted to take part: 'Whatever you do, do not insult the Japanese. Do not throw stones. Do not hit with your fist. For these are the acts of barbarians.'

The leading patriots read their proclamation at noon at the Bright Moon Café in Seoul on 1 March 1919 (3.1, *Sam-il* in Korean) and then calmly submitted to arrest. Their plan appears to have been to swamp the Japanese authorities with so many peaceful, responsible Koreans that acceptance of the demonstration would be unavoidable. Around the country, an estimated one million Koreans – some say almost two million – took part on marches and parades, shouting '*Manzei!*' – 'May Korea live ten thousand years!'

Unfortunately, some Korean toughs used the cover of the demonstrations to brawl with Japanese police and smash Japanese stores and shops. Several Japanese were killed – a fact never mentioned in most Korean accounts of what happened next. The police riot that followed this brief episode of looting and probably accidental killing shocked the American missionaries, astounded the Korean demonstrators, and permanently destroyed any hope of harmony between Japanese and Koreans.

Reverend Edward Twing of Boston was traveling in Korea and was a witness to the suppression of the Sam-il Revolt. He saw Korean girls of school age shout '*Manzei!*' at some Japanese soldiers. The soldiers splattered them with bullets. Other girls, walking peaceably beside a road, were knocked down with rifle butts and had their clothes torn off and 'the soldiers treated them in a most shameful fashion.'[4] At Suwon, Japanese soldiers chased 23 fleeing Korean demonstrators into a Christian church, set the church on fire, and then fired on anyone who tried to clamber out until all 23 trapped inside were dead.

'The odor of burned flesh in the vicinity of the church was sickening,' wrote Horace Underwood, a missionary who saw the charred church a few days later. Houses and villages were burned all over the vicinity – 31 houses in Suwon alone, and 315 in the region. All over Korea, those who urged independence were shot down or bayoneted at unarmed protests, girls were beaten and sometimes raped. The Korean National Police – at this point about half Korean and half Japanese – staged marathon public floggings of Korean patriots.

'The beating goes on, day after day,' an American who worked for the Japanese wrote in disgust. 'The victims are tied down on a frame and beaten on the naked body with rods till they become unconscious. Then cold water is poured on them until they revive, when the process is repeated. It is sometimes repeated many times... Men, women, and children are shot down and bayoneted. The Christian Church is especially chosen as an object of fury, and to the Christians is meted out special severity.'

The Japanese reported 533 Korean dead and 1,409 wounded in putting down the Revolt, along with 12,522 arrests. Korean sources estimate 7,500 killed, 15,000 injured and 45,000 arrested. Later, when the dead of became martyrs for various Korean patriot groups and anti-Japanese propaganda, the disparity between the official figures and the estimates soared still further. Robert Tarbell Oliver, Syngman Rhee's biographer, who met Rhee in the 1940s, gave the 'official' – thus Japanese – figure as 7,645 Koreans killed. Instead of the documented burning of one Korean church with 23 Koreans taking cover inside, Oliver reports the burning of 30 churches, 'some with their congregations inside.'⁵ T.R. Fehrenbach, a decorated US Army officer writing in the 1960s, and no friend of Japan, said that 'more than fifty thousand were killed or at least hospitalized by the lesson.'

The Japanese figures are probably closer to the reality than the hyperbole produced by outraged Koreans and indignant Americans, but that reality was awful enough. Every respectable Korean gunned down, raped, or beaten half to death left a family committed to a blood feud with Japan and all things Japanese except for Princess Nashimoto. The line between those Koreans who were willing to cooperate with the Japanese and those pledged to resist them at all costs became a flaming trench between collaborators and heroes.

On March 13, Kimm Kyu-sic, a Korean patriot whose father had once loaned Syngman Rhee the use of a printing press, arrived at the Versailles Peace Conference in Paris and was told that 'self-determination' would be extended only to those people who had actually participated in World War I.

'If we deal out justice in Europe and punish the criminals here it may prove a leaven of righteousness in other fields,' Colonel Edward House, Woodrow Wilson's confidant, told the baffled Korean. 'Perhaps the League [of Nations] will be able to curb Japan when it has less pressing matters nearer at hand to deal with.'

Translated into *realpolitik,* the Americans and the British were far more worried about the Bolsheviks in Siberia than they were about the problems of the people who had killed Durham White Stevens and Hirobumi Ito. The Japanese had already been offended when they tried to insert a clause in the League of Nations charter asserting that all races were equal – and were rebuffed by the British and French, who controlled huge empires of Asians, Africans, and recently Arabs 'liberated' from the Turks.

'The President presented the amendments to the original draft which had been approved by the Commission and then the Japanese delegates stated their objection with a good argument about the equal treatment of all races, etc., but stated they would not press the issue at this time,' Arthur S. Link reported in *The Papers of Woodrow Wilson*. The Japanese also had the largest and most reliable contingent of troops in Siberia watching the Reds, and sometimes fighting against them. Everybody else wanted to go home. The Japanese soldiers didn't get to vote on when they went back. Masatake Terauchi, the *samurai* who had pulverized the Korean rebels of the Righteous Army and co-opted the majority of the Korean *yangban* class with Japanese patents of nobility, was now prime minister of Japan. Terauchi and his wife were both ailing when the Americans spent a year trying to talk him into intervention in Siberia. He had agreed only when the Americans, the British, and the French all agreed to send both troops and money to augment the Japanese contingent. Goro Miura, who had engineered the murder of Queen Min with her father-in-law, was a respected elder statesman of the *Genro,* the counsel or elders, and was agitating for the complete separation of the civil government and the military. Back of it all, of course, was the still-secret Taft-Katsura Treaty in which the US had handed Korea to Japan in return for a free hand in the Philippines and Hawaii, and the Root-Takahira Agreement that handed Japan special rights in Manchuria in return for protecting China, in essence, from Russia. Woodrow Wilson's 14 Points had demanded 'open covenants openly agreed upon.' The closed covenants of Taft-Katsura and Root-Takahita were the last word on Korean hope for American help against Japan.

6

THE CHINA CARD

The harrowing brutality with which the Sam-il Revolt of March 1919 was put down affected different people in different ways. Yoshimichi Hasegawa, the Japanese governor-general who had replaced Terauchi, resigned in the middle of the revolt. The Japanese Diet, or parliament, demanded an investigation of the extreme brutality involved in crushing the demonstration. Admiral Makoto Saito, the new governor-general, was given a policy guide drafted by Japanese experts which said in part: 'The study of Korean history shows that Korean people, if they are oppressed, cannot be obedient to their rulers... If they are treated with kindness they are a docile race.' Admiral Saito instituted a policy of 'harmony between Japan and Korea.'

Even the Korean patriotic histories indicate that conditions in Korea continued to improve somewhat between 1921 and the Depression of the 1930s. Ku Kim, the avenger who had killed Tsuchida, was, oddly enough, not involved in the Sam-il Revolt. Finally released from prison, he was in the remote countryside running a school to teach Western learning and Korean patriotism when word of the revolt and the savage repression reached him. Ku Kim took a train for Shanghai and presented himself to Ahn Chang Ho, also known as Dosan, Hirobumi Ito's reluctant admirer and stalwart critic in the days before the Protectorate had turned into annexation. Koreans there had already begun to form their own faction in the spectrum of settlers in Shanghai, the most cosmopolitan city in Asia.

The original walled city of Shanghai belonged to the Chinese, but the British and Americans shared control of the International Settlement, a zone where Chinese laws couldn't touch offenders and where Europeans and Americans felt they were in their own country, except for the cheap labor and the under-age prostitutes. The French Concession maintained French laws and customs. The city flourished by trading in silk, opium, rice, and prostitution, especially child prostitution. The Koreans, most of them highly moral people in the first stages of conversion to Christianity and Western political thought, kept themselves apart from Shanghai's endemic climate of vice, and most of them worked at skilled or manual jobs to support their extended families.

Ku Kim, who seemed eager to humble himself in his conviction that his own *yangban* class had betrayed the Korean people to the West and to the Japanese, said that he wanted to be a janitor. Ahn Chang Ho said that he had better things in mind for the man who killed Tsuchida. Ku Kim became the leader of an elite assassination squad whose members were pledged to rid the world of Japanese dignitaries adjudged guilty of the oppression of Korea.

In Hawaii, Kilsoo Haan was a teenager when the Sam-il Revolt took place, and the stories of how Korean girls were raped and of how Koreans were shot down in the streets or beaten half to death made a traumatic impression on him. The damage to Korean lives and the insult to Korean culture– especially to people in Hawaii who heard about the Japanese brutality, and never heard that Japanese had been killed and shops and stores had been looted to trigger the police response – confirmed him and his peers in his hatred of Japan.

More to the point, Kilsoo Haan was faced with the problem of obtaining an education without much help from his family. He first joined the Hawaiian National Guard, where he picked up a complete fluency in English and a knowledge of American slang and American opinions. His next stop was the Salvation Army.

Modern Americans know the Salvation Army, founded by a devout Christian reformer from England, 'General' William Booth, as a rehabilitation agency for people with alcohol and drug

abuse problems. But in Asia, the Salvation Army at the turn of the
20th century took great pride in liberating Asians from ignorance
and cultural oppression. In India, Salvation Army missionaries
told the Untouchables, the lowest social class of outcasts, that if
they became Christians they were the equals of all other men and
women, whatever the color of their skins. In Japan, the Salvation
Army contingent led by General Booth's daughters touched off
riots when they told Japanese girls who had been sold into brothels
that the contracts their parents made for them were null and void.
Geisha may have glamorized themselves but the girls who worked
in brothels were desperate. The girls themselves were delighted
to learn they were free from the squalid life and paraded through
the streets holding hands and singing about their liberation. The
brothel-keepers petitioned the Japanese government to make the
Salvation Army go away.

The courage of the Booths and their impact on institutions
which many intelligent Asians regarded as unsavory, or at least
embarrassing, made an excellent impression on the more respectable
Japanese. Maresuke Nogi, the general who had conquered the
Russians at Port Arthur in the Russo-Japanese War, became a
headmaster of a school for upper-class boys after Japan's victory.
He had lost both of his own sons in battle and was revered as
Japan's greatest living hero. One day, a new boy, Tarao Saito, was
brought to school and introduced to the national hero.

'What do you want to be when you grow up?' General Nogi
asked the little boy.

'I want to be a general,' Tarao Saito said.

'Like whom?' Nogi asked eagerly.

'Like General Booth.'

Kilsoo Haan was also inspired by General Booth's message of
salvation in Heaven and of social mobility through clean habits
and intense hard work on Earth. He joined the Salvation Army
and by 1924 had worked his way up to the rank of captain. He
also obtained a thorough and rigorous education. He was now
utterly fluent in spoken English and a confident speaker before
any audience. His written English, while somewhat short of
perfect, was on a grammatical level with that of the average college
graduate – and his speaking and writing was far sharper in terms

of wit and insight. He was a natural story-teller. The clean habits he learned in the Salvation Army appear to have remained with him though his career: Koreans love political scandals, but no one ever appears to have accused Kilsoo Haan of being a drunkard or a philanderer. His only vice – usually kept under control – was a hot temper.

'My Mom told me that one time they were at a meeting with Korean people,' his son Stan remembered. 'Dad got into an argument with one of the people at the meeting and Dad punched him and the guy rolled down the flight of stairs.'[1]

Kilsoo Haan met and married his wife Stella Yoon in Hawaii. She appears to have been a model wife. Stella kept her job as schoolteacher to make ends meet while her husband tried his hand at real estate, first in Hawaii, then in California. His Korean political enemies left his marriage out of the equation, but at one point they claimed that his real estate license had been revoked. The charge was bogus. He was never charged with any offenses in relation to his real estate activities – and considering the volatile nature of the real estate business, this in itself is a sort of recommendation. The only charge against Kilsoo Haan that wasn't of a political nature was a familiar one leveled against Asian males – he didn't spend enough time with his family because he was too busy trying to earn a living, or later, to change the world.

'Sometimes he gave ten speeches in a week, sometimes two or three in a day,' his son Stan said. 'We had missed the early years when a father and son bond... I was not real close to my Dad.'[2]

While Kilsoo Haan was experiencing the stress and strain of earning a living in a society that was still officially racist, but otherwise rich in opportunity, the Korean-American community in Hawaii received several more thumping shocks from overseas. A scuffle between Japanese and Korean schoolboys over some Korean girls was about the worst that took place during Saito's conciliatory regime. But another disaster struck those Koreans who had left Korea to seek work in Japan.

On 1 September 1923, the great Kanto earthquake devastated Tokyo and Yokohama. Modern buildings crashed onto the street in what many Japanese thought must be the end of the world. Fires broke out to destroy those houses not shattered by the earthquake.

The earthquake killed or seriously injured 140,000 people and collapsed 120,000 buildings. Another 450,000 wooden buildings burned in the fire that followed.

Tokyo at the time was crowded with two types of slum-dwellers: Japanese from the lowest classes or from rural areas, impervious to the educational reforms that by now had made most Japanese literate, and Korean men from the poorest classes who competed for their jobs. Just as Koreans had blamed the Europeans and the Japanese for the drought and failed harvests of 1894, the Japanese *soshi,* or slum dwellers, blamed the Koreans for the Tokyo earthquake of 1923. Japanese folklore told of two Gargantuan carp that lived far beneath the sea, supporting Japan on their backs. The gibbering chatter of the Koreans, the *soshi* were told, had disrupted the carp and led to the earthquake that destroyed Tokyo. How many people actually believed this absurdity is anybody's guess. But the Korean immigrants were economic threats to the poorest Japanese of Tokyo. The urban riot that followed, concealed by the even larger damage from the earthquake itself, was immensely savage and brutal. Nobody knows how many Korean immigrants were slaughtered by Japanese street thugs and superstitious city dwellers, but the estimates range from 800 to almost 5,000. Thousands of surviving Koreans fled Japan in poverty and took the word of the massacre – largely ignored elsewhere – back to Korea. Korean patriots had another factual tale of Japanese brutality to weight against the visible material and educational progress of Korea under Japanese administration.

Hostile as they often were to each other, the Japanese and the Koreans both took a hit from American labor in 1924, when the United States revised its immigration standards. In 1922, American influence, seconded by Canadian influence, caused the British to fail to renew the military-naval alliance with Japan – a move that British subjects in Australia and New Zealand opposed. The Japanese Navy had protected ANZAC troop convoys during World War I and later gave the British a valuable component of security in the Pacific. The Americans and Canadians, however, had opposed ties between Britain and Japan because of concerns about immigration to the West Coast – still a hot topic with organized labor in the US and Canada. Congress changed the immigration standards two years after Japan had been insulted by Britain's scrapping of the treaty under American pressure.

The 1924 quotas were based on the number of immigrants who had arrived from foreign lands in past years: Germany received an annual quota of 51,227, Great Britain of 34,007, and Ireland (newly independent of Britain) of 28,567. But China, with 400 million occupants, received a quota of exactly 100, and Japan – including Korea and Taiwan – which had a collective population of about 100 million, also received a quota of 100. Other countries which received a quota of 100 included Andorra, Bhutan, Liechtenstein, Luxemburg, and Monaco. The Free City of Danzig – a German-speaking enclave in the middle of Poland – received a quota of 228, Estonia received a quota of 124, and Lithuania a quota of 334.

White workingmen, saved from the menace of economic competition from 'Chinks' and 'Japs,' breathed a sigh of relief. The wise guys coined a phrase that covered hopeless situations in sports and love: 'He hasn't got a Chinaman's chance.' In Tokyo, offended patriots threatened *hara kiri* in front of the American embassy. Japanese newspapers, which had recently praised Americans for their help after the Kanto Earthquake, exploded with hatred for the United States.

In California, the only state other than Hawaii with a large population of either Japanese or Koreans, the 1924 immigration law followed hard on the heels of a 1921 state law which limited Chinese, Japanese or Korean immigrants to 3 per cent per year of the existing population – which kept Korean immigration to a trickle, since their base population was only about 3,000 in 1920. California law also forbade intermarriage with whites – to the relief of some Chinese and Korean parents, though the Japanese found this miscegenation law insulting. California forbade Chinese, Japanese or Koreans from owning farm land. Japanese and Korean farmers raised vegetables for Los Angeles and San Francisco on land they leased because they couldn't buy it. Their white competitors warned food shoppers that the Orientals used 'night soil' for fertilizer, a practice that Hiram Bingham King had noted with approval in *Farmers for Forty Centuries*. King was more worried about smoking.

By the 1920s, Koreans in Los Angeles owned one restaurant, one hotel, two grocery stories, a photographic shop and an auto repair shop. There were a tiny handful of professionals including a doctor and a dentist and some shopkeepers: three-quarters of Korean-Americans were working people or farm laborers. Racism was endemic, though most racists called the Koreans 'Chinks' or 'Japs' because they didn't know where Korea was – or, in legal terms, had been. The Japanese formed the Japanese-American Citizens League in 1929 to protest racism and oppose anti-Asian legislation, but the bad blood between the Koreans and the Japanese since the annexation of 1910 and the Revolt of 1919 dissuaded most Koreans from seeking help from Japanese, even those who were Christians and American citizens.

The Japanese and the Koreans including Kilsoo Haan all took a broadside hit from Wall Street. Few Japanese and even fewer Koreans played the stock market, but the stock market crash of October 1929 sent its reverberations through the lives of millions of Japanese and Koreans on both sides of the Pacific who had barely heard of buying on margin. As the Great Depression began, millions of Americans lost their jobs. Farm prices plummeted because of too much food and not enough buyers, Congress reacted with the Smoot-Hawley Tariff – the legislation, according to some experts, that led to World War II. Reed Smoot was a member, elder, and official of the Mormon Church – and the third son of his father's fifth wife, a Norwegian immigrant who had come to America to find a respectable husband and was willing to share him with four other wives. Smoot had been born in 1862, and he was a grown man and a father himself by the time Congress outlawed American polygamy in 1890. The new law threw many Mormon husbands in jail for refusing to divorce their second wives. The Mormon community was rocked by the polygamy ban, which impacted on their highly moral lifestyle in a way perhaps even more harsh than the way that the Japanese Protectorate had impacted on Korea. (The Japanese banned harems, but multiple wives remained a fact of life for many rural or rich Koreans, just as concubines remained a fact of life for many prosperous or powerful Japanese.)

Reed Smoot had been elected to the United States Senate in 1903 by the Utah legislature, and survived a bitter three-year debate over whether or not he could be seated. Some observers saw the debate as a trial not of Reed Smooth but of Mormonism. Smoot, who was himself monogamous and not especially devout, had in fact supported the ban on polygamy, but opponents said he was part of a ruling church elite that continued secretly to support plural marriage, and that somewhere in the sinister depths of Salt Lake City he had taken 'a secret pledge of disloyalty to the American government.' A Senate committee actually voted for his expulsion from the US Senate. But Theodore Roosevelt used his influence to ensure that Smoot would be seated. Smoot was re-elected by the Utah legislature in 1908. After the passage of the 17th Amendment provided for direct voting for senators, he was elected by Utah's citizens in 1914, 1920, and 1926.[3]

Despite the dose of bigotry he had experienced at the hands of his fellow Americans, or more probably because of it, Reed Smoot was ardently committed to the interests of American business and industry against all foreign influences. The Mormon church at this point was strictly segregated – though their honesty in keeping their word made Mormons popular with Native Americans. The whiteness of the Mormon Church in the 1920s gave an added spin to the hostility many Westerns felt towards 'cheap Oriental labor.' Reed Smoot also had personal axes to grind: two of the imports he wanted to build barriers against were the woolen industry and the sugar industry – he was invested in both. His real concerns, however, were protecting American business, American jobs, and his own questioned status as a 'real' American. Smoot became chairman of the US Senate's Finance Committee in 1923, and he was still in place when the Wall Street Crash of 1929 plunged America into depression.

The Great Depression started, most experts agree, due to excessive speculation on the New York Stock Exchange, added to the problem that too many goods and too much food had been produced, leading to inventories of materials and produce that couldn't be sold. One American worker in four was thrown out of work, college graduates couldn't find jobs meant for high school drop-outs, and farms were being foreclosed all over the US.

The 'protectionists' in Congress responded with the Smoot–Hawley Tariff, named for Reed Smoot and his colleague in the House of Representatives, Willis C. Hawley, an Oregon Republican, farm boy, teacher, lawyer, and frantic flag-waver from a state where the residents were not fond of Japanese immigration.[4]

Japan been a self-sufficient agricultural society in the 1850s with a population of about 30 million when Commodore Perry arrived with his 'black ships' and pushed the door open. In 1930 Japan's population had more than doubled and was on the verge of tripling, yet food production had not kept pace with population. During times of bad harvest, the Japanese authorities sometimes took the rice from Korean peasants and left them to subsist on millet – birdseed, the pauper's grain of Asia, as barley was once the pauper's grain of Europe. During good times, everybody had enough to eat, since manufacturing in Japan and export on Japanese merchant ships brought in enough revenue to support a growing economy both in Japan and Korea. The collapse of Wall Street and the American market for Japanese goods, especially silk, porcelain and other luxury items, followed by the Smoot-Hawley Tariff, plunged Japan's tightly knit economy into a catastrophe that was not of Japan's making.

Coming on top of the American influence in scrapping Japan's alliance with Britain in 1922 and the blatantly racist US immigration laws of 1924, the Smoot-Hawley Tariff added injury to insult. The Japanese, once charmed by 'Victorian' American honesty outside the political sphere and marriage for love, now came to see the Americans of the Jazz Age as a cold, decadent, deeply racist people who exploited all Asians. The quota of 100 immigrants from Japan and Korea put together had slammed America's door in their faces. Soviet Russia remained Japan's bugbear, but American racism and European colonialism became the basis of a propaganda campaign that those Asians with no political axe to grind with Japan found extremely plausible. From India, from Indochina, from Burma, and even from Manchuria and Korea, nationalists traveled to Japan to ponder the Asian society that had defeated the predatory Russians, exiled the predatory Germans, and now confronted the exploitation of British, the French, the Dutch and the Americans – and the ultimate menace of Russia.

7

THE RIPPLE EFFECT

Even before the economic catastrophe inflicted on the Japanese economy by the Smoot-Hawley Tariff, Hirohito, the Japanese emperor after 1926, had not enjoyed absolute popularity or approval by his own people. The idea that he was worshipped as a god with a small g was largely a product of American wartime propaganda.

Hirohito's father was Yoshihito, known as the Taisho Emperor after his death, son of Mutsuhito, the Meiji Emperor by one of his subsidiary wives when Haruko, the favorite wife, failed to produce offspring. Yoshihito was an emulator of European elegance – his favorite outfit was a tight-fitting German-style hussar's uniform that showed off his trim physique – and he was an epic drunkard, though otherwise a tolerant and likable man. He maintained a regular harem, somewhat smaller than his father Meiji's. The fact that he died of a stroke at the age of 46 suggests that nobody dared to tell him it was time to quit.

The tale is told of how, during one epic binge, the courtiers were running low on liquor and Taisho told a couple of his underlings that the party was too much fun to end so abruptly.

'Go to the French embassy and tell them to give you a case of cognac.' He told two courtiers. 'We'll pay them on Monday... You can take my own horse.'

A few hours later the liquor finally ran out and Yoshihito demanded that the two courtiers bring him the French cognac. They came in, bowing profusely by way of apology.

'Where's the cognac? – did they refuse my request?' Yoshihito demanded.

'Great One... Neither of us could get on the horse!'

Yoshihito laughed and there were no repercussions. Unfortunately, his bibulous administration lacked the kind of rigor that is sometimes needed to cope with bad times. Toward the end of his visible reign, he began to roll up a map and use it as an imaginary telescope without a lens to stare at anyone who wished to speak to him, remarking 'Yes... I can see you...' He was an honest enough human to see his exalted role as slightly ridiculous.

Hirohito, the crown prince, was shortly named as regent. He was in place when the Kanto Earthquake struck and a mob surrounded the palace seeking shelter from the huge fire after the earthquake. A Japanese Communist named Sakac Osugi stood before the terrified, confused crowd and shouted: 'Remember Russia, and never lay down your arms!' The wind turned the flames away from them and the crowd were spared. Some of them credited the proximity of the palace. Most Japanese still feared and hated Russia after the 100,000 dead of 1904-05. The Japanese police soon had a full description of Osugi. Hirohito proclaimed martial law and showed up in uniform in the crumbling ruins of Tokyo. The police looked up Osugi and shortly after his arrest a police captain slipped into his cell and strangled him. Then he strangled Osugi's wife and eight-year-old nephew in a nearby cell. The murder of the child outraged Japanese women and hundreds of protests were filed by mail and by demonstration. The police captain got three years in prison for the triple murder.

On 27 December 1923, Hirohito was riding in his horse-drawn carriage to deliver his annual address at the Diet on 27 December 1923, when a Japanese Communist named Daisuke Namba fired at him with a shooting cane. The odd shooting cane was one of the weapons that had been stockpiled to assassinate Tsarist officials if things went bad during the Russo-Japanese War two decades before. A chamberlain riding with Hirohito was hit by shattered glass but Hirohito himself was untouched. The attack worried the whole Diet – especially since the would-be assassin was the son of a delegate. Some Diet members urged the need for economic reform. When Namba himself was put on trial, he bluntly asked the judge if the judge really believed that Hirohito was of divine origin – and the judge declined to answer.

'I've proved the joy of living for the truth,' Namba told the embarrassed judge. 'Go ahead and hang me! Banzai for the working people and the Communist Party of Japan! Banzai for Russian socialism and the Soviet Republic! Banzai for the Communist International!' Namba was executed two days later and buried in a secret grave so that Japanese Communists – a significant party in the 1920s – couldn't turn his final resting place into a political shrine. His disgraced father, the Diet delegate, shut himself up in his room and starved himself to death.

Hirohito tried to deal with his unpopularity. In 1926, now officially the Emperor after his father's death, he learned that a Korean dissident named Pak Yol and his Japanese wife, Fumiko Kaneko, had been sentenced to death for plotting to assassinate him in a separate incident three years before when he was still crown prince. A photograph was circulated showing the loyal Fumiko sitting on her husband's lap while they both waited to be interrogated – tortured – at police headquarters. Hirohito stepped in and had their sentences commuted to life in prison, which kept them from becoming martyrs and may not have made them happy.

The act of clemency did little or nothing for Hirohito's popularity in Korea, still restive under Japanese administration despite some significant material progress. Many Koreans actually liked Princess Nashiamoto. They liked the Japanese women teachers who came to Japanese-built Korean schools to foster literacy and modern education and a gentle feminism at the same time. The Koreans respected the skills of Japanese physicians and engineers, and some of the Koreans themselves were given scholarships to study medicine and engineering. But the memories of the destruction of the Korean Righteous Army under Meiji and of the drastic suppression of the Sam-il demonstrations of 1919 under Yoshihito – now the Taisho Emperor – filled the Koreans with a bitter hatred of the Japanese Army and the rest of the Japanese Imperial Family.

On 8 January 1932, when Hirohito was returning from a military review, a Korean patriot named Pang-Chang Yi dramatized these feelings by throwing a hand grenade at Hirohito in his horse-drawn carriage. Yi had spent the night before the grenade attempt sheltered in a Japanese brothel stocked with Korean girls sold for debt by their families. He no doubt had time for bitter reflection on what the Japanese presence had done to Korea: there were few brothels in Korea before the Japanese arrived, but plenty of harems, which was probably better for the girls. Once again, Hirohito was unhurt when the grenade exploded under the carriage Pang- Chan Yi thought was Hirohito's. The grenade fragments caused some injuries to the horses. Newspapers reported that Hirohito sent 10 pounds of carrots to the injured horses. He also asked his cabinet not to resign, as the cabinet customarily did when someone attacked the Emperor. He passed the whole thing off with a clumsy-Korean joke – Korean and Japanese peasants both enjoy charades about bumpkins tripping over their own feet, and the Japanese apparently thought this sort of thing was typical of the people who invented the mariner's compass, the astrolabe, central heating and the world's best phonetic alphabet. The Korean Yi Pang-chang died in police custody some nine months later. Oddly enough, nobody attacked Japan's Korean community because of the attempt on Hirohito's life. But when some Chinese newspapers dryly suggested that it was too bad the 'clumsy Korean' hit the wrong carriage, Japanese settlers in Shanghai trashed the Chinese newspaper offices. This vandalism may not have been spontaneous.

While Korean patriots were throwing grenades at Hirohito – after an earlier Korean had become a national hero by killing Hirobumi Ito – Soviet forgeries were being created. 'The Tanaka Memorial,' was a fake Japanese plan to take over the world. It was a somewhat more adept forgery than the pre-Soviet Russian forgery known as The Protocol of the Learned Elders of Zion, in which the Jews were supposedly scheming to do the same. The methodology was similar: take a few undoubted facts and build a towering false edifice on top of them. One of the silliest aspects of the Tanaka Memorial was that the Japanese of the 1920s were planning to use Koreans as a Fifth Column to take over China. Most Koreans who had any interest in politics were staunchly and bitterly anti-Japanese. But since most Korean patriots were Christians, the Soviets probably saw them as subversive and expendable.

The Roosevelt and Taft administrations had given a key role in the development of Manchuria to Japan by the secret Root-Takahira Agreement. But the re-adjustments after the Chinese Revolution of 1911 and after World War I had essentially allowed China to supervise Manchuria through the control of local war lords, who swayed in their allegiance between China and Japan with indifference.

The Japanese continued to operate the South Manchurian Railroad, one of their proudest assets after the Russo-Japanese War. On 18 September 1931, a bomb went off under the track. The Japanese Kwantung Army, which operated in a semi-independent manner, sent in seven trains loaded with soldiers and took over political control of Manchuria to protect Japanese settlers and railroad workers. Four more trains followed. More Japanese soldiers rumbled through Manchuria in trucks and took over an area the size of France and Germany put together, with a population of 30 million. Manchuria was now administered by Japan. The Chinese government protested to the League of Nations, which backed China against Japan – but not to the point of countering Japanese aggression. The Japanese dropped out of the League of Nations.[1]

By 1932, the full brunt of the Smoot–Hawley Tariff had fallen on Japan. The United States under President Herbert Hoover had already begun infrastructure projects – notably the Hoover Dam on the Colorado River – to provide jobs but also actual, measurable electricity and effective irrigation, because the Republicans had qualms about 'make-work' projects. This gave jobs to 4,000 Americans – all but a handful of them white – and helped develop Las Vegas and Los Angeles, but it didn't solve the Depression or restore the kind of prosperity needed to improve the Japanese export economy. Japanese exports of the 1920s and early 1930s were mostly luxury items – silk and porcelain in particular – and these were the first things that hard-pressed Americans and Europeans stopped buying when things got tough, especially when the 50 per cent duty drove the prices so high that practically nobody on either side of the Pacific could afford them. Japanese farmers whose sons couldn't take ship to California or Hawaii to find work and send back most of their money were forced to sell their daughters as geisha, as prostitutes, or more often as housemaids, factory workers or agricultural serfs to those land-owners who still made a living growing rice and vegetables. Bankers, who seemed to do well no matter what happened, became the stock-company villains for the junior officers and sergeants who saw themselves as the defenders of the common people against the exploiters who were, in their turn, dupes of the whites.

Most Japanese were unrepentant after the seizure of Manchuria on a clumsy pretext, but a Chinese boycott of Japanese manufactured goods, on top of the Smooth-Hawley Traffic, was deemed insufferable. In Shanghai, an international city with a substantial number of Japanese residents, Chinese shop-keepers left Japanese toys, photograph records, luxury foods and other products piled in the streets outside Chinese shops rather than accept delivery. Some Japanese and some Chinese with Japanese friends were beaten up on the street. Japanese children were escorted to school by armed guards because Chinese gangsters had threatened to kidnap and torture them.

On 18 January 1932, a Chinese mob beat up five Japanese Buddhist priests and two of the priests died. A Japanese mob burned down a Chinese towel factory and two Chinese died. The Japanese then bombed Chapei – the section of Shanghai where the menacing gangsters reportedly came from – and killed about 100 Chinese, few of whom were gangsters. Japanese troops from naval vessels on the Yangtze River landed 'to restore order' and most of the European settlers actually backed the Japanese, though the Christian missionaries and some Germans were horrified by the bombing of civilians. On the international level, the Japanese were reviled. Japanese reservists who lived in Shanghai sometimes responded by beating up Europeans, including women, whom they met on the street.[2]

The battles between Chinese and Japanese troops in Shanghai killed about 14,000 people, most of them soldiers or armed partisans on one side or the other, but the result was a foregone conclusion. The Chinese soldiers, many of them kids of Boy Scout age, put up a much better fight than anybody expected, but the Chinese were humbled once again. Then a couple of Koreans stepped in to avenge the defeat.

Ku Kim had relocated to China after his last confrontation with the Japanese authorities and formed a Korean Patriotic Corps. The 'athletic organization' was actually a group of political activities committed to assassination until the Japanese got out of Korea. One of Ku Kim's recruits was Yun Bong-gil, born in Korea in 1908 and relocated to Shanghai. In 1930, Ku Kim's bearish bulk and beaver teeth made him too conspicuous to attempt any assassinations at close range himself, but Yun Bong-gil had volunteered to fill in for Ku Kim.

On 29 April 1932 the victorious Japanese in Shanghai were celebrating the Emperor's birthday with speeches by dignitaries from a grandstand in Hongkou Park. Outside the perimeter of the crowd and the police, Ku Kim and Yun Bong-gil bowed to one another with tears in their eyes. Then Yun handed Ku Kim his watch and his pocket change. He would not be needing them again.[3]

'The Japanese National Anthem was being played, when a youth was seen to step forward and place a cylinder on the front of the dais and then dart backwards,' *The Illustrated London News* reported.[4] 'A dull explosion immediately followed, but it attracted so little attention that the music continued playing.'

The cylinder was a bomb disguised as a water bottle. The explosion killed General Yoshinori Shirakawa and Kawabata Sadaji, the government minister for Japanese residents in Shanghai. Mamoru Shigemitsu, the Japanese envoy to Shanghai, lost a leg, and Admiral Kisaburo Nomura – the target of Kilsoo Haan's sarcastic car purchase offer just before Pearl Harbor – lost an eye, as Kilsoo Haan reminded him. 'Others were seen to collapse wounded and bleeding while soldiers seized the youth and battered him. Subsequently, another bomb of the same type was found near the dais.' Yun, in fact, had attempted to detonate a second bomb disguised as a lunchbox to kill himself and the soldiers arresting him. The detonator failed. Yun was severely beaten, put on trial and convicted on 5 May. Yun Bong-gil was executed by a firing squad in Japan on 19 December, and his body was buried in a Japanese cemetery, perhaps to keep the Koreans from turning his grave into a shrine.

Chiang Kai-shek, angry after his defeat by the Japanese, called Yun Bong-gil 'a young Korean patriot who has accomplished something tens of thousands of Chinese soldiers could not do.'[5] Syngman Rhee, however, disapproved of the incident and of Ku Kim's assassination policy because he said that the Japanese would use the assassinations as a pretext for further oppression. Ku Kim has retained more respect than Syngman Rhee among modern Koreans, but in the short term, Rhee had a point: before the assassination in Shanghai, the Japanese-run schools in Korea had been bilingual. After the Shanghai grandstand assassination, the Korean language was forbidden. Koreans were given to understand that if they wanted to make anything of their lives, they should not speak Korean in public and adopt Japanese names as quickly as possible.

The deletion of the Korean language from the curriculum of Japanese-supervised Korean schools can only have angered Kilsoo Haan, and the celebrity that cost Yun Bong-gil his brave young life undoubtedly caught his attention. He began to cultivate active members of the Korean resistance against Japan, now based largely in China. One of the leaders was Kiusik Kim – one of several spellings – who had been raised by the Underwood missionary family after being orphaned at the age of six. Kiusic Kimm, as Kilsoo Haan called him, was a graduate of Roanoke College with a master's degree from Princeton. After his studies Kimm had returned to Korea and worked as a schoolteacher before the Japanese annexation. Unlike Syngman Rhee, Kiusic Kimm was actually able to gain admittance to the Paris Peace Conference after World War I in 1919, but he had been deliberately ignored, since Japan – designated as Korea's new owner by the still-secret Taft-Katsura Agreement – was at that time an important Anglo-American ally. Kimm's legislative attempts to win independence for Korea marked the first part of his career. But as the League of Nations and the United States showed no real interest in an independent Korea, Kimm and his supporters fell back on gathering intelligence that might help them undermine Japan and win the respect of America.[6]

The Korean independence advocates had two pieces of good luck. The terrifying Terauchi's Japan, having been cajoled into fighting the Bolsheviks in Siberia, was substantially abandoned by the Americans, the British, and the French, which led to disaffection on both sides. The Anglo-Saxons and France – afraid of the growth of Bolshevism in China – soon forced Japan to return Shantung, the prize booty from the Japanese victory over Germany in World War I, to the rightful Chinese owners, who had declared war on Germany and had supplied 200,000 laborers to work behind the Western Front, but no warships or combat troops as Japan had supplied. The Japanese felt jilted and old acquaintance was gradually being forgot.

On 20 April 1933, KIlsoo Haan – given the code name W.K. Lyhan – was designated by Kiusic Kimm, the Shanghai-based head of the Sino-Korean People's League, to participate at a conference with US Army Intelligence at Fort Shafter near Honolulu on 21 July 1933.[7] On 6 March 1934 Kilsoo Haan under his real name confidently wrote a letter to First Lady Eleanor Roosevelt and presented her with a report he had prepared about the problems with the Japanese in Hawaii, or as he came to call it, 'The Japanization of Hawaii.'[8] Haan probably selected Eleanor Roosevelt because she was famously more sympathetic to minorities than her patrician husband Franklin Delano Roosevelt.

Haan was objecting in particular to the use of free Japanese textbooks donated by the Japanese government to the after-hours schools operated for Japanese and Japanese-American youngsters in public school buildings. Japanese schoolteachers – according for future US Medal of Honor winner and US Senator Daniel Inouye – were sometimes fanatical Japanese nationalists. The Japanese teachers tried to inculcate this attitude into any students of Japanese ancestry. Inouye also noted that the Japanese-language schools encouraged feelings of contempt for the Chinese, which he himself refused to share. He grew up in a Chinese neighborhood and had many friends there. George S. Patton had noted the same fiercely nationalistic attitude on the part of the Japanese-language teachers when he was stationed in Hawaii. Patton said that in case of a war with Japan he would have arrested the Japanese-language schoolteachers – but not the general population.

Kilsoo Haan's complaint (this time written under the name of W.K. Lyhan) brought some cautious agreement from the Superintendent of Public Instruction for the Territory of Hawaii, Oren E. Long, who wrote on 21 January 1935:

> The whole issue of the Japanese language schools will doubtless remain a controversial issue for a great many years. I am familiar with opinions expressed some years ago by a number of public school leaders and university professors. They agreed at the time that the language schools were not a particular detriment to the best development of the community. At the same time I think that each of these educational leaders looks forward to the day when the schools will be eliminated.
>
> My own opinion is that all these schools have a direct bearing on Hawaii's standing before the American bar of public opinion, and for this reason I should like to see them eliminated.
>
> I am not in a position to state definitely that they interfere with either the problem of spoken English or of citizenship. Further study on these important phases of the question will doubtless be made.[9]

Other school officials requested more information without venturing an opinion. Harry Carr, a columnist with *the Los Angeles Times*, visited Hawaii in the summer of 1936, had dinner with Kilsoo Haan and his wife Estelle Yoon – traditional Korean wives keep their last names after marriage – and examined his notes on the Japanese schools in Hawaii.

'It was his confidential assessment that I was fighting a losing battle against the "Combined Big Five" [the sugar plantation owners] and the Japanese Consulate,' Haan wrote in a memo to himself in 1936. He quoted Carr: 'The Japanese consulate influence seems to be in position to use the Big Five against you and your work. When the chips fly, I don't think the military and the Navy boys will help you.'

'He suggested that I concentrate on obtaining documentary evidence,' Kilsoo Haan noted.[10]

Kilsoo Haan took some criticism from Kiusic Kimm, who still believed in peaceful agitation for Korean independence, and agreed to tone down his hostility to Japan – or so it seemed. In 1936, he was one of a number of Koreans who actually signed on for some part-time work with the Japanese Consulate in Honolulu. Data collected by the Clausen Committee investigating Pearl Harbor discovered that 'Kylsoo Haan' had been paid $60.00 on 25 May 1936, $40 on 15 August 1936, and $10 on 25 August 1936.[11] Kilsoo Haan's detractors briefly used this schedule of payments to assure people he had actually been a Japanese agent. What happened next would seem to prove otherwise.

On 27 February 1937, Kilsoo Haan, using the name W.K. Lyhan of the Sino-Korean Peoples League of Hawaii, sent a letter to the Legislature of the Territory of Hawaii following up on a petition about the Japanese-language schools sent in 1935. Haan charged that the Japanese government was now trying to unite Asians against whites in Hawaii – always the dream of the Black Dragon Society – and to push for statehood under Japanese leadership. Japanese Vice-Consul Tsueneshiro Yamazaki termed the accusation 'ridiculous.'[12]

This was a key issue to the Asian community – and to their enemies. Since Hawaii was a territory, Asian laborers were still allowed to reside in Hawaii without the restrictions of the 1924 immigration law: that restriction to 100 Chinese and 100 Japanese, including Koreans, who were often reluctant nationals of the Japanese Empire. Kilsoo Haan portrayed himself and the Korean community at large as friends of the Hawaiian Sugar Planters Association in an extended letter, written long-hand, on 5 December 1937.

The Koreans during the past 35 years have positive demonstrated their sincerity in the belief that the Hawaiian Sugar Planters are the stabilizing industries in Hawaii.

May I remind your Association that the Koreans fearlessly took the leading role to break the two major strikes in the past aiding the Planters to bring about stability and security? It further more saved millions of dollars for HSPA because of that belief...

Hawaii is our home and thus United States of America, our adopted country. We want to do what we can and all we can to offset any activity that jeopardizes our economic and national welfare and that the prosperity and security in these island be insured.

My activities during the past years have been called anti-Japanese by prominent sugar officials. In spite of this biased and prejudiced attitude of their acts toward me I have continued to make efforts to call their attention of the dangers lurking in the so-called *cultural* activities of the Japanese through the cooperation of many of the leading men of Hawaii…

May I sincerely call your attention to the probable danger, namely the curtailment of Hawaii's alien supply to the sugar and the pineapple industries if and when Hawaii becomes the 49th State of the Union?

In searching for opinions I have found there are strong doubts whether Hawaii can stop or prohibit alien laborers from migrating to the mainland. Today any alien Japanese or a Filipino is permitted to travel from one state to all parts of the 48 States in the Union. Under the international treaties and in the act granting independence to the Philippines, aliens are given the right to travel and reside wherever within the USA.

When Hawaii becomes a State, the laws applicable to the 48 states regarding aliens will automatically be enforced in the state of Hawaii. Hence Hawaii labor supply under statehood will be precarious and subjected to a last resort, namely the importation of Filipinos in large numbers again.

If and when the Sugar Planters resort to this there will be an unfavorable racial question raised not only by the Americans in the Pacific Coast but by laborers in Hawaii.

Furthermore, the evidence presented to the Statehood Committee revealed that the object of the Institute for Education of Overseas Japanese is:

To educate the children of Japanese living abroad in order to establish a foundation for their future overseas development and solving the education of these children to encourage overseas expansion.

In essence, it shows Japan's expansion toward Hawaii will inevitably compel the HSPA to face Japanization of Hawaii and Japan's political and economic influences over Hawaii.

HSPA and the pineapple industries are going to face only the benefits of a temporary nature. However to Japan and the Japanese-Americans this becomes permanent.

Unfortunately Japan will use this opportunity to set a firmer foothold, aiding Japan's future expansion of her Empire in the Pacific.

It is not a secret when the Japanese leaders predict that within a decade or more years, there will be many of the Japanese sitting with the directors of the Big Five not as observers but as directors. These Japanized trained men [entering] into the directorship of the Big Five will be a matter of time and when Hawaii becomes the 49th State it will hasten and strength[en] Japan's influence over Hawaii.

Toward the end of the letter, Kilsoo Haan began to repeat himself as he urged the Big Five to discuss all matters publicly and act in the interest of all residents of Hawaii and not just the sugar companies.[13] His obvious intention was to alert the sugar companies to the threat of what he himself feared most – a Japanese take-over aided by Japanese settlers, as had happened in Korea and had started to happen in Shanghai.

8

THE 'CHINA INCIDENT'

Two weeks after Kilsoo Haan summarized his beliefs that the
Japanese were scheming to take over Hawaii, the Japanese Army
took over Nanking, the capital of Nationalist China, and committed
a series of war crimes that horrified Europeans of every political
persuasion. One hero of Nanking, John Rabe of Siemens AEG,
was an admirer of Adolf Hitler. An American commentator, Edgar
Snow, a Leftist who once got rich on Wall Street, was an intense
admirer of Mao Tse-tung. A third witness, Georg Rosen, was a
Rhodes Scholar and a German Jew who had been temporarily
retained in the Nazi diplomatic corps. The disparate background
of key witnesses, and the fact that some other witnesses were on
the Chinese payroll, make for a very difficult analysis of what
actually happened at Nanking and why. Frank Tillman Durdin,
an honest Texan who was respected by both sides, summed up the
surest statement about Nanking: neither side had anything to be
proud of.[1]

Most Americans were far more upset about the strafing and
bombing of the USS *Panay*, an American gunboat on patrol on the
Yangtze River – three US sailors killed and 20 seriously wounded –
than they were about a huge but disputed number of murders of
civilians inside the city.

The numbers were controversial due to the sources. Iris
Chang's 300,000 Chinese dead and 20,000 to 80,000 rapes came
directly from Communist sources. Harold Timperley, an English

newsman who was both a pacifist and a paid propagandist for Chiang Kai-shek, claimed 200,000 Chinese dead from battle or murder.[2] Edgar Snow, a devoted Communist sympathizer, cited 42,000 dead and claimed that the Japanese had raped every Chinese female from 10 to 70 and that the outrage had gone on for six weeks.[3] During this time, Japanese newspapers published photographs of Chinese women and children laughing while Japanese translators gave them emergency food. Minnie Vautrin, a devout Christian missionary teacher and frequent rescuer of rape victims, glumly vouched for the Japanese photographs as authentic and probably not taken under coercion.[4] Minnie Vautrin had also sheltered Chinese girls during the 1926 take-over of Nanking by the National Chinese and she was at first astounded and then furious at Japanese outrages, which were regarded as completely out of character after the decent record that Japanese had established in Jack London's day. Her health broke down due to overwork and depression and she committed suicide after her return to the United States.

The German businessman John Rabe, though he was an admirer of Hitler, was regarded, as Minnie Vautrin was, as a hero by the Chinese. Rabe personally broke up several rape attempts with the help of Japanese officers: he initially estimated the Chinese dead at 50,000 to 60.000 from all causes and guessed at about 1,000 rapes.[5] Georg Rosen of the German embassy, the Jewish veteran of World War I, also reported numerous Japanese atrocities. The Reverend John Magee, an Episcopal priest, was able to photograph some outrages.

No responsible person denied that atrocities had taken place at Nanking – but only one American reporter told both sides of the story. His name was Frank Tillman Durbin and he worked for the *New York Times*. Durdin had covered China for the past seven years as a correspondent for the *New York Times* when Nanking fell on 13 December 1937.[6]

Chiang Kai Shek's German military advisors told him that Nanking couldn't be defended but he let his army take shelter behind the walls, where many of the undisciplined conscripts made the lives of the Chinese citizens miserable by stealing food. The Japanese dropped surrender leaflets by air on 10 December and urged the Chinese to surrender or to evacuate and declare Nanking an open city. As the Japanese closed in, Chiang and his command party fled in a seaplane and left General Tang Sheng-shih in charge. Durbin wrote:

> The Chinese command, fully realizing the practical certainty that the Chinese Army would be completely surrounded in the walled city of Nanking – trapped like rats ... chose voluntarily to place themselves in just such a situation, apparently with the intention of making the capture of the city as costly to the Japanese as possible in a final heroic gesture of the kind so dear to the Chinese heart. The disgraceful part of the whole business is that the Chinese command proved lacking in the courage needed to carry through their oft-announced and apparent intentions. When Japanese troops had succeeded in breaking over the southwestern wall and while the Hsiakwan back door was still open ... General Tang and a few close associates fled, leaving subordinate commanders and wellnigh leaderless troops to the mercy of a hopeless situation, which probably had never been explained to them in the first place... The Chinese burned nearly all the suburbs, including fine buildings and homes in Mausoleum Park... The Japanese even avoided bombing Chinese troop concentrations in built-up areas, apparently to preserve the buildings. The fine Ministry of Communications building was the only big government structure destroyed inside the city. It was fired by the Chinese.

When the Japanese broke in, those Chinese troops who were still committed to battle reportedly turned their machine guns on their own troops who broke and ran. The Japanese killed the Chinese who fought to the death, and then began to slaughter the military fugitives they caught in civilian clothes. The Japanese Army rated the fighting as far less fierce than at Shanghai, where the Chinese had held out longer than anyone thought possible. Arthur Menken of Paramount Newsreels, embedded with the Japanese Army, filmed Nanking residents cheering the Japanese as liberators from the constant looting and threats of the abandoned Chinese soldiers. He also told the Associated Press that he saw large numbers of

Chinese soldiers changing into civilian clothes and of looting by both the Chinese and the Japanese troops. Then things got really ugly. Durdin dispatch published on 18 December:

> The helpless Chinese troops, disarmed for the most part and ready to surrender, were systematically rounded up and executed. The Japanese had not shelled the Safety Zone established by Americans and Europeans, but they dragged off many Chinese males of military age they found there, and executed them.
>
> Chinese women were freely molested by Japanese soldiers, and American missionaries personally know of cases where many were taken from refugee camps and violated.

Durdin, respected by both sides for his blunt journalistic integrity, estimated a week after the fall of Nanking that the Chinese Army had lost about 13,000 men in battle and another 20,000 to execution. Japanese casualties were about 1,000. Looting, arson, and rape continued sporadically for the next six weeks. The Japanese military commander, General Iwame Matsui, was long known as a friend of China in pre-war days. When he rode his horse into the city in triumph and discovered the carnage and rubble left in the wake of the capture, Matsui was horrified. He angrily rebuked his subordinates – and then his health collapsed and he took to his sickbed. The violence flickered on for weeks afterwards. Matsui adopted a Chinese baby girl and raised her as his own daughter, Matsuko – Matsui's Girl. Some Japanese played with Chinese children while other Japanese raped their sisters.

'There was little glory for either side in the battle of Nanking,' Durdin concluded. There was also little hope that Japan's original intention of uniting and modernizing Asia would survive the documented brutality at Nanking and – perhaps even more important – the humiliation that the one-sided battle and the massacre that followed had inflicted on Chiang Kai Shek and his Nationalist government. The Chinese Nationalists were now incapable of following their pre-war intention of destroying the Chinese Communists. The Chinese Nationalists inflated the number of killings and rapes in an attempt to win the sympathy of the American public. Most Americans were indifferent. Chinese propaganda led most Americans to believe the entire population had been exterminated, as at Homer's Troy or at Carthage or Jerusalem in Roman times. In fact, the vast majority of citizens of Nanking survived and six months after the battle there was a reasonably effective Chinese collaborationist government operating out of Nanking. The population was soon larger than it had been at the time of the battle. But the Japanese were now stuck with a war they couldn't win militarily and politically couldn't afford to lose.

One of the real puzzles of Nanking is that many of the Japanese troops were recalled reservists, men in their 30s or even in their 40s, some of whom believed that Japan's real mission in Asia was to construct a barrier against Russian Communism and Chinese banditry. Other Japanese soldiers were outright humanitarians before they were conscripted.

In 1937, Sadao Yamanaka, 27, one of Japan's greatest film directors, released his last movie, *Humanity and Paper Balloons*. It tells the story of a *samurai* who has had to sell his sword to buy rice to feed his family, and of his wife, who makes paper balloons to help earn a living – both violations of the rigid *samurai* code. The plot proceeds to a tragic ending. Critics who saw the film hailed it as a masterpiece, a condemnation of those who would inflict the *samurai* ethic on people who were too poor to afford the trappings and caste-related work restrictions. Sadao Yamanaka received his Army draft notice the day film opened. A year later, he was dead of intestinal disorders he contracted serving in China.[7]

Before Yamanaka died in China, he encountered another great Japanese film director, Yasujiro Ozu, then 34, also recalled into service after making sensitive movies about family life and its disappointments from a woman's point of view. Ozu had apparent homosexual leanings as an adolescent but sublimated his instincts with heavy drinking while he lived out his single life with his mother and sister. He seems an unlikely mass murderer. Even social protestors like the trade unionist Ashihei Hino or the fearless feminist author Fumiko Hayashi said that the Chinese had committed far more atrocities against one another than the

Japanese had committed in China.[8] The numbers at Nanking remained elusive. The Red Swastika Society, a Chinese benevolent group, claimed to have buried 42,000 Chinese – only 1.2 per cent of the dead were reported as women or children – but the Japanese thought the numbers were exaggerated because the Chinese laborers were paid by the corpse. George Rosen, the German Jewish diplomat who hated Japanese militarism, agreed with the Japanese about the padded burial figures. The Safety Zone Committee signed off on 49 murders and 360 rapes, but eight of the rape victims had been murdered – along with uncounted others – and other victims may have been too ashamed to claim damages.

At the Tokyo Trials in 1946, a lone Chinese named Lu Su claimed he had seen the Japanese 7th Infantry regiment round up exactly 57,418 Chinese deserters and stragglers, truss them up with barbed wire, machine gun them at Straw Shoe Gorge, burn the bodies with kerosene, and float the remnants down the Yangtze. Nobody else in the Safety Zone heard the machine guns or saw the corpse fires. But the Tokyo Trials had to contend with 800,000 Japanese burned to death in American air raids so the number 50,000 went in the books along with the battle deaths reported by Frank Tillman Durdin. The numbers at Nanking, unreliable as they are from both the Chinese and the Japanese side, were expressions of injured national pride or shame rather than accurate statistics.

Revulsion against Nanking, and even against the sinking of the USS *Panay*, certainly didn't stop American companies from selling war materiel to the Japanese – not just steel and gasoline, but aircraft. In 1938, the year after Nanking and the sinking of the USS *Panay* by Japanese aircraft, Seversky Aircraft Corporation of Farmingdale, New York, accepted an order for 20 two-seater versions of the P-35, then the first-line American fighter plane. The P-35s flew with Japanese pilots at their controls in World War II. For some Americans, the war in China was a business opportunity. Chiang Kai-shek bought most of his military equipment from Nazi Germany before Hitler and the Japanese signed the Anti-Comintern Pact, but Americans sold military hardware to both sides until the embargo on selling weapons to any nation but Great Britain was adopted on 18 July 1940.[9] The war in China may have helped relieve the Great Depression in the United States but it was a tragedy for both the Chinese and, eventually, for the Japanese and the Koreans.

The Second Sino-Japanese War was Sophocles in reverse: the Greeks would have put the farce at the end after the three tragedies, but the Chinese- Japanese catastrophe started with the farce and ended with three tragedies unrivalled in terms of victims killed and opportunities lost. By 1937, some Japanese felt they needed a war to save the national economy – and perhaps to save the emperor. In 1933, as the Depression had deepened, all of Japan was singing a song made famous by a geisha named Katsutaro, played on the newly popular phonograph or radio, about the transient nature of the pleasures of life.

Japanese officers and sergeants were also singing the song with new lyrics in their mess halls:

Those in power are swollen with pride
But have no real concern for the country
The wealthy show off their riches,
But care nothing for the good of the country.

The author of the song, Takashi Mikami, was a lieutenant in the Japanese Navy. The officers and sergeants of the Japanese Army sang his song too, and agreed with him. The sentiment echoed that of of an American ditty from a decade before: 'There's nothing surer, the rich get rich and the poor get poorer.

Some Japanese knew this song from studying English and most agreed. The seizure of Manchuria from China had brought some brief hope to the struggling Japanese economy, beset by the Great Depression and the tsunami-like ripple effect of the Smoot-Hawley Tariff. The Japanese now had affordable raw materials but the markets were still closed by tariffs and economic stagnation. Now the Chinese, too, were boycotting Japanese products in rage and shame over their inability to take back Manchuria. China was plagued by wars between the Nationalist Chinese government – supported by officers who reported, however reluctantly, to Adolf Hitler – and by Mao's Chinese Communists. From the Japanese perspective. China might well be better off under Japanese administration – just as most Japanese felt Taiwan and Korea were better off under Japanese administration.

Chiang Kai-Shek, who had been a rebel against the Manchu tyrants as a young man, became the brother-in-law of Sun Yat-sen, the liberator of China from the opiate-soaked Manchu Dynasty. Chiang had received his military training in Japan. Chiang and his top German military advisor, Alexander von Falkenhausen, routinely communicated in Japanese, which Falkenhausen had learned as an attaché in Tokyo before World War I. Chiang had dumped his first two humble Chinese wives and married Mei Ling Soong, American-educated daughter of the richest man in China. Chiang became a conservative. In 1926, he put down a revolt in Nanking by Chinese trade unionists, shot the leaders, and sent their wives and daughters to the brothels.[10]

Mei Ling Chiang was no shrinking plum blossom. She made something of a career out of captivating a considerable part of the entire US State Department, including President Roosevelt, at a safe distance. Chiang, meanwhile, dropped some of his advocacy of reform and hired 40 German military advisors to keep the Communists at bay. Alexander von Falkenhausen, a Prussian royalist distantly related to the former Kaiser, also hated Communists. Falkenhausen Germans showed Chiang how to stop the Communists. He authorised the construction of a network of large pill-boxes – 'turtle houses' – constructed in depth and supplied with food and ammunition by truck all over Northern China so that the Nationalist troops controlled the roads and were independent of the support of the peasants. Communism in Northern China began to shrivel.

As Falkenhausen was gaining the upper hand over the Communists, the mutual enemies of the Chinese Nationalist and the Japanese, a rebellion was also brewing in Japan. In July 1933, 44 members of two obscure and short-lived Japanese groups, the Love County Labor Society and the Japan Production Society, were arrested and charged with planning to stage an uprising and wipe out the bankers, the industrialist, and those members of Hirohito's cabinet and diplomatic corps who had shown such indifference to the poor. Plans to put Hirohito's more affable younger brother

Chichibu on the throne in his place were revealed only a decade later but were known to the secret police at the time.

Hirohito wasn't popular with a great many Japanese working people or his own junior officers, but he took a long time to get the message. In February of 1934, Hirohito was shown the statistics of poverty: in 1932, 12,108 farm girls from northern Honshu, Japan's biggest island, had been sold to Tokyo labor contractors by families who could no longer feed them or find husbands for them. By 1934, the figure calculated for 1933 had reached 58,172 – 2,196 of the prettiest and smartest as *maiko,* apprentice geisha who might hope to better themselves as rich men's mistresses, 4,512 as common prostitutes, 5,952 as bar girls who tried to act like the American girls they saw in Hollywood movies, 5,279 as casual laborers, 17,260 as factory workers, and 19,244 as nursemaids for families which demonstrably still had money.

'The farmers should not talk on and on about the unpleasant aspects of their life but should concentrate on the enjoyment of nature around them,' Hirohito blandly told his advisors.[11]

Hirohito was clearly a man of limited perspective. Members of the old nobility, not in awe of the 'divine' role of emperor manufactured by Hirobumi Ito in the late 19th century as an antidote to European colonialism and more of Japan's feudal wars, sometimes wondered if all those cousin-marriages hadn't flawed his genes. Hirohito may have wondered about this himself: His own personal crisis before 1935 was that he had failed to father a male heir, and since Hirohito was the first Japanese emperor in history to be whole-heartedly monogamous, the fact that he and the Empress Nagako had four daughters but no son at this time was a serious worry. Some Japanese may have seen it as a curse, or at least a supernatural omen. More educated Japanese simply thought the dynasty was inbred, and perhaps an anachronism.

Hirohito, as a symbol of Japan's spiritual claims, was bulletproof except to Communists and Korean nationalists. But young officers formed a number of plots to eliminate the bankers and senior statesmen they blamed for widespread poverty and a lack of defiance toward Russia and the Anglo-Saxons. In February of 1936, a group of junior officers and sergeants led 1,359 confused troops in a take-over of Tokyo and a wave of assassinations that rocked the cabinet.[12] Hirohito appointed Koki Hirota, a stone-mason's son, as prime minister and urged him to try to save the dynasty. Hirota began some New Deal-style plans for extended school years and rural electrification, but the Japanese economy still lagged.

Japan's army in China – permitted by the treaty at the end of the Russo-Japanese War – including one garrison near the Marco Polo Bridge, a landmark already standing when Marco Polo told all of Europe about the wonders of China's ancient culture – paper money, movable type, eyeglasses, noodles and silk were just some of the marvels – when Europe was still recovering from the loss of the Crusades during the waning of the Middle Ages. The bridge was a fabulous site for viewing the phases of the moon, a favorite pastime of Chinese and Japanese alike in gentler times.

On 7 July 1937, a Japanese infantry company, part of the garrison authorised after the Boxer Rebellion in 1900, was staging night maneuvers in a gravel pit near the Marco Polo Bridge. The soldiers set up their machinegun, loaded with blanks, and enlivened the night with gunfire and a bugle call. They were abruptly sprayed with a dozen real bullets from the Chinese garrison stationed nearby – but none of the Japanese was hit. This incident has never been conclusively explained: Chinese historians said, plausibly, that the Chinese Nationalist troops mistook the Japanese machinegun shooting off blanks for the real thing. One Japanese historian has asserted that the Chinese who actually did the shooting were random gangsters siphoned into the Nationalist Chinese Army: the Chinese gangsters had supposedly been paid by Communists to touch off trouble with the Japanese. In a fight between Chiang Kai Shek's Chinese anti- Communists and Hirohito's Japanese anti-Communists, the Communists were the obvious winners.

In the confusion of a peacetime unit taking real gunfire, one Japanese enlisted man disappeared. As soon as both sides determined by telephone calls and personal conversations that they weren't at war, the Japanese asked the Chinese if they had the missing soldier, and the Chinese replied that they didn't. The Japanese enlisted man showed up later that night, alive and unhurt. Accounts differ as to whether he had dropped out of formation to urinate, had slipped away to a brothel, or had fallen into the gravel pit while intoxicated. In any case, he hadn't been murdered by sinister Chinese villains. The Chinese and Japanese junior officers on both sides had behaved responsibly. The farce was over. The tragedy was about to begin.

Word of the bloodless gunfire at the Marco Polo Bridge triggered responses from both the Chinese and the Japanese. The hotheads on both sides demanded action. A Japanese airplane bombed a Chinese barracks – manned by puppet troops who were actually in Japanese pay. The angry puppet Chinese troops believed the accidental Japanese bombing was deliberate and spilled over into a nearby Japanese settlement and murdered 260 Japanese and Koreans. Now Japanese and Korean blood had been spilled, and the Japanese dispatched three divisions to China as reinforcements. The Chinese responded with their own reinforcements.

Those Japanese who still followed Black Dragon Society precepts of Asia for the Asians, and a common defense against Russia in particular, made one last bid for peace. The Black Dragon supporters, including the leery Prime Minister Fumimaro Konoye, located Ryusuke Miyazaki, son of the giant samurai Toten Miyazaki who had fought with Sun Yat Sun for a modernized and progressive China. Miyazaki's father was a hero remembered to the Chinese as Americans remembered Lafayette, Steuben, and Pulaski. The younger Miyazaki was also respected by the Chinese as a man of vision who favored the Asian brotherhood that the older Miyazaki has risked his life for so many times.

Unfortunately, the younger Miyazaki was arrested by the Japanese secret police when he attempted to take ship at Kobe and bring the Chinese and the Japanese back into the harmony that his father and Sun Yat Sen had risked their lives for. China and Japan were soon at war.

Chiang was a man with a dagger at his back. His own people wanted him to stop fighting with Mao and to fight the Japanese. Chiang did not personally agree: 'The Japanese are a disease of the skin – the Communists are a disease of the heart.' But Chiang agreed to fight, believing he could throw away three Chinese divisions to take out one Japanese division. Compared to Chiang, Alexander von Falkenhausen, a Prussian militarist who detested Hitler and had protected Palestinian Jews from the Turks during World War I, was an outright humanitarian. He told Chiang to withdraw from Northern China where food was scarce and Communists were plentiful, retreat southward where food was plentiful and Chinese loyalties more stable, and let the Japanese wear themselves out fighting transportation problems instead of predictably destroying unprepared Chinese conscripts in huge numbers and ruining Chinese morale. Chiang ordered Falkenhausen to defend Shanghai for political reasons. Falkenhausen, unwilling to run out on the Chinese he had trained, subsisted on cognac and hard-boiled eggs as he led some very brave young Chinese soldiers in a tougher battle than the Japanese expected.

When Falkenhausen lost Shanghai as he knew he would, he felt back toward the capital at Nanking and told Chiang not to attempt a defense. The Nanking Massacre was a result of Japanese rage and also of Chiang's obtuse refusal to give ground and save lives. Falkenhausen indirectly saved some of his Chinese soldiers: he knew the Japanese had been trained by Germans and he warned his Chinese soldiers to surrender only in uniform if things went badly. The Japanese actually accepted (and photographed) the surrender of the German-trained, uniformed troops. The Chinese troops who threw away their uniforms were wantonly but lawfully executed – though the executions were cruel and stupid, since the captured Chinese could have been used as laborers or even released without much fear of retribution,

Falkenhausen was outraged and disgusted by what happened to the civilians and even to the deserters at Nanking, and he may have had the last word on the future defense of China before he was called back to Germany at the end of 1938. He suggested to his Chinese officers that Japanese officers could be picked out by their *samurai* swords, map cases and binoculars and picked off by Chinese snipers. Suicidal bayonet charges were a waste of Chinese lives.

The Chinese troops Falkenhausen had trained actually won a local victory at Taierzhuang where the Chinese used a night attack to off-set Japan's edge in artillery. Then Chiang tried to slow to a stop the Japanese advance by blowing up the Yellow River dikes that irrigated Chinese rice lands. The Japanese slogged forward through the mud or paddled in small boats. The destruction of the dikes – by Chiang's own forces –.probably killed more Chinese through famine than all the bombs, bullets and bayonets the Japanese imported to China, though the Japanese themselves fought mercilessly when they encountered Chinese guerillas.

The Second Sino-Japanese War that started in 1937 was a disaster for China and ultimately, once the United States and Britain were drawn in, a disaster for Japan. But for the Korean independence movements, the war was an opportunity. Koreans now understood, after discoveries by Korean scholars in the 1920s, that Theodore Roosevelt had sold their country to Japan with the Taft-Katsura Agreement of 1905 and the Root-Takahira Agreement of 1908 in return for Japan's protection of Open Door China from Tsarist Russia. But by 1937 Japan was no longer protecting China for anyone but Japan. Korean agents committed to the Chinese Nationalist cause could now hope to win the support of the United States – with some Nationalist Chinese influence – and overturn Japan's privileged role, in American eyes, as Korea's rightful owner.

9

THE AMERICAN CARD

The capture of Shanghai and the catastrophe at Nanking was followed by the recall of Chiang Kai-shek's 40 Prussian military advisers back to Nazi Germany as Hitler dropped his alliance with China. Hitler had now switched to the Anti-Comintern Pact with Japan – soon to be known as the Axis. The visible decline of Chinese fighting power meant that the Korean nationalists could no longer hope to use Nationalist China to win their independence from Japan. China could barely help itself. The Koreans – Ku Kim and Syngman Rhee now bonded and leading the largest faction – fell back on the idea of winning the gratitude of the US. So did Kilsoo Haan.

Kilsoo Haan's first move was to become as important as possible to US Military Intelligence and to influential politicians. He charged – for the benefit of the Americans and to the horror of the Japanese diplomatic corps – that the Japanese were attempting to organize Korean students to act as Japanese secret agents and that Japanese-American advocacy of statehood for Hawaii would help introduce Japanese settlers to the US mainland. The Japanese indignantly denied any such intention and subjected Kilsoo Haan to whatever ridicule they could muster in a world where neither Koreans nor Japanese were taken very seriously.

Kilsoo Haan, however, used his friendship with Senator Guy Gillette of Iowa, a traditional Populist wary of Franklin D. Roosevelt's New Deal and its implications of excessive government control, to convince at least some legislators to take him seriously and not write him off as a silly little guy from a silly little country that no longer existed. Guy Gillette was known through his life as a friend of the little guy. Gillette had supported FDR's New Deal until Roosevelt was accused of trying to 'pack' the Supreme Court and centralize government powers. Gillette and his buddy Senator Ed Johnson from Colorado had also come up against British objections when they tried to rush food and medical aide to displaced refugees in Europe after the Nazi victories in 1939 and 1940. The British claimed that the Germans would use the American food and medicine to supply their own armies. Gillette's wife, the former Rose Freeman, was Jewish, and he wasn't having any of this argument while Jewish fugitives from the Nazi regime were going hungry in Nazi-occupied northern France and the Netherlands, along with members of the pre-war population who couldn't afford the black market. During the post-war years, Gillette became known as the best friend Israel ever had in politics, but in wartime his advocacy was limited to sending food and medicine – not troops. He voted with the 'isolationists,' or as they called themselves, the 'non-interventionists.'

'I had occasion to become acquainted with Mr Haan on the visit to the Territory [Hawaii] last year made by the Hawaiian Territory Commission, appointed from both houses of Congress pursuant to a resolution creating it and whose duties were to investigate conditions in the Territory relative to statehood,' Gillette wrote in a letter of introduction to Secretary of State Cordell Hull on 6 April 1939. 'In our hearings which were much extended, Mr Haan was a valuable and helpful witness and it seemed to me and several of us that he was in possession of information and in control of certain channels of information that not only aided the Committee but would be of interest to the State Department. I am informed that he is now in Washington and I am sending this letter in the hopeful anticipation that you will accord him every courtesy and consideration to which he is entitled.'[1]

The Taft-Katsura Agreement, by this time, had been revealed to Koreans as an American betrayal of Korea to Japan and Kilsoo Haan threw a veil over the seething outrage he and other Koreans felt about it, as he tried to make the Americans believe that they too were threatened by Japanese expansion.

Cordell Hull and Guy Gillette had a lot in common. Both had served in the Spanish-American War – Gillette also served overseas during World War I – and both were advocates of ordinary Americans rather than internationalists, bankers, and major manufacturers. Both could be described as liberals but not as Leftists. They were Christians who had no use for Communism or extreme Socialism. Neither was a bigot. Gillette had married his wife, the former Rose Freeman, under a *chuppah* at a Jewish ceremony with a rabbi who took the train from Des Moines, but she was later active in his own Presbyterian church. Jealous rivals – Guy was quite a catch – sometimes called Rose 'Mrs Jew-lette' – but she gradually won most people over. She was a schoolteacher, and during World War I she took a summer job in a gas mask factory to help the war effort.

Cordell Hull's wife was the daughter of a rich Jewish father and an Episcopalian mother. She was raised as an Episcopalian but Hull was reluctant to talk about her father because he had presidential aspirations and anti-Semitism was a force in American politics. Both marriages were childless, though Guy and Rose adopted a son. Gillette was deeply suspicious of FDR's ambition. Hull was from Tennessee and not as liberal as FDR might have liked. Kilsoo Haan probably received a more sympathetic audience thanks to Guy Gillette than he would have otherwise.

Kilsoo Haan's first approach to the Senate Foreign Relations Committee with the endorsement of Senator Guy Gillette was to urge the Committee to take Hawaii seriously in strategic terms: 'We believe the strategic value of Hawaii cannot be too highly stressed,' Hann said on behalf of the Sino-Korean Peoples League of Hawaii. He also urged the Americans to protect the island of Guam from what he saw as a Japanese threat.

Recent report of Dr. Laura Thompson, research associate in anthropology at the University of Hawaii, after eight months study of Guam, says that the people of Guam, too, fear Japanese domination and that they do not wish to come under Japan. Hence they 'strongly desire American fortification.'

It is interesting to note the parallel of strategic importance of these islands with Korea.

The Koreans feared Japan's domination and justly warned the Powers that their diplomatic action, turning Korea over to Japan, was contrary to their best interests.

In spite of repeated warnings in the name of 'Peace in the Far East,' the Powers applied the 'Munich' on Korea, forcefully sacrificing their freedom and independence.

We trust that Guam and Hawaii will escape the fare of Korea.[2]

Kilsoo Haan's attribution of the Taft-Katsura Agreement to 'the Powers' as opposed to Theodore Roosevelt and William Howard Taft was a fudge. Russia and China certainly had no desire whatsoever to see Japan take over Korea. Korea's foreign policy had been pro-German during World War I, which gave American diplomats an excuse for just about anything. Forcefully citing America's secret betrayal of Korea between 1905 and 1910 would not have been politic, but it would have been accurate. This would lead to problems down the road.

Kilsoo Haan cited Japanese insistence that Korean students in Japanese-run schools be required to visit Shinto shrines as part of their education and that many of the students and their parents had objected.

'This declaration was a direct violation against the Christian religion and the so called religious freedom granted under the Japanese constitution. Hence many protests were made,' Kilsoo Haan wrote in a letter circulated to Protestant denominations in the United States with missions in Korea. 'Even the Japanese Christians in the beginning made joint protests with the missionaries and the Koreans. However, protests were of no use. The Shinto militarists were bent on performing an operation on the heart of Christianity. The design of the Japanese government was to Japanize Christianity as they did Buddhism, "Ryobu Shinto," half Christian and half Shinto.'[3]

Haan noted that before 1935, missionaries had discouraged Korean-style ancestor worship – very similar to Japanese Shinto minus the intense Japanese nationalism – and worried that they might now accede to Japanese demands for what is called syncretism, an unauthorised merger of religions.

'Christianity must be saved – it is the only hope for the world,' Kilsoo Haan wrote. He was undoubtedly sincere but he made some enemies as well as friends. Bishop Herbert Welch of the Methodist Church wrote to criticize the inclusion of a statement by Haan in the US Congressional Record that implied that the Presbyterians were standing up to the Japanese demands for Shinto shrine attendance better than the Methodists were:

The only American Christian Churches of any size represented in Korea are the Presbyterian & the Methodist. The two have not agreed in their judgment on the shrine question. Mr Haan has a perfect right to his own opinion but how did he secure the right to promulgate it in this way? His letter casts serious reflections on the Korean missionaries in general and, on the Methodist Church, & on me personally.

Was it wise, was it fair to take such a case into a Government publication? I think I am calling to your attention a real grievance.[4]

On 19 February, Kilson Haan received a warm endorsement for his efforts to protect Christians from mandatory Shinto worship from T. Stanley Soltau of the Scripture League Church of Evanston, a church in Illinois that also had missions in Korea.

I would like to give you all the encouragement possible in the work you are doing in Washington;" Dr. Soltau wrote. 'I realize it is no easy task and that you must often feel lonely and discouraged, but nevertheless the Lord has called you to this particular work and will daily give you the needed grace and strength for it. You have already accomplished a good deal and I pray God that you will be used to accomplish still more.'[5]

Kilsoo Haan penned in the lower margin: 'US State Department avoided the Shinto Shrine questions like small-pox.'

Kilsoo Haan and his friends were marginally successful with their support of legislation to allow students admitted to the US as students to remain 'until there is a change in political conditions in

Chosen (Korea).' The legislation had been introduced as Senate Bill 2870 by his friend Senator Guy Gillette on 24 July 1939. KIlsoo Haan had brought individual cases to the attention of Guy Gillette and had received a thank-you note from the Korean Student Club of Los Angeles on 20 December 1939.

Dear Mr. Haan;

We are informed that through your effort, Mr. C.H. Lee, one of our club members [was] released from the immigration authority some time ago. In knowing the fact, every one of our members requests me to tell you his appreciation for the cause.

We are indeed, proud of you. You are doing 'something' that none of our past leaders have even thought of. Naturally, we value so much of your work.

We hope you success in whatever you may undertake,

Yours most cordially,
S.Y. Chang, President
Korean Students Club[6]

KIlsoo Haan also received a letter from Senator William H. King of Utah describing the progress of the proposed legislation on 13 May 1940.

My dear Mr. Haan:

As you are aware, S. 2870 is before the Committee on Immigration of the Senate. It calls for relief in a number of cases which make a strong appeal from the humanitarian standpoint. I am sure the Committee was greatly impressed with the object of the bill and the humane purposes which it seek to accomplish. After full consideration by the Committee and conferences with representatives of the United States Department of Labor, the conclusion was reached that the status quo be maintained for the period which the exigencies of the case require.

From the views expressed by the Committee and representatives of the United States Department of Labor, I am assuming to state that the persons interested will be permitted to remain in the United States it is to be hoped until there is a change in the situation in which they find themselves and their freedom from punishment or arrest would not be jeopardized if they returned to their own country.

Sincerely yours,
William King[7]

The resolution was not an actual act of legislation, but a sort of informal agreement that Koreans who might be in jeopardy would be allowed to reside in the US even though they were legally – if reluctantly – citizens of the Japanese Empire. Since the Depressian-era the US had brusquely deported *Tejanos* – Mexicans who had been born in Texas.—and had denied citizenship to Filipinos even though they had been born in a US Territory. The safe status of Korean students born in the Japanese Empire was a considerable triumph for Kilsoo Hann and his friends, including Senator Guy Gillette. It was distinctly informal but it was also binding. A letter to Kilsoo Haan from Marshall E. Dimock, an administrative assistant to the Immigration and Naturalization Service dated 5 September 1940, sketched out some of the details.

...As Mr. Shaugnessy has already told you, the Immigration and Naturalization Service cannot consider the possibility of giving any group a blanket agreement without specific authorization of Congress. We are bound by law to consider each case on its merits in conformity with the immigration laws of the United States.

I am informed by the head of our warrant branch that no Korean student has been forced to leave this country since the meeting of the Immigration Subcommittee referred to above. This being the case it would seem to be that the situation should be satisfactory to ever one concerned.

I am sure that the efforts of you and your group on behalf of democracy are appreciated by every one loyally attached to the principals of democratic government.

I trust that the above statement will be satisfactory to you in every respect.[8]

Senator Guy Gillette received a similar letter at the Senate Office Building.

Kilsoo Haan's first Pearl Harbor breakthrough – at least in retrospect – had come through a few days before. Through sources in the Korean underground, either at the Japanese consulate in Honolulu or in shipyards in Japan, he had learned that the Japanese Navy was engaged in the secret construction of midget submarines. Haan first tried to explain the importance of the submarines to General George Marshall and to Admiral William Leahy at the US State Department, who separately questioned him. The meetings were held in Washington DC at the Munitions Building in June of 1940. Haan's files contain no acknowledgement from the military men or the State Department. Haan then offered the story to Henry H. Douglas, a newsman, and on Tuesday, 3 September 1940, the *Washington Post* and the *New York Herald Tribune* both ran stories that made the Japanese midget submarines a matter of record. Henry H. Douglas wrote to Kilsoo Haan on 3 September 1940:

I got back this morning to find us on the front page of today's paper and on the back of the first section of the *Washington Post*. This of course means that it was syndicated and you may have already seen an abbreviated version of it. *The Tribune* printed it in full but the *Post* left out some parts. I got hold of as many copies as possible today and am sending you two of the *Tribune* and one of the *Post*. Syndication means that we will get more money for it, though I don't as yet know how much. I suppose I won't know for several days.

I was completely flabbergasted when I saw that they put it on the front page. The first I knew of it was when Greene called to congratulate me on it. He seemed as pleased as I was.

Let me know if you want more copies of the article.

Good luck,
Douglas.[9]

The article itself under Henry H. Douglas's byline mentions the midget subs only briefly:

At the present writing Japanese naval strength closely approximates that of the United States in some categories.

Since 1934 Japan has had a policy of strict secrecy with regard to her naval construction, and so far has been unusually successful in keeping her building a secret. Her shipyards are cities of silence, surrounded by high walls and charged wire, from which no workman ever emerges, into which no foreigner ever goes.

In spite of this secrecy it was been recently ascertained from reliable sources that in the three and a half years since the beginning of 1937 Japan has commissioned:

A 10,000-ton cruiser
2 7,500-ton cruisers
22 1,600-ton destroyers
12 1,600-tion submarines.

These additions to Japan's Navy since the end of the Washington Naval Treaty at the close of 1936 because of the denunciation of the treaty by Japan, place the comparative strength of the two fleets as follows (official United States figures from the Navy Department)

	Japan	U.S.	Japan	U.S.
Aircraft Carriers	11	6	146,520	134,500
Battleships	10	15	301, 400	464,300
Cruisers, Heavy	20	18	183,000	171,000
Cruisers, Light	24	19	144,515	157,775
Destroyers	141	201	190,148	260,600
Destroyers, Converted	...	46	...	52,620
Submarines	74	102	102,063	102,060
Total	280	407	1,067,063	1,343,155

This table brings out the fact that while we exceed Japan in number of submarines, the submarine tonnages are almost exactly equal. Also, to be added to the Japanese tonnage is their fleet of midget submarines, not included in the present figures, and concerning which a brief report recently appeared in the press. Our destroyer tonnage is considerable greater than that of Japan, while Japan has forty-four cruisers to our thirty-seven, with tonnage practically equal.[10]

The existence of the midget submarines was, as Kilsoo Haan said 'ominous'[11] because midget submarines had one purpose in modern warfare: surprise attack on moored ships or other stationary targets. John Holland, an Irish-American engineer, had originally designed his prototype submarines for harbor attacks on the Royal Navy, and had only shifted over to designing submarine cruisers with crews of dozens of sailors and deck guns after a quarrel with his original financial backers, the Irish revolutionary patriots who wanted to liberate Ireland from British rule. The emphasis that the Japanese were placing on midget submarines – they ultimately constructed about 50 of them – told Kilsoo Haan that when war came, it would begin with a surprise attack against moored ships.

At the end of 1940, Kilsoo Haan claimed another breakthrough that at first sight can only be called sensational:

On Dec, 27, 1940 in Los Angeles, California, the Korean Underground Workers purloined the Japanese War Plan – the Japanese *Mein Kampf* – from the Japanese agents from Japan. In Dec. 1940 I informed Senator Guy M. Gillette and our advisor, the retired US Navy Capt. Willis Bradley. On Jan. 8, 1941, I submitted the information – the Japanese war plan, the strategy to attack Hawaii, to President Roosevelt. On January 22, 1941, I conferred with the FBI Special Agent Mr Alex Le Grand and informed him of Japan's war plan and the need for tightening US internal security.[12]

Kilsoo Haan was engaging in melodrama: 'The Three-Power Alliance and the United States-Japanese War' by Matsuo Kinoaki was not a top-secret document. The book was a work of pro-Japanese propaganda published in Tokyo in October of 1940 to assure wary Japanese that an alliance with Hitler and Mussolini would not draw Japan – as many Japanese feared – into a hopeless war with the United States and certain defeat. Americans were told after war broke out that the Japanese dared to attack a 'decadent democracy' with twice their population and 20 times their natural resources because they thought Americans were too soft to defend themselves. But Matsuo Kinoaki, whoever he was, extolled the valor of American soldiers as seen in World War I. 'The soldiers of the American Army do not seem to be weaklings ... there is something astonishing about their excellent fighting spirit.'

Kinoaki said that American tanks, armored cars and trucks were better than Japan's. Kinoaki also said – contrary to Frank Capra's propaganda film *Why We Fight* – that a Japanese landing on the North American continent would be doomed from the start.[13]

Kinoaki, in fact, saw Japan as the target of American aggression, as Japan had been in the 1860s in the days of the USS *Wyoming*, and as Korea had been in the days of the *General Sherman*. Courageous Japanese *samurai* and Korean Tiger Hunters – coupled with the conscience of the much-maligned but honorable Ulysses S. Grant – apparently convinced the Americans that conquest of either Japan or Korea was not worth the cost. Kinoaki saw Americans a little differently than they saw themselves: he mentioned bluntly that a third of the United States had once belonged to Mexico and added that 'the United States is in possession of territories such as the Philippines and Guam, which are near Japan's eyes and nose...'[14]

Kinoaki described the conditions that would indicate an imminent American attack on Japan:

> If the war clouds between the United States and Japan become intense, the United States will make up her mind to remove the Atlantic Fleet and combine it with her Pacific Fleet.
>
> From Japan's standpoint this fact is of the utmost significance. As a matter of fact, many military experts are of

the opinion that Japan will act at last before the combination of the United States Atlantic Fleet with the United States Pacific Fleet.

If Japan acts at this period, it may be said that she has chosen the best time.

We do not think, however, that military action, no matter how quick Japan's action may be, can be carried out before the combination of the two fleets. But I certainly think that the time for Japanese action will come when the United States Fleet departs for Pearl Harbor after its combination, or when it is finally on the point of carrying out its successful action in Hawaii.

In the former case, Japan will not be directly menaced, but in the latter case, Japan will feel a great menace.

Suppose that Japan, with generosity and farsightedness as her principle, clings hopefully to her diplomatic conversations with the United States and confines her action to scouting the movements of the United States Fleets concentrated in Hawaii – if these United States Fleets depart westward from Pearl Harbor, Japan cannot lose even a second; she should launch a Naval attack like a lighting flash.[15]

Kilsoo Haan had the book translated into English and it was published by Little, Brown and Company in Boston in 1942 as *How Japan Plans To Win*. He said he had submitted the information to President Roosevelt in January of 1941 and had confirmed it to the FBI in the same month.

WAR PLAN ORANGE UPDATE

America's contingency plan for the rise of Japan as a modern military power was War Plan Orange. First conceived as early as 1897, after Japan humbled Manchu China in the first war for Korea, War Plan Orange was substantially revised in 1919, after Japan had helped round up and deport the Germans from the Pacific and had gained control of the Marianas Islands, later to become famous as Saipan and Tinian. The plan was updated on a regular basis to reflect the size of the US and Japanese fleets. War Plan Orange was a factor in the Washington Naval Conference and Treaty when the United States and Britain joined hands in 1921–1922 to preserve the Open Door policy of free trade with China and to demand that Japan accept a limit of three capital ships for every five British battleships or battle cruisers or five American battleships. The Japanese had wanted equality – as they had wanted racial equality in the League of Nations Charter – but had to settle for an inferior status in both cases. They were not happy. The article written by Henry H. Douglas with information supplied by Kilsoo Haan indicates that they were not acquiescing either.

War Plan Orange predicted that the war in the Pacific would be triggered by a Japanese attack on United States territory, which would be stimulated by America's interference with Japan's global ambition. Homer Lea, an eccentric American militarist from Virginia who had served as a general for Dr. Sun Yat-sen's Chinese revolutionaries, had predicted in 1911 that the war would be triggered by American racism, as Jack London had predicted before him in 'The Yellow Peril'. In 1905, War Plan Orange predicted that the US would be unable to protect its territories in the Western Pacific, and Japan would be unable to affect a landing on the West Coast of the United States. Since Japan had about one-half of America's population and one-tenth of America's industrial might, the outcome was obvious: the United States would push Japan back through a war of attrition, with both sides inflicting and taking losses, until the Japanese and the Americans met in a single great naval battle near Japan. The Japanese would lose.

About a hundred US Naval officers held written copies of War Plan Orange at any given time, sometimes referred to as 'Estimates of the Situation Blue-Orange'. (*Blue* was the United States and *Orange* was Japan.) The US Secretary of War and the US Secretary of the Navy each received, and presumably also read and signed, copies of War Plan Orange on their assumption of office. Most senior naval officers were familiar with the plan.

One of the naval officers who worked on War Plan Orange was Admiral James O. Richardson. Admiral Richardson knew War Plan Orange backwards and forwards but obviously hadn't seen the Japanese counter-plan, which probably led Matsuo Kinoaki to write the book that Kilsoo Haan's men bought or stole later in 1940 and introduced to the FBI and the White House in January of 1941. When he was ordered to take the US Pacific Fleet from San Diego to Pearl Harbor in early April of 1940, Richardson didn't understand from the outset the reason for what he was ordered to do, or what he was supposed to accomplish. But Richardson understood, both intuitively and intellectually, that sending the major portion of the United States Fleet, less the Atlantic Squadron, to Hawaii, starting on 2 April 1940, would be seen as a threatening move in Japan.

The original orders called for the fleet to remain in Hawaiian waters until 9 May 1940, as a brief training operation, and then return to San Diego and the other bases on the West Coast. But Richardson received a dispatch from Chief of Naval Operations Harold Stark on 29 April 1940, telling him not to take the fleet out of Hawaiian waters because Italy might enter the war against England and France.

Richardson was understandably puzzled and sent a letter to Admiral Stark on 1 May in which he voiced his 'firm conviction that we urgently need a re-estimate of the situation of the United States in world affairs and a reconsideration of our basic war plans based on such an estimate. I strongly believe that such a re-estimate and reconsideration will result in a firm determination to remain out of the present conflict in Europe and Asia. I hope that nothing will delay the arrival of the Fleet at its normal bases on the Pacific coast.'

On 4 May 1940, Richardson received a dispatch from Stark, who, as a young naval officer under Theodore Roosevelt's presidency, had sailed with the Great White Fleet in a round-the-world voyage whose tacit purpose was to intimidate Japan:

IT LOOKS PROBABLE BUT NOT FINAL THAT THE FLEET WILL REMAIN IN HAWAIIAN WATERS FOR SHORT TIME AFTER MAY 9TH. WILL EXPECT TO APPRISE YOU FURTHER MONDAY OR TUESDAY NEXT.

This would have been 6 or 7 May.[1] On 7 May, Admiral Stark sent another dispatch to Admiral Richardson:

CINCUS (RICHARDSON) MAKE IMMEDIATE PRESS RELEASE IN SUBSTANCE AS FOLLOWS: I HAVE REQUESTED PERMISSION TO REMAIN IN HAWAIIAN WATERS TO ACCOMPLISH SOME THINGS I WANTED TO DO WHILE HERE X THE DEPARTMENT HAS APPROVED THIS REQUEST PARAGRAPH – DELAY FLEET DEPARTURE HAWAIIAN AREA FOR ABOUT TWO WEEKS PRIOR TO END OF WHICH TIME YOU WILL BE FURTHER ADVISED REGARDING FUTURE MOVEMENTS X CARRY OUT REGULARLY SCHEDULED OVERHAULS OF INDIVIDUAL UNITS, MOVEMENTS OF BASEFORCE UNITS AT YOUR DISCRETION. 7 MAY 1940[2]

On 22 May, Richardson wrote Stark a letter in which he bluntly asked to be told, once and for all, what he and the Fleet were doing in the Hawaiian Islands while Hitler was over-running Europe and Japan was showing no signs of overt hostility.

(a) Are we here primarily to influence the actions of other nations by our presence, and if so, what effect would the carrying out of normal training (insofar as we can under the limitations on anchorages, air fields, facilities and services) have on this purpose? The effect of the emergency docking program and the consequent absence of task forces during the training period must also be considered.

(b) Are we here as a stepping off place for belligerent activity? If so, we should devote all our time and energies to preparing for war. This could more effectively and expeditiously be accomplished by an immediate return to the West Coast, with 'freezing' of personnel, filling up complements, docking and all the rest of it. We could return here upon completion.[3]

Stark finally sent Richardson a reply that was 'one of the most direct replies to any of my letters to him, although it was far from being as definite as I would have liked'.

Why are you in the Hawaiian Area? You are there because of the deterrent effect which it is thought your presence may have on the Japs going into the East Indies. In previous letters I have hooked this up with the Italians going into the war. The connection is that with Italy in, it is thought that the Japs might feel just that much freer to take independent action. We believe that both the Germans and the Italians have told the Japs that so far as they are concerned she, Japan, has a free hand in the Dutch East Indies.[4]

Stark told Richardson, who had recently worked as his top assistant, that he himself didn't know how long Richardson was supposed to remain in Hawaii, but that he was trying to find out. He also said he was 'moving Heaven and Earth to get our figure boosted to 170,000 enlisted men (or even possibly 172,300) and 34,000 marines. If we get these authorised I believe you will be comfortable as regards numbers of men for the coming years.'

A month later, on 22 June – the day France acknowledged that it had lost the war to Hitler and signed an armistice that was actually tantamount to an alliance – Stark wrote Richardson and told him, 'Tentatively decision has been made for the fleet to remain where it is. This decision may be changed at any time.'

Stark and Richardson were able to work out an arrangement so that married sailors and petty officers could sail back to the West Coast with returning ships to spend some time with their families. But the bulk of the Fleet remained in Hawaii. Richardson later said that Stark had agreed with him that the Fleet could better be prepared for any eventual war at San Diego and the other West Coast bases, but that Stark had quietly been told by FDR that the Fleet was staying in Hawaii. Richardson continued to send memos to Stark and to the Secretary of the Navy, Frank Knox, listing reasons why the Fleet would be better off on the West Coast: lack of sea-going target sleds for large-bore gunnery practice, lack of ranges for machinegun practice, and perhaps most important, the fact that it was difficult to get enlisted men to re-enlist when they were based so far from their families. Richardson noted that while the re-enlistment rate had been 80.81 per cent, it had fallen to 75.45 per cent during the fiscal year 1940 and to 71.49 per cent in fiscal year 1941. Enlisted men, one of Richardson's subordinates told him, did not want duty in the Hawaiian Islands.[5]

As the US Fleet lingered in Hawaii, Admiral Kichisaburo Nomura was brought in as ambassador to the US. Nomura, a Japanese giant at 6 feet tall, had met Franklin D. Roosevelt when FDR was Assistant Secretary of the Navy during World War I and had been unimpressed with his intelligence. Later, as previously outlined, he had lost an eye when Ku Kim's patriot assassin had exploded his bomb on the grandstand at Shanghai in 1932. Nomura didn't think much of FDR but he liked Americans in general, knew the vast industrial power of the nation, and wanted peace with the United States. Nomura, pro-American in temperament, had to deal with the fact that America's fleet in Hawaii was the menace that Japanese war planners had seen as the catalyst for a Pacific War in the book that Kilsoo Haan had publicised.

On 2 July Admiral Richardson had lunch with Clarence Gauss, US Consul-General in Shanghai, and Admiral Claude Bloch, Richardson's predecessor as commander of the Fleet and a specialist in Naval Intelligence. Gauss had just come from Washington and told Richardson and Bloch that, in his opinion, 'FDR and Hornbeck are handling the Far East policy and the disposition of the Fleet.'

Hornbeck was Stanley K. Hornbeck, the state department's indestructible expert on Far Eastern affairs. In 1909, through the help of his mentor, German-born Paul Reinsch, Hornbeck, a newly minted Ph. D., landed a teaching position in Chekiang Provincial College in Hangkow, China, an attractive and cultured city still going through the throes of warlord resistance to the Chinese Republic. Hornbeck's Chinese biographer, Shizang Hu, who generally admired his subject, pointed out that the American's lack of language skills – he never learned to speak Chinese – made it doubtful that he was an expert on China. But Hornbeck favored the Open Door policy of John Hay, Teddy Roosevelt's secretary of state in the first decade of the century: China should not be colonized by foreign powers, official spheres of exclusive European or Japanese influence should not be recognized, but Americans should not be subject to Chinese courts of law or police until China was completely stabilized – the policies, in short, that the United States had always practised in China and had practised in Japan until the Japanese defeated Russia and evicted Germany from Asia. Much as Hornbeck claimed to love China, China's minister to the United States, Y.N. Wen, didn't love Hornbeck and called him 'a reactionary'. Chinese scholars then and now have always considered him condescending and racist.[6]

But Hornbeck hated Japan. As early as 1916, when Japan was a useful ally of Britain, Hornbeck was writing that Japan was a threat.

'Twenty years ago the oldest, the largest, the most populous country in the world – a huge continental empire long accustomed to esteem itself the sole repository of national strength and substance – was defeated in war and invaded by the armed forces of a little insular neighbor,' Hornbeck wrote in *Contemporary Politics In The Far East*. 'In the treaty that followed, the partitioning of China was begun.'[8]

Hornbeck's knowledge of history was selective. The British and French had seized Chinese territory including Shanghai in 1842, following the first Opium War, which forced the reluctant Chinese Empire to accept British opium raised for export in British-owned India. This seizure began the partition of China a decade before isolated Japan was opened to the West at gunpoint by Commodore Perry. The French, the Russians, and finally the Germans had all made inroads into China long before the Japanese had. But Britain, France and Germany were white nations and Hornbeck was Anglo-Saxon, Dutch and German by ancestry.

When America entered World War I, Hornbeck joined the US Army and Woodrow Wilson summoned him to become his expert on the Far East, where he did everything he could to thwart Japan's sphere of influence after the Japanese took Shantung from Germany. Hornbeck was an advisor at the Treaty of Versailles Conference and the Washington Naval Conference of 1921–1922. After lecturing at Harvard, Hornbeck joined the US State Department as the chief of the Far Eastern division responsible for both China and Japan. The Chinese saw Hornbeck as an agent of American merchantile colonialism and the Japanese saw him as hostile and potentially dangerous.

Oddly enough, a lot of Americans didn't like Hornbeck either. He survived the drastic shift from the Republican hegemony of the taciturn Calvin Coolidge to the warmer, more scholarly Herbert Hoover – a Quaker, like many Japanese Christians and the American wives of some Japanese diplomats. Hoover actually spoke some Chinese and he knew both China and Japan. He had been trapped in Peking during the Boxer Rebellion of 1900, when the Japanese joined the rescue mission that saved the Western diplomats and those missionaries and Chinese Christians who hadn't already been butchered by the

Boxers. Hornbeck impressed Hoover because he considered the Chinese to be fellow humans, even if his affection was seen as condescending by the Chinese.

When FDR became president, Hornbeck became one of four special advisors to FDR's secretary of state, Cordell Hull, and was the leading expert on China and Japan of the Roosevelt administration. Many people in the State Department thought Hornbeck was out of kilter. Joseph K. Grew, ambassador to Japan, said Hornbeck was pro-Chinese and 'the epitome of that all-embracing American conscience' that made Grew's own job difficult. Assistant Secretary of State Breckenridge Long considered Hornbeck anti-Japanese with 'a rather violent mentality ... a rather dangerous man where delicate matters are concerned in which he has a violence prejudice'. One of Hornbeck's own subordinates said that Hornbeck was 'irascible and pigheaded. He antagonized people in any meeting.' Clark Howell, FDR's personal friend and editor of the *Atlanta Constitution*, said that Hornbeck was 'intensely pro-Chinese and anti-Japanese. He lived and taught school in China and his attitude is largely controlled by his former affiliations there.'⁹

Hornbeck was not a warmonger. He was a believing Christian, an anti-Communist, and a man of conscience. He actually believed that intimidating the Japanese with economic sanctions, and above all with American naval power, could keep them in their place and allow the US to maintain a status quo in which America would protect China militarily and quietly dominate the huge Chinese market economically. He opposed committing American troops to any clash between China and Japan – the threat of force, he honestly believed, would make the use of troops unnecessary.

Admiral Richardson, also a religious man of conscience, may have shared some of Hornbeck's convictions but was unimpressed by his unconsciously racist and condescending brand of diplomacy. Considering the situation in mid-1940, he wrote:

If I am a small man, and after an unfriendly argument my big-man opponent takes a threatening position in regard to me, I may be restrained thereafter in what I say or do. If, however, the man with whom I have had my unfriendly argument is smaller than I am and known to be less capable in the manly art of fisticuffs than I, then his moving in close may well be welcomed by me as an opportunity to settle the matter by a quick punch to my jaw ... that part of the United States Fleet in the Pacific, in its state of unpreparedness and in a peace posture, was the small man vis-à-vis the Japanese Fleet. This was true because the Japanese Fleet was superior to the Pacific contingent of the US Fleet in all categories, except possibly battleships, and was in a war posture as a result of its continuing war with China.[10]

In late September of 1940, when the Fleet had been in Hawaii for five months, the world received an object lesson in the failed intimidation of Japan when the Japanese landed a dozen tanks and 4,500 troops near Haiphong in French Indo-China. The Vichy government asked Japan for an armistice and the railroad to China was as good as closed. The battle for Tonkin ended on 26 September 1940. On 27 September, Japan signed an alliance with Nazi Germany and Fascist Italy – but made no overt move against the British, Dutch, or American colonies in the Pacific.

The United States responded to an incursion into a European colony – even one allied with Hitler – by placing an embargo on the sale of US steel and scrap iron to Japan. The Japanese, however, were more worried at having their supply of oil cut off, and they began to negotiate with the Dutch East Indies' government in Batavia to increase the commitment of Dutch oil to Japan in case of an oil embargo by the United States, Japan's main supplier.

On 12 September 1940, a 24-man Japanese diplomatic party including Rear Admiral Tadashi Maeda arrived in Batavia, the capital of the Dutch East Indies located on the island of Java, to demand that the Dutch in the Indies increase the authorised sale of 750,000 tons of petroleum to 3,750,000 tons – about 50 per cent of Java's total production. The Dutch, whose nation had been overrun by Nazi Germany in May of 1940, offered 1,800,000 tons. The Japanese accepted – there was, as yet, no US oil embargo on Japan – but when they returned to Japan the agreement was revoked. Another Japanese delegation arrived in Batavia in

November of 1940 and demanded 80 per cent of the total Dutch output, or 3,800,000-plus tons. The negotiations continued.

The scrap iron and steel embargo made the situation even more problematical, and Admiral Richardson made the second of his two trips from Washington to Hawaii in October 1940. On the first trip, Richardson had told FDR that the Fleet wasn't ready for any war that might break out – though Richardson himself didn't want a war with Japan. On the October trip, Richardson was explicit, or, as he put it later: 'The discussion waxed hot and heavy.' Richardson said that FDR seemed more concerned with winning the November election than he did in preparing the Fleet for a possible war with Japan. Finally, when it became apparent that Roosevelt had no intention of accepting his recommendations for an increase in the strength of the Fleet, Richardson put it on the line.

'Mister President, I feel that I must tell you that the senior officers of the Navy do not have the trust and confidence in the civilian leadership of this country that is essential for the successful prosecution of a war in the Pacific,' Richardson said.

'Jim, you just don't understand that this is an election year and there are certain things that can't be done, no matter what, until the election is over and won.'

While Hitler was bombing London and U-boats was sinking British ships in the Atlantic, FDR was running for his unprecedented third term as president of the United States – and 80 per cent of Americans polled said they wanted to stay out of war unless the United States was attacked. The Selective Service Act, the first peacetime conscription in American history, had been approved a few weeks before over the protests of pacifists and conservatives alike. Devout Christians cited the Biblical invocations against bloodshed. Literary pacifists hated all wars, in the spirit of *All Quiet on the Western Front* by Remarque and *The Paths of Glory* by Humphrey Cobb. On college campuses students solemnly took the pledge not to go. Old-style progressive and populist historians like Charles Austin Beard and rock-ribbed Republicans who remembered that Britain had backed the Confederacy saw no reason to spill American blood. Irishmen who had lost relatives in The Troubles that led up to Irish independence in the first two decades of the century were livid at the idea of fighting for England. German-Americans found Hitler an embarrassment but saw the plundering of stricken Germany after the Treaty of Versailles as an insult and an injury perpetrated by France, Belgium, and Britain that they didn't want to defend or support. Black people pointed out that far more victims of prejudice had died in Southern lynchings than in Nazi outrages before 1940. Perhaps most important, worried parents saw the draft as a prelude to another war in Europe that would slaughter their sons.

The first 12-month draft notices had gone out in October. Roosevelt desperately wanted to help the Mother Country – but he also desperately wanted to get elected. The speech that probably clinched his election came on 30 October 1940, in Boston: 'And while I am talking to you mothers and fathers, I give you one more assurance. Your boys are not going to be sent into any foreign wars. They are going into training to form a force so strong that, by its very existence, it will keep the threat of war far away from our shores.'

In Brooklyn, on 1 November 1940: 'I am fighting to keep our people out of foreign wars. And I will keep fighting...'

In Buffalo, New York, on 2 November: 'Your president says this country is not going to war!'

FDR was re-elected handily. The Fleet that wasn't going to war, however, also wasn't leaving Hawaii.

The next shock came from Great Britain. The British had begun to refine their airborne torpedo tactics in secret even before the war in Europe began. On the night of 11/12 November 1940, in an operation plagued by constant accidents but saved by great courage and skill, 24 two-man Swordfish biplanes of the Royal Navy were launched to attack the Italian Fleet anchored at Taranto in Italy with a mixture of flares, dive bombing and aerial torpedoes. Three of the Swordfish didn't make the target due to mechanical problems. Two British aircraft were shot down by antiaircraft fire. Two aviators were killed and two were captured. The Italian Navy lost half its strength in one night. Three battleships were damaged so badly it took months to make them seaworthy. One was out of the war permanently. This was the first air-only attack on capital ships and it stunned the world.

Richardson behaved responsibly. Before Taranto, the Pacific Fleet had spent most of its time in Hawaii anchored off-shore in the open sea at Lahaina off the island of Maui. Alerted to the danger of torpedo attack, he moved the fleet to Pearl Harbor, where the shallow depth of the harbor would make aerial torpedo attacks as he understood them impossible. 'Torpedoes ... could not be used against berthed ships. Our then operating air torpedoes dove very deep when launched, and took some hundreds of yards before rising to their desired running depths. They did not arm until about back at running depth.' Pearl Harbor was only 35 to 40 feet deep, and the torpedoes that Richardson knew about would crash uselessly into the bottom of the harbor.

In vulnerable situations, anchored ships were sometimes screened by torpedo nets, heavy-duty mesh that dangled underwater from floats to detonate or entangle torpedoes launched from destroyers or submarines. Richardson didn't think these were called for at Pearl Harbor. He even put it in writing on 28 November 1940 in a memo to Admiral Stark: 'I think torpedo nets within the Harbor are neither necessary nor practicable. The area is too restricted and ships, at present, are not moored within torpedo range of the entrances.'

Early in January of 1941 – about the time that Kilsoo Haan was trying to warn the White House and the FBI that the Pacific Fleet at Pearl Harbor constituted a harbinger of war as far as Japan was concerned – Admiral Richardson took a break from his struggle to bring the Fleet up-to-date to welcome Japan's Ambassador Nomura to Hawaii, who on his way to Washington. The two men knew one another casually and Richardson cheerfully provided a US Navy destroyer to escort the Japanese merchant ship Admiral Nomura was traveling on into Pearl Harbor so that they could have lunch together.

'I express the professional gratitude which we feel in having a Japanese Naval Officer appointed to such a high diplomatic post,' Richardson said at the luncheon for American and Japanese officers.

'The first time I had come to the United States I had come as a young midshipman just learning the rudiments of being a professional naval officer,' Nomura said, exuding his bearish charm with a little traditional self-deprecation. 'I have been back to the United States several more times, and each time I became more qualified than before. But this return finds me again a midshipman, in the diplomatic profession, just learning the rudiments of my profession.'

The two veteran admirals – Nomura was 60, Richardson 62 – each looked back with satisfaction on four decades of peaceful if not always harmonious relations between their countries, punctuated by a victorious alliance against Germany in World War I. Neither looked forward to a war between the United States and Japan.[11]

On 31 January 1941 – perhaps after the White House had a chance to digest Kilsoo Haan's warning about Japanese perceptions of the Pacific Flee at Pearl Harbor – Admiral James Otto Richardson found out, to his complete surprise, that he had suddenly been relieved as commander of the Pacific Fleet.

'My orders had been a real shock to me,' Richardson wrote years later, after waiting in vain for an explanation of why he had been terminated when he had been led to expect a two-year tour of duty. 'I was deeply disappointed in my detachment, yet there was some feeling of prospective relief, for I had never liked to work with people whom I could not trust, and I did not trust Franklin D. Roosevelt.'[12]

Kilsoo Haan saw which way things were going when the Fleet stayed in Pearl Harbor: he knew that war was more than likely. The government was not convinced. On 27 February, Kilsoo Haan wrote a letter to the Treasury Department, headed by Henry Morgenthau Jr., one of FDR's best friends and richest neighbors, trying to secure the position of the Koreans as an independent people rather than reluctant citizens of the Japanese Empire.

In view of the precarious situation which exists in the Pacific .area, and in view of the strained relations between the Imperial Government of Japan and the United States, the Sino-Korean Peoples' League requests that your department help us to clarify some of the apprehensions which exist among the Korean people in the Hawaiian Islands and in

America, We understand if and when America freezes all the Japanese financial holdings or confiscates the Japanese financial holdings in time of war, all such properties and financial holdings belonging to the Koreans too may be frozen or confiscated.

May we humbly request that the Department of Treasury take the attitude of sympathetic understanding and refrain from freezing or confiscating the financial holdings of the Koreans in America, even though internationally speaking, we are [a] subject race of Japan.

Last August 19th, the Justice Department Director of Registration, Hon. Earl G. Harrison, ruled Koreans can register as Koreans and not as Japanese subjects when registering under the Alien Registration Act.

We humbly plead that your Department give us the same consideration and rule that the Koreans are Koreans and not to be considered as Japanese, hence Korean properties and holdings to be exempted from freezing or confiscation.[13]

J.W. Pehle, assistant to the Secretary of the Treasury, wrote back on 10 May that Kilsoo Haan's request was premature. 'I regret to advise you that this Department is not in a position to answer your inquiry since it is not felt to be appropriate to anticipate courses of action to be followed in hypothetical situations.'[15]

Korean agents supplied Kilsoo Haan with another piece of intelligence that led to a contact with the Secretary of the Navy, in which Haan reported that the Soviet Union and Japan would sign a mutual non-aggression pact no later than 29 April 1941. The Russians and the Japanese had clashed twice in Mongolia in battles the Japanese referred to as *Nomonhan* and the Russians called *Khalkin Gol*. The Soviet border troops had taken a serious beating by the Japanese in the first stages of the battle. Then Stalin had sent in hundreds of BT tanks and elite Guards units from western Russia – poised to invade Poland – and defeated the Japanese, who had no tanks comparable to the high-speed BT. The attack made such an impression on the Russians that they held back on the invasion of Poland as allies of Nazi Germany. The Nazis attacked on 1 September 1939. The Russians waited until they had an armistice with Japan on 17 September before they joined Hitler's forces in crushing Poland after the Germans had done most of the fighting.

Secretary of the Navy Frank Knox thanked Kilsoo Haan for this information in a letter of 26 April. 'Your letter of April 15, 1941 and its very interesting enclosure are much appreciated,' Knox wrote over his personal signature: 'Some of your facts and predictions have indeed been borne out by the passages of time and I assure you that the information that you have given us has always been highly appreciated,' Frank Knox[15]

On 15 April 1941, Kilsoon Haan reported that he took part on a confidential conference with Sidney Sherwood of the Advisory Commission to the Council of National Defense at the Federal Reserve Building. Haan was representing both the Sino-Korean People's League and the Korean Volunteer Army in China – those Korean patriots who served Chiang Kai-shek rather than Mao Tse-tung, who also had Korean auxiliaries. Sherwood and Haan discussed both Haan's report on the Soviet-Japanese non-aggression pact, which had convinced at least some American officials to take his intelligence abilities serious, and the possibility of US aid to the Korean Volunteer Army.

'Hon. Sherwood promised and assured me that "If Japan attacks Pearl Harbor. Obviously the US government will help the Korean Volunteer Army in China and the Korean Underground Intelligence",' Haan wrote in his notes.[16]

The *New York Times* reported that the US State Department had been taken by surprise by the Soviet-Japanese non-aggression Pact but that the Sino-Korean People's League had reported that it would happen. Kilsoo Haan also received a note from the War Department thanking the League for its interest in National Defense.[17]

Gen. George Marshall also took an interest in Kilsoo Haan's information. 'Late in June 1941, Gen. George C. Marshall wanted me to be at the old Munitions Building for a conference related to our January 8, 1941 [warning?] to FDR, Japan's War Plan, the Sneak Attack on Hawaii,' Haan wrote in marginal notes. 'I told him that Japan's occupation of French Indo-China can be the prelude to Japan's attack on Pearl Harbor. He replied; "What do you think we'll be doing while the Japs attack fleet sails for Hawaii? Twiddling our thumbs?"[18] White House Secretary [Stephen] Early told me that the State Department told him that our reports were "the product of Haan's imagination – anti-Japan propaganda".'[19]

Kilsoo Haan next got into a squabble with Togo Tanaka, editor of *Rafu Shimpo,* and some other leaders of the Japanese-American community. Haan had asserted that some Nisei – second-generation Japanese – had complained to him that they were being recruited as Japanese agents but wished to remain loyal to the US. Togo Tanaka denied that this was true – and in fact the Japanese-Americans subsequently proved to be overwhelming loyal to the United States – but some Americans bought into the idea of a Japanese-American Fifth Column and asked Kilsoo Haan for more information. He provided copies of the Kinoaki book and his own report on the Nisei. The report on the Nisei was essentially a description by Japanese from Japan who wished to win the Nisei over to their cause but provided no real documentation that they had done so.[20]

One war warning missed Kilsoo Haan completely. In the spring of 1941, Communist waiters in German-occupied Belgium began to hear drunken German officers talking about a projected Nazi invasion of the Soviet Union. The Hitler-Stalin Pact was in force and Stalin had even agreed to provide Hitler with troops for the war against Britain. Stalin refused to believe the information – but the NKVD believed it.[21]

In early May of 1941, Vitalii Pavlov, a 27-year-old NKVD agent, called Harry Dexter White, a senior official in the US Treasury Department. White was a committed Soviet sympathizer who had supplied the NKVD with government papers until his courier, Whittaker Chambers, defected and warned White to drop out of the espionage network or be exposed. White was terrified at the time and dropped out of Soviet intelligence. Pavlov, however, tracked Harry Dexter White down and met him for lunch at the Old Ebbitt Grill in Washington DC. Pavlov handed over a written note from 'Bill' – Iskhak Abdulovich Ahkmerov – his own boss until Akhmerov had been demoted for marrying an American Communist, a violation of NKVD protocol. The note was an order to provoke a war between the United States and Japan – the secret goal of Soviet intelligence since the 1930s. White had visualized a cut-off of Japan's credit and oil supply as early as 1938, when he dropped out of the Soviet network. All he needed now was an excuse.[22]

On 21 June 1941, the Japanese occupied all of French Indo-China without a fight and shut off China's access to supplies from the sea. The idea that any European country had lost a colony, even if it was Vichy France, appears to have been upsetting. The greater shock came the next day. On 22 June 1941 – the date is important – Nazi German invaded the Soviet Union: Operation Barbarossa. On 28 June 1941, the US and Britain asked the Dutch to join with them in a reduction of oil supplies to Japan, promising the Dutch East Indies American and British help in case of a Japanese invasion. After two Japanese tankers had been filled up at the Dutch East Indies oil port of Tarakan, a third tanker was sent back to Japan empty.

Roosevelt had originally intended to restrict the sale of oil to Japan without an actual embargo. He told a group of civil defense workers that the plan was to make it difficult, but not impossible, for the Japanese to purchase outside oil because he did not want a war in the Pacific. He was interested, he said, in '...our own good, for the defense of Great Britain, and the freedom of the seas.'

Unfortunately, while Roosevelt was on vacation after the death of his mother Sara in early September of 1941, and while Secretary of State Cordell Hull was also out of town, a State Department lawyer named Dean Acheson turned the restriction into an outright ban. Japan could no long purchase oil from the United States.

The Dutch military commander in the East Indies was General Gerardus Johannes Berenschot. The general was an Indo – a Eurasian of Dutch and Malay ancestry – and a realist. He knew that most of the native Indonesian people were either pro-Japanese or apathetic and that no total defense of the Dutch East Indies was possible. The British wanted him to defend he island of Borneo because it covered the approaches to British-held Malaya. General Berenschot told them that he might be able to hold the southern part of Java until he received help from Australia but that defending Borneo or the other islands was militarily impossible.

Berenschot was more concerned with the war in Europe and the safety of his occupied Netherlands homeland than he was about US foreign policy.

On 13 October 1941, Berenshot's twin-engine Lockheed Lodestar took off from Batavia, the capital of the Dutch East Indies, after a conference with British officials who had agreed to back the American embargo against Japan. Five minutes after take-off, the left engine of the Lodestar – a famously reliable aircraft – began to flame. The pilot attempted a controlled crashlanding but the Lodestar's wing struck a palm tree and pivoted into a Malay village, killing everyone on board and 25 hapless Malays.

Dutch newspapers reported that General Berenschot's death was due to Berenschot's refusal 'to walk on a British leash,' though a British officer was among those passengers killed. Many years later, an elderly Malay told Berenschot's grandson that he had seen a white man tampering with the left engine just before take-off.[23]

As the oil reduction hardened into an embargo, Prince Fumimaro Konoye, appointed as prime minister, was given a month to get the embargo lifted. Konoye asked Ambassador Joseph Grew to arrange a personal meeting with FDR. Konoye knew Japan could not win a war with the United States. He was prepared to drop the alliance with Nazi Germany and agreed to a gradual withdrawal from China. The State Department talked Roosevelt out of meeting with Konoye and the oil embargo was kept in full force.

General Hideki Tojo, noted for his fanatical loyalty to the Emperor, was appointed after Konoye resigned as prime minister. When Cordell Hull suggested, apparently in response to FDR's own concern, that the US might release oil for domestic use only if Japan gradually evacuated China, Harry Dexter White wrote a letter for Henry Morgenthau to sign and give to FDR.

I must apologize for intruding on your pressing schedule with this hurried note. I have been so alarmed by information reaching me last night – information which I hope and trust to be mistaken – that my deep admiration for your leadership in world affairs forces me respectfully to call your attention to the matter that has kept me from sleep last night.

Mr. President, word was brought to me yesterday evening that persons in our country's government are hoping to betray the cause of the heroic Chinese people and strike a deadly blow at all your plans for a world-wide democratic victory. I was told that the Japanese Embassy staff is openly boasting of a great triumph for the 'New Order.' Oil – rivers of oil – will soon be flowing to the Japanese war machines. A humiliated democracy of the Far East, China, Holland, Great Britain will soon be facing a Fascist coalition emboldened and strengthened by diplomatic victory – so the Japanese are saying.

Mr. President, I am aware that many honest individuals agree that a Far East Munich is necessary at the moment. But I write this letter because millions of human beings everywhere in the world share with me the profound conviction that you will lead a suffering world to victory over the menace to all our lives and all our liberties. To sell China to her enemies for the thirty blood-stained coins of gold will not only weaken our national policy in Europe as well as the Far East, but will dim the bright luster of America's world leadership in the great democratic fight against Fascism,

On this day, Mr. President, the whole country looks to you to save America's power as well as her sacred honor. I know – I have the most perfect confidence – that should these stories be true, should there be Americans who seek to destroy your declared policy in world affairs, that you will succeed in circumventing these plotters of a new Munich.[24]

The State Department's last bid, the Hull note on 26 November, was drafted based on the memorandum the Soviet agent of influence Harry Dexter White sent FDR the day after his hysterical letter. The Hull note bluntly told Japan to get out of China immediately—with no instructions as to how to get out while a war was in progress – and to give up Manchuria, which was a mainstay of the Japanese economy and a bequest from Theodore Roosevelt in the Taft-Katsura Agreement. Japanese newspapers quoted on the front pages of American newspapers said that the demands of the Hull note caused 'shocked surprise and extreme pessimism' and that they were 'utterly impossible.' The *St Paul Pioneer Press* carried at AP story under a banner headline on 5 December saying that the Japanese found the terms unacceptable and were closing their embassy in Mexico. American code-breakers picked up a pre-arranged message – *haruna,* the name of a dormant Japanese volcano – that told Japanese consulates in British and US cities to burn their confidential files and break up their decoding machines.

Later that night, Kilsoo Haan picked up on the discount-price auto sale from the Japanese Embassy at the Chinese Lantern restaurant in Washington and understood perfectly what it meant. Kilsoo Haan's newspaper coverage expanded exponentially after 7 December 1941.

II

THE DAY OF INFAMY

While Kilsoo Haan was contacting eight different government agencies trying to warn that the Japanese would attack Hawaii, the Japanese attacked Hawaii. Admiral Husband Kimmel had taken over the Pacific Fleet from Admiral James Richardson. Like Richardson, Kimmel had tried to warn the White House that the fleet was a tempting target, and he had asked for more patrol planes, which he never received. The available twin-engine Catalina flying boats had been sent to Britain and most of the four-engine B-17 bombers had been sent to the Philippines. An ill-advised interview with General George Marshall on 15 November, not published at the time, had told US reporters that in case of war, Japan's wood-and-paper cities would be incinerated and civilians would not be spared. Reporters kept the secret after Marshall's interview on November until the war actually began, but a two-page pictogram cartoon and map in *United States News* showed American bombers attacking Japan from Guam and the Philippines in case of war. The Pictogram ran on Halloween – five weeks before 7 December.

At about 6:45 on 7 December, the crew of the USS *Antares*, pulling a barge into Pearl Harbor, spotted what looked like a submarine trying to shadow the World War I-vintage transport ship into the harbor mouth. One of the midget submarines that Kilsoo Haan had reported as being under construction in 1940, obviously designed to operate in shallow water against anchored ships, was sneaking into Pearl Harbor ahead of the air strike. The USS *Antares* put out a submarine alert. A twin-engine Catalina PBY seaplane dropped smoke pots. The USS *Ward*, a destroyer, spotted the midget submarine. The *Ward*'s 4-inch deck guns hit the conning tower twice and the midget submarine submerged. The USS *Ward* dropped depth charges that lifted the midget sub out of the water. Both the *Antares* and the *Ward* radioed messages. Incredibly nobody ashore paid any attention.

Kilsoo Haan's warnings about midget submarines were a matter of record, but had probably never been forwarded to Pearl Harbor. The newspaper headlines predicting a probable war with Japan in the near future and the fact that the Japanese were known to be building midget submarines for a harbor attack, taken together, could have provided some warning for what happened next.

At 7:55 a.m. Japanese aircraft from four carriers appeared over Pearl Harbor. The sailors first saw the airplanes in the distance at about 7:50 am as they waited to raise the American flag over Battleship Row at Ford Island.

'The Army must be having maneuvers,' one young sailor said.

Another saw the red sun insignias on the wings of the hundreds of single-engine monoplanes thundering in neat formations over the calm American fleet and mistook it for the Soviet red star.

'What are the Russians doing in Hawaii?' he asked his buddies.

Only one enlisted man instinctively knew what was about to happen. In 1937, he had served on the USS *Panay*, an American gunboat sunk by Japanese aircraft while patrolling the Yangtze River near the ravaged city of Nanking. As soon as he saw the Japanese insignia, he broke open the ammunition magazine on the USS Battleship *Pennsylvania* and began to dole out ammunition to the younger sailors.

Without a shot fired, the sailors and their officers stood gazing upward in amazement. American soldiers watched from the island of Oahu as 40 Japanese Nakajima-97 torpedo planes began to make their runs a few feet over the flat surface of Pearl Harbor against the anchored American battleships. The torpedoes beneath their bellies were fitted with wooden fins to enable them to function in the shallow water of the harbor. Climbing higher over the harbor, 48 Nakajima B5N1 horizontal bombers carried armor-piercing bombs improvised from 16-inch Japanese naval shells. Starting their dives, the 51 Aichi dive bombers, whose pilots were said to be best trained dive-bomber pilots in the world, carried 500-pound bombs they could drop down a ship's smokestack. Overhead, 43 Mitsubishi A6 fighters armed with machine guns and automatic cannon – the aircraft Americans called the 'Jap Zero' – flew top cover. The Zero, at this point in time, was rated as the best fighter plane in the world.

7:51 a.m. Wheeler Field, the Army's biggest air base at Pearl Harbor came under attack. The Army base, protecting the Navy ships, had 87 P-40 fighter aircraft lined up wingtip-to-wingtip. The Army had feared sabotage by the local Japanese population, the largest ethnic group in the Hawaiian Islands. The Japanese from Japan attacked the parked planes with 26 Aichi dive-bombers and eight Zero fighters. Parked aircraft burst into flames as pilots and ground crewmen stared in disbelief. Some pilots were killed trying to start their planes or taxi for take-off. None got into the air.

7:53 a.m. The United States Marine Corps had 48 aircraft, including the new F4F Wildcat fighters and Douglas SBD dive-bombers along with obsolescent aircraft at Ewa Field. Torpedo bombers zoomed overhead without dropping anything, and headed for the fleet at Battleship Row. Six Zero fighters came in, firing machine guns and automatic cannon at the densely parked Marine fighters and bombs. Most Marine aircraft went up in flames or were riddled with bullets before their crews could start the engines.

Two American Army pilots, Kenneth Taylor and George Welch, were sleeping off an all-night poker game after an early Christmas party the night before. Tuxedoes had been mandatory and they were wearing tuxedo pants when the bombs began to fall. Taylor and Welch telephoned ahead to Haleiwa Field and had two P-40s gassed up. They drove at 100 miles an hour, dodging Japanese strafing attacks, jumped in the P-40s – armed only with .30-caliber machine gun ammunition – and took off. Taylor and Welch flew back to Pearl Harbor and attacked a flight of Nakajima torpedo planes. Taylor shot down two of them and Welch damaged one.

7:55 a.m. While the American sailors and soldiers watched in disbelief at Ford Island Naval Air Station, a single Aichi dive-bomber hit the seaplane ramp with a 500-pounder. The explosion jarred Pearl Harbor awake. Commander Logan Ramsey – who had described an imaginary Japanese attack on Pearl Harbor five years before – looked up in astonishment. 'It's a Jap!' he said.

7:56 a.m. Torpedoes slammed into the USS *Raleigh*, a cruiser, and the USS *Utah*, a retired battleship now used as a target ship. Mistaking the *Utah* for an aircraft carrier because of the planks on the old ship's deck in place of the discarded gun turrets, the Japanese wasted torpedoes and bombs on the obsolete ship throughout the entire attack.

7:57 a.m. A torpedo struck the USS *Helena*, another cruiser, and broke the back of the USS *Oglala*, an aging mine-layer anchored beside the cruiser. The USS *Oglala* began to sink.

7:58 a.m. Rear Admiral Patrick Bellinger, the Navy's commander of shore-based aircraft, issued a signal to all ships in the harbor: AIR RAID ON PEARL HARBOR THIS IS NO DRILL.

8 a.m. Kaneohe, the Navy's seaplane base, came under strafing attack by Aichi diver bombers with machine guns blazing. The Navy lost 33 seaplanes, vital for reconnaissance and rescue missions and communications between bases. At Ewa Marine Corps Air Station, Japanese strafing had now set fire to 47 of the 48 Marine Corps fighter and diver bombers.

Incredibly, the military band was still playing the National Anthem as the flag was raised over the USS *Nevada* at 8 a.m. Pacific time. A Japanese torpedo plane dropped its torpedo aimed at the USS *Arizona*, flew over and sprayed the bandsmen with its machine guns. The sailors in dress white uniforms kept playing right through the last note of *The Star-Spangled Banner* and the machine gun bullets. Then they scampered for cover to find their battle stations as alarms all over Pearl Harbor began to sound 'general quarters' – the signal to man the guns and the fire hoses.

While the Japanese torpedo planes and some of the dive bombers concentrated on the Pacific Fleet, the Zero fighters and other dive bombers continued to attack the Navy and Army aircraft parked on the landing fields within sight of the battleships. Most of the American P-40s and the older, outmoded US fighters were blown up on the landing strips without a chance to fire a shot.

Phil Rasmussen, an Army lieutenant, was one of four Army pilots who took off under fire in obsolete P-36 Hawk fighters. Rasmussen's guns stuck open, spraying bullets, and a Zero flew in front of him and blew up. The other Zero pilots used Rasmussen's obsolete fighter for target practice in revenge. When Rasmussen landed, he had no brakes, no tail wheel, and no control over his rudder. Mechanics counted almost 500 bullet holes in his P-36.

8:02 a.m. Two torpedoes had hit the USS *Arizona*; three torpedoes had hit the USS *Oklahoma*. Japanese aerial photographs showed the rooster tail kicked up by a Japanese midget submarine as the 'long lance torpedo' left the torpedo tube and the wake of one torpedo headed for the USS *Oklahoma*, which capsized.

8:05 a.m. Struck by four torpedoes and a bomb, the USS *West Virginia* sank at her moorings and took part of her crew down with her still alive. Some of the trapped men, locked in airtight compartments within the bowels of the battleship, did not die for three weeks. Their bodies were not recovered for a year.

8:07 a.m. The USS *Vestal*, a repair ship moored beside the USS *Arizona*, once host to Jack London, America's top exponent of the menace of the Japanese, was hit by two bombs aimed at the battleship. One blew a big hole in her bottom.

Five two-man miniature submarines of the type that Kilsoo Haan had warned about in 1940 had been launched from Japanese mother submarines outside Pearl Harbor. One had been intercepted, one had foundered at the harbor mouth, but three of them apparently entered Pearl Harbor. Unseen except by Japanese air photographs, one of the two-man submarines launched two standard-size 'long lance' torpedoes at Battleship Row. One of these 'long lances' with its thousand-pound warhead struck and helped cripple the USS *West Virginia*. The other plowed into the USS *Oklahoma*.

8:08 a.m. Struck by as many as 10 torpedoes on the same side including the double-sized 'long lance,' the USS *Oklahoma* heeled over and capsized. Father Aloysius Schmitt, the Catholic chaplain, led 100 men trapped below decks in a prayer, then led them up a ladder until he found an undamaged watertight compartment. He shepherded as many of the frightened young sailors as would fit, many of them teenagers, into the watertight compartment, and locked the watertight door from the outside. Father Schmitt led the other men to a porthole facing the sky. Unable to fit through himself, he slid back out of the porthole and pushed other men to safety.

Chief Carpenter John Arnold Austin, another big man who weighed over 200 pounds, also stood by a porthole, pushing skinny young sailors and an officer through to safety. Chief Watertender Francis Day stood aside for 15 men at a porthole, but didn't try to go through himself. The USS *Oklahoma*, her huge bottom turned slowly up to face the sky like a beached dead whale, rolled over with more than 300 of her sailors trapped inside the steel hull. Ensign Francis Flaherty and Seaman James Ward, already underwater in one of the gun turrets, helped others escape upside down out the submerged turret door. Father Schmitt, Carpenter Austin, Watertender Day, Ensign Flaherty and Seaman Ward all went down with the ship. Some trapped sailors were later rescued by the frantic effort of other sailors and civilian shipyard workers functioning as rescue crews. All of the men Father Schmitt stuffed in the watertight compartment survived. Most of the other 300 men aboard USS *Oklahoma* drowned or suffocated. The 'long lance' torpedo from the midget submarine Kilsoo Haan had warned about probably caused most of these deaths, since the heroic last-minute evacuations could have saved many more men trapped below decks had the ship not sunk so quickly.

8:11 a.m. A Japanese Aichi dive bomber hit the USS *Arizona* with a 500-pound bomb dropped directly down the battleship's smokestack. The bomb burst the ship's boilers and flames reached the forward magazine. The explosion almost knocked some of the Japanese planes out of the sky and killed more than 1,100 US officers, marines and sailors. Americans were blown off the decks of nearby ships into the water. The USS *Arizona* sank at her moorings. Two bombs hit the USS *Maryland* and three hit the USS *Tennessee*. Both ships were seriously damaged and out of combat readiness for months. The USS *Pennsylvania*, warned by the gunner's mate who survived the Japanese attack on the USS *Panay* in China in 1937, was now blazing away with her antiaircraft guns. The battleship was in drydock and could not be torpedoed, but bombs aimed at her wrecked the destroyers USS *Cassin* and USS *Downes*, also in drydock nearby.

Fires set by bombs reached the fuel tanks of the USS *California*, already hit by two torpedoes. Some sailors were burned to death while manning their antiaircraft guns. The ship was abandoned and burned for three days, casting a cloud of black smoke over the harbor.

8:17 a.m. The USS *Helm*, a destroyer, escaped from the channel of Pearl Harbor and spotted another one of the miniature submarines that Kilsoo Haan had warned about at the harbor entrance. The American destroyer opened fire from a thousand yards but the miniature submarine escaped. The USS *Vestal*, leaking badly, was taken in tow by a tugboat. Her captain, blown over the side by the cataclysmic magazine blast of the USS *Arizona*, had swum back to the ship, clambered aboard, and had taken over efforts to save his ship.

8:20 a.m. A flight of 11 B-17s, big four-engine Army Air Corps bombers, began to arrive at Pearl Harbor and found themselves in the middle of a war. With minimum crews and their machine guns covered with protective grease, the B-17s were unarmed and helpless as Japanese fighter planes attacked them. But the big bombers were so mechanically tough that most of them made safe landings despite bullet holes and minor fires.

8:25 a.m. The Japanese planes dropped a final bomb on the USS *California*, already burning, and then regrouped and left Pearl Harbor. The first wave of the Japanese attack on Pearl Harbor had lost one dive-bomber, three Zero fighters, and five torpedo planes. The Americans had lost two battleships totally destroyed, three others sunk but later salvaged, three others damaged, two cruisers seriously damaged and out of action and two destroyers wrecked. The Navy had lost 112 combat aircraft out of the 148 which were destroyed at Pearl Harbor, and the Army had lost most of the 52 planes which were destroyed out of 129 Army aircraft on Oahu.

8:32 a.m. With the big ships sinking or burning and the Japanese planes gone, American destroyer USS *Monaghan* and USS seaplane tender *Curtiss* spotted and sank another Japanese miniature submarine. Already damaged, the USS *Nevada* made a run for the mouth of the harbor in the hopes of reaching the open sea and striking back at the Japanese carriers. Sailors all over the harbor cheered, some of them in tears, as the only battleship to get up steam sailed past the submerged wreck of the USS *Arizona* and the dozens of dead sailors and marines floating in the water.

8:45 a.m. The second wave of Japanese carrier planes rumbled over Pearl Harbor. The Japanese had 78 more bombers, 54 more torpedo planes, and 35 more Zero fighters. Their pilots, eager to sink another American battleship, swarmed around the USS *Nevada* like angry bees. Four bombs hit the USS *Nevada* – but this time, the Americans knew they were in a war. The battleship blazed away with antiaircraft guns, hitting several attackers. Sailors, marines and soldiers with 3-inch and 1.1-inch antiaircraft cannon, 50-caliber and 30-caliber machine guns, hand-held Browning Automatic Rifles and bolt-action 1903 Springfields let fly at the Japanese. Some officers fired their .45-caliber pistols. A crane operator, perched on the drydock near the USS *Pennsylvania* and the destroyers USS *Cassin* and USS *Downes*, swung the hook of his crane into the paths of the Japanese airplanes to disrupt their torpedo runs. The Americans were furious – and the Japanese noticed the intense fire as the second wave sought targets amid the smoke from burning ships and the clouds of anti-aircraft bursts.

8:40 a.m. Taylor and Welch, having landed after taking fire from their own anti-aircraft guns – which missed – were airborne again, this time with all their guns loaded. Taylor closed on a Japanese dive bomber. The rear gunner opened fire and missed Taylor's head by about an inch and put another bullet through his arm. Welch shot down the dive bomber whose gunner had injured Taylor. Welch and Taylor each damaged another Japanese plane. They were attacked by a Zero – a far more maneuverable airplane than the P-40. After an inconclusive dogfight, the Zero turned back for its carrier and Taylor and Welch returned to Haleiwa.

9 a.m. The 14th Naval District officers spotted the USS *Nevada's* run for the sea as a potential disaster if the Japanese planes sank her in the channel. Flags went up at the signal tower: KEEP CLEAR OF THE CHANNEL! The USS *Nevada*, obeying orders, grounded herself in the mud, her antiaircraft guns still firing.

9:10 a.m. Caught in the drydock, the USS *Pennsylvania* took a direct hit. The destroyers USS *Cassin* and USS *Downes*, shattered by repeated near-misses, both burst into flames.

9:12 a.m. The USS *Shaw*, another destroyer in drydock, was hit by a bomb and began to burn. The seaplane tender USS *Curtiss* and the cruiser USS *Honolulu* were also hit and damaged.

9:30 a.m. The USS *Shaw* exploded in an enormous fireball that sprayed shells all over Pearl Harbor. Some of the shells fell in Ford Island, the center of Battleship Row, adding to the damage of Japanese bombs and bullets.

9:37 a.m. The USS *Cassin*, burning in drydock near the USS *Pennsylvania*, blew up and rolled onto the USS *Downes*, leaving both destroyers totally wrecked.

9:45 a.m. The Japanese planes regrouped and left with Pearl Harbor burning and exploding in their slipstreams. The second wave finished off the two wrecked destroyers in drydock, damaged the USS *Pennsylvania*, and blew up the USS *Shaw*, with damage to three or four other ships and a handful of aircraft. The second wave had lost six Zero fighters and 14 dive bombers, due to Taylor and Welch and to heavier antiaircraft fire. When Taylor and Welch got out of their damaged P-40s and drove back to Wheeler Field, still wearing some of their glad rags, a ground officer shouted at them: 'Get back to Haleiwa!. You know there's a war on?' Both flew in combat later in the war, and Welch – whose father had changed the family name from Schwartz to duck prejudice against German-Americans – later became a test pilot and arguably the first man to break the sound barrier. Taylor, interviewed many years after the war, said he had no lasting hatred for the Japanese but hated the men who started the war.

Pearl Harbor was the worst day in the history of the US Navy in terms of human losses and ship damage. The Japanese had lost 29 airplanes and 55 flyers and all ten two-man submariners. One submariner, Kazuo Sakamaki, blacked out after he swam to the beach from his foundered sub and became the first Japanese prisoner-of-war of World War II.

Sorting out the pieces, the United States Army had gotten fourteen planes off the ground during the attack – there was no air cover in the sky at all when the Japanese arrived – and these fighters accounted for ten of the Japanese attackers. One full-sized Japanese submarine used to launch the miniature submarines had disappeared, not in combat. The United States had lost eighteen ships sunk or damaged. The Navy had lost 2,008 sailors and officers killed and 710 wounded, with 109 marines killed and 69 wounded. The Army had lost 218 killed and 364 wounded. The civilian losses were 68 killed and 35 wounded, all but eight of them hit by stray bullets and shells from the fleet's antiaircraft fire or shells thrown off by exploding ships. Only one Japanese bomb fell on the city of Honolulu, by mistake, but forty Navy and Army antiaircraft shells blew up homes, shops, and a school and did about $500,000 worth of damage.

One case was emblematic: civilian workers at Pearl Harbor were called by telephone and ordered to come to their jobs for damage control work. Four riggers – Joseph Adams and his son John Adams, Joe McCabe, a mixed-blood Irish-Hawaiian, and McCabe's nephew, David Kahookele – were headed toward the clouds of smoke over Pearl Harbor when a misplaced Navy antiaircraft shell hit near their car in Judd Street. The riddled car pivoted and stopped dead on four flat tires. Joseph and Fata Kekahuna ran to help and found three of the civilians dead and the fourth dying. A fragment from the same shell struck 12-year-old Matilda Faufata over the heart while she was standing at her front door watching. She died in a matter of moments. Everybody in the neighborhood knew that the four riggers and the girl had been killed by a stray US shell, but for the next 40 years, photographs of the riddled car with two dead men visible in the front seat would be shown as 'evidence' of Japanese strafing of civilians.

Most victims were Japanese-American, Chinese-American, Korean-American or Hawaiian. Many were children. All were killed by stray American shells except for three off-duty soldiers taking civilian flying lessons, a Japanese-American airfield plumber who brought his own gun to fight Japanese parachutists, and four Honolulu firemen who were handling a hose when a Japanese fighter machine-gunned them. The myth that the Japanese had wantonly strafed women and children – like the myth of treachery by large numbers of American-born Japanese – was frantically promoted by newspapers and Hollywood for decades afterward.

In strategic terms, half the gun power in the Pacific Fleet was at the bottom of Pearl Harbor and the United States didn't have a single functional battleship in the Pacific Ocean to face the Japanese Navy. Incredibly, Japanese Admiral Chuichi Nagumo had failed to launch a third wave that would have destroyed the Navy's oil tanks and the dry docks. If the oil tanks had exploded, most experts believe that the United States would have lost Hawaii to Japan. For months afterwards, US currency issued to servicemen at Oahu was stamped 'HAWAII' so the Japanese couldn't spend it anywhere else if they overwhelmed the garrison and seized the islands.

That afternoon, Kilsoo Haan, who hadn't been able to break through to most of the federal officials he tried to reach, even with the help of Senator Guy Gillette, got a telephone call from Maxwell Hamilton of the State Department. Hamilton told Kilsoo Haan that if his 5 December warning of a Pearl Harbor attack were released to the press, Haan would be 'put away for the duration.' On 8 December, the FBI told him not to leave Washington DC until further notice.

This Japanese print made from a woodcut by the artist Kobayashi Kiyochika (1847–1915) shows a Japanese soldier bending slightly under the weight of a fortress, from which Russian soldiers fall, which he has pierced with his bayonet. Two men in the background, representing Korea and China, are in awe of the strength of the Japanese soldier. To this day the North Koreans express hostility towards Japan. (Library of Congress)

Above, below and opposite above: The papers – international, national and local – knew the writing was on the wall; and they were taking it down and printing it.

Rafu Shimpo editor Togo Tanaka (left) looks over a copy with pressman Yasuhei Nakanishi (right) in Los Angeles in 1941. Tanaka disparaged Kilsoo Haan's war warnings until just before the actual attack on Pearl Harbor. Tanaka was one of the first Japanese-Americans arrested after the attack.

Korea's King Kojong was a shy, kindly man who refused to sign away his country's independence, but his protests to the outside world were largely ignored.

Durham White Stevens was dubbed the American Dictator of Korea before his murder by Korean nationalists in San Francisco in 1908. The assassins became popular heroes in Korea. On 23 March 1908, an American diplomat in the service of the Korean government became a celebrity for a few moments and then disappeared from history.

Franco-American soldier-adventurer Charles William Le Gendre, shown as a colonel in the Civil War before his frightful mutilation by two Confederate muskets that destroyed his nose and one eye, had also moved from America to Japan and then to Korea, with service in all three governments.

Ahn Jong Gun threw his own life away to assassinate Hirobumi Ito. But Ito had actually opposed the outright annexation of Korea – which took place after Ito's assassination.

A company of women soldiers march through the streets of a Kwangsi town during the rebellion against Chiang Kai-shek in 1936. The Kwangsi leadership was promoted at the time as being progressive in all matters and the recruitment of women was part of this policy. It is doubtful that any of these young women would get near the frontline but they could be used in support roles. They are mostly armed with rifles, which may be being carried purely for propaganda purposes. (Courtesy of Philip S. Jowett, from *The Bitter Peace: Conflict in China 1928–37*)

Red Army troops march over mountainous terrain during an operation in the mid-1930s carrying all their equipment on their backs. The survivors of the Long March were joined by new recruits to expand the Red Army ready to face the Nationalists in 1936 and 1937. These same men would be expected to serve in units that were officially part of the Nationalist Army after the formation of the United Front in 1937. (Courtesy of Philip S. Jowett)

Chiang Kai-shek and his 'ally' Chang Hsueh-liang are photographed in the period of the Sian Incident in 1936. Chang was in turmoil about his betrayal of Chiang and his kidnapping by his North-Eastern Army. He was driven by his patriotism and his wish eventually to liberate his homeland in Manchuria, now under Japanese occupation. (Courtesy of Philip S. Jowett)

The corpses of massacre victims on the shore of the Qinhuai River, 1937, with a Japanese soldier standing nearby.

USS *Shaw* ablaze after the Pearl Harbor attack. (Library of Congress)

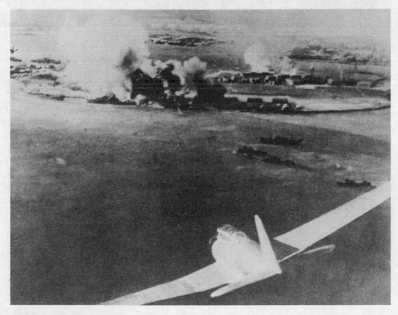

A Japanese bird's-eye view of the devastating attack. (Library of Congress)

The wreckage of USS *Arizona*. (Library of Congress)

Joseph and John Adams, Joe McCabe and David Kahookele were killed when a stray US Navy shell struck the road near their car as they were rushing to help save damaged ships at Pearl Harbor. Matilda Faufata, a 12-year-old girl in a doorway nearby, was also killed by the same shell burst. Newspapers ran this photo as proof of Japanese strafing of civilians through the war and for years afterward. Newspapers in Hawaii printed the real story with quotes from eye-witnesses in the 1980s. (Library of Congress)

Kilsoo Haan's warning about Japanese midget submarines like this one salvaged from the waters of Pearl Harbor turned out to be absolutely correct – and a joint US-Japanese underwater expedition in the 21st century provided plausible evidence that one of the midget submarines had torpedoed both the USS *Oklahoma* and the USS *West Virginia* for a loss of about 600 American sailors trapped inside the battleships when they sank. Haan's 1940 warning was ignored.

Japanese and Japanese-Americans were evacuated from California, Oregon and Washington state by Presidential Order 9066 at the instigation of Henry Morgenthau Jr., a mouthpiece for the Soviet agent Harry Dexter White. Morgenthau later fronted Harry Dexter White's plan for the national destruction of post-war Germany. (NARA)

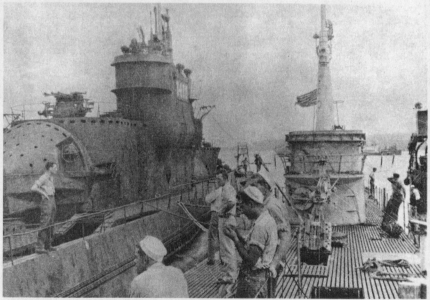

Blower (SS-325) in Tokyo Bay next to captured Japanese submarine I-400, c. September 1945. Bigger than any US subs until the nuclear program of the 1960s, the I-400 submarines were designed to launch aircraft attacks on the West Coast. Her six-inch deck gun (actually 5.5 inches), described precisely by Korean intelligence agents through Kilsoo Haan's report to the *New York Times* in October of 1942, was probably the biggest gun ever mounted on a wartime submarine.

A Japanese type 97 tank crew of the 3rd Tank Division. The Japanese used 800 tanks and Japanese and Korean troops indoctrinated to befriend and conciliate the war weary Chinese peasants in Operation Ichi Go starting in April of 1944. Kilsoo Haan had predicted the attack while testifying before a Congressional Committee chaired by Republican Samuel Dickstein of New York – a paid Soviet agent – almost a year before it happened.

Korean Is Sharply Critical Of U. S. Retention of Japs

(The following article on America's Korean policy of the moment was written for The Standard-Times by Kilsoo K. Haan.

By KILSOO K. HAAN

On the heels of shooting by Japanese police of peaceful Koreans who tried to welcome the American occupation forces, Lieutenant-General John R. Hodge announced that all Jap officials in Korea will be retained to rule the zone of occupation.

One cannot lightheartedly dismiss General MacArthur's decree as merely a policy of expediency. Past events in Japan and Korea raise many pertinent questions which demand careful examination of American policy in Korea.

It has been a well-known fact that for more than a generation, Anglo-American investors have loaned hundreds of millions of dollars to the Japanese to exploit the helpless Koreans and other Orientals. Some students of the Far East say, "This policy, to protect the Japanese properties in Korea, is in reality an indirect attempt to save as much as possible of the Anglo-American investment."

A recent London report says: "British investors are scrambling to buy Japanese sterling loans—Japanese stock companies' bond issues. Japanese sterling bonds of 1924 spiraled up £6¼ to 38. Jap loans of 1930 advanced £6 to 39 and loans of 1910 and 1907 advanced £5¾ each to 32 and 36, respectively." Obviously the British investors have every reason to rejoice and be hopeful.

SEPTEMBER 16, 1945.

Could their jubilation be largely due to this advance knowledge of U. S. policy in Korea and Japan? Since Dec. 7, 1941, the Japan societies in America have kept up an astute and steady campaign to save their investments in Asia through saving the Japanese Emperor.

It is the writer's opinion that the present unfortunate event in Korea is the direct result of political and economic psychological reaction created by the pro-Jap Americans.

KILSOO K. HAAN

Protest to Truman

Last Sunday, when Mr. Haan learned the U. S. decision to permit the Japanese to continue to govern Southern Korea, he sent the following message to President Truman:

"Obviously the temporary appointment of the former Jap Governor-General as Governor-General of Korea by the U. S. occupation commander may be considered the U. S. policy of expediency.

"We are forced to look upon this act as highly ill-advised, to say the least, and we fear that it will have a far-reaching psychological repercussion unfavorable toward democracy and toward the U. S. A. This act, in effect, may be construed by millions of subjugated Koreans as an unfriendly act toward the 26,000,000 Koreans.

"This first step is in reality a violation of the spirit of the Cairo Declaration.

Haan Urges Preparation For Quick Korea Freedom

Special to The Standard-Times

WASHINGTON, Oct. 11—Creation of an interim provisional commission of Koreans, Americans and Russians to prepare for freedom of Korea was proposed today by Kilsoo K. Haan, Washington representative of the Sino-Korean Peoples League, in a statement given to The New Bedford Standard-Times.

OCTOBER 11, 1945.

Might Cause War

He predicted the present setup would cause international friction and might result in war.

He said he was submitting the proposal to Secretary of State James F. Byrnes for consideration.

Mr. Haan suggested that the interim commission hold office for one year, beginning next Jan. 1.

Duties of the commission would be:

TO ELIMINATE the zones of occupation and unite Korea under a joint Soviet-U. S. command.

Asks Election

TO PREPARE for a general election next May to elect 13 States Government officials.

TO CALL for a constitutional convention immediately after the election and form a provisional representative Government not later than next Aug. 14, Atlantic Charter Day.

TO CREATE a hearing board to weed out collaborationists—Koreans, Americans and other foreign agents—who have acquired land and other properties in Korea with the aid of the Japanese.

TO FORM a provisional Land Holding Co-operative to take over all Japanese-owned land and wealth, and to hold in escrow the properties of Koreans and foreigners found guilty of collaborating with the Japanese. Property held in escrow later would be returned to the rightful owners.

Between the Japanese surrender and the beginning of the Korean War in 1950, Kilsoo Haan became a frequent newspaper commentator about Korea and proposed a number of actions that led to a reasonably democratic government in South Korea.

Ruth Bryan Owens, daughter of three-time US presidential candidate and former Secretary of State William Jennings Bryan, first woman member of Congress from the South and first US woman ambassador (seated left of center in hat), shares a joke with Kilsoo Haan (right) at the San Francisco Conference that founded the United Nations at the end of World War II.

Soviet T-34 tanks were urged to invade Japanese-held Manchuria by US policy makers but did so only after the atomic bomb had doomed Japan. Five years later, Secretary of State Dean Acheson's defense perimeter statement excluded South Korea and doomed the South Koreans to a Soviet-backed invasion that killed millions of Koreans and 53,000 US soldiers and Marines.

The brutal North Korean murders of American prisoners, like this soldier from the 21st Infantry who was bound and shot during the invasion of 1950, made a quick withdrawal from South Korea politically unacceptable. The courageous refusal of most Koreans to live under Communism led to a seismic shift in world opinion. Dean Acheson lost his job.

Men of the 3rd Battalion, 34th Infantry Regiment, 35th Infantry Division, covering up behind rocks to shield themselves from exploding mortar shells near the Hantan River in central Korea, 11 April 1951. (Library of Congress)

COMSTOCK
CLUB *presents*

"THE SOVIET 30 YEAR MASTER PLAN"

KILSOO HAAN

Kilsoo Haan kept up his anti-Soviet message, as seen here from a 1971 lecture brochure, for the rest of his life. His anti-Soviet message at this point was – arguably – largely redundant and his Pearl Harbor warning little more than an embarrassment.

Korean War Memorial, Washington, D.C. (Library of Congress)

12

THE USUAL SUSPECTS

Everybody in the Roosevelt White House had expected war with Japan. Pearl Harbor, however, had been an incredibly obvious target – that was why John Huston was directing the movie mentioned earlier, *Across the Pacific*, about a fictional Japanese air attack on Pearl Harbor at the time the real attack took place. The film was a vehicle to re-unite Humphrey Bogart, Sydney Greenstreet and Mary Astor, who had captivated audiences the year before in *The Maltese Falcon*. Huston quickly changed the scripted Japanese target in the film from Pearl Harbor to the Panama Canal. The new ending improvised some ridiculous second-unit scenes with a toy airplane taking off from a jungle landing strip lugging twin torpedoes until Bogart shot it down on take-off. The Asian assassins who are trying to thwart Japan's designs on world conquest are 'Filipinos,' who had a zero profile in assassinating Japanese leaders, rather than Koreans, who did that sort of thing a lot. Possibly because the film was almost completed when the real Pearl Harbor attack took place, the title remained *Across the Pacific* – even though none of the film takes place in the Pacific. Had the film been released with a simulated attack on Pearl Harbor depicted by Warner Brothers and finished before the attack – which could have happened – FDR's embarrassment might have been even deeper than it was.[1]

The week before the attack, newspapers around the United States featured six-column and eight-column banner headlines: *San Francisco Chronicle*, 1 December – F.D.R. RUSHES TO CAPITAL; FAR EAST CRISIS GRAVE. *Dallas Morning News*, 3 December, with map – F.D.R. ASKS JAPAN WHY TROOPS SENT TO INDO-CHINA. *Des Moines Register*, 5 December – ACTION LIKELY IN PACIFIC. *St Paul Pioneer Press*, 5 December – JAPS ANSWER TODAY: BREAK NEAR, with the sub-headline beneath, 'Hull's Terms For Peace Denounced.' *The Honolulu Advertiser*, Sunday morning 7 December, printed before the attack – F.D.R. WILL SEND MESSAGE TO EMPEROR ON WAR CRISIS. *The Baltimore American*, 7 December, printed before the attack – ROOSEVELT SENDS PERSONAL MESSAGE TO JAP EMPEROR with a sub-headline, 'Tokyo Ponders "Blood Or Oil"'.[2]

When the news about Pearl Harbor reached Washington, Franklin Delano Roosevelt was thunderstruck, not because he was surprised at the attack itself – someone must have seen some of the eight-column newspaper headlines – but because the attack had been far more dreadful than anything Washington had expected. Secretary of Labor Frances Perkins, who saw him at a cabinet meeting that night said that FDR 'could hardly bring himself to describe the devastation. His pride in the Navy was so terrific that he was having actual physical difficulty in getting out the words that put on the record him knowing that the Navy was caught unawares.'[3]

At 12:45 on 8 December in the Philippines, the second act of the tragedy took place, little noticed outside the Philippines, as thousands of Americans rushed to volunteer and avenge the unexpected 'sneak attack' forecast for seven days in mainland newspapers.

The Americans had hoped for at least 100 B-17s before the war everyone knew was coming broke out. They had received 35 B-17s – the four-engine bombers that Admiral Kimmel had wanted for long-range armed reconnaissance around Hawaii and had never received. The Americans didn't want to be caught on the ground so they kept the B-17s in the air. Then they decided to attack the Japanese on Formosa, Japanese territory since 1895. The B-17s were called down to Clark Field to refuel and arm. Most of the airmen went to lunch while they waited to make their first bombing attack on Japanese territory. A formation of two-engine Japanese bombers arrived and carried out a precision bombing run from 20,000 feet. Clark Field exploded in flame and smoke and eighteen of the 21 B-17s were destroyed in a matter of minutes.

Japanese A-6 Mitsubishi Zero fighters zoomed in to strafe the P-40 and P-36 fighters at Eba and Nichols Fields. The Japanese destroyed 18 B-17s, 53 of the 107 US fighters in the Philippines and 35 other supply and training aircraft, for a loss of seven Japanese fighters. Not a single US fighter plane had been aloft to oppose them. Many of the surviving fighters were obsolete P-36 Seversky fighters, second-string aircraft that stood no chance at all against a Zero in a dogfight. Most of the P-36 fighters were destroyed in the next few days and the nose-heavy P-40s – themselves obsolescent if not obsolete – were whittled down until there were two left. The American infantrymen who called themselves 'the battling bastards of Bataan – no Mama, no Papa, no Uncle Sam' – referred to their two-plane air cover as The Lone Ranger and Tonto.

The *United States News* pictogram had shown the Philippines as one of the bomber bases that would burn Japan's wood and paper cities in case of trouble. The pictogram also depicted the island of Guam. The Japanese took Guam on 10 December.

Faced with losses and humiliations they hadn't anticipated when they dictated unacceptable conditions to a proud but threatened nation – now enraged and filled with ferocious self-confidence – FDR and the men around him began a frantic search for scapegoats.

The 26 November Hull note had made war all but unavoidable. Henry Stimson, the Secretary of War, looking over the flurry of decoded documents, clearly knew war was about to break out, But Stimson said that the main thing was to make sure the Japanese fired the first shot so Japan, and not the United States, would be branded the aggressor by world opinion.

The last tip-off came in a decoded order from Tokyo to the Japanese Consulate in Hawaii: the Japanese Embassy staffers ordered the Japanese Consulate to break up their decoding machine and burn their files. Incredibly, nobody bothered to inform Admiral Husband Kimmel or General Walter Short of this virtual declaration that the attack was coming and Hawaii was the target. At Pearl Harbor Admiral Kimmel, in fact, had been told that there would be no ultimatum to the Japanese – and the Hull note was nothing if not an ultimatum. Radhabinod Pal of India, observing the Tokyo Trials at the end of the war, commented: 'As far as the present war, the Principality of Monaco, the Grand Duchy of Luxemburg, would have taken up arms against the United States on receipt of such a note as the State Department sent the Japanese Government on the eve of Pearl Harbor.'4

Kilsoo Haan had provided a wealth of information that the target would be Pearl Harbor. The target was now confirmed by decoded messages from Japan's own diplomatic corps. Washington sat on the information – apparently because they wanted some sort of war but didn't expect anything like what they got.

The last act of the tragedy was a farce: Counseled by the Japanese elder statesmen like Hirota and Yonai to behave in such a way as to make an early peace possible, the Japanese Embassy had proposed to issue a formal declaration of war in Washington a half-hour before the actual attack on Pearl Harbor. The note had been postponed until the last few hours in the vain hope that something would head off a war that the Japanese diplomats in America knew would be a catastrophe for Japan. Because the American decoders stayed on duty all night, the White House knew about the 14-part messages before the Japanese did. As Roosevelt read Part 13 of the decoded message, he turned to his ultra-liberal alter ego, Harry Hopkins – a Communist sympathizer according to the Soviet agent 'Bill' Akmerov – and said, 'This means war.' This was at 9 p.m. on 6 December – ample time to get a warning to Kimmel and Short at Pearl Harbor – but nobody telephoned Hawaii from the White House. General Marshall was supposedly out riding his horse when the decoded messages reached his office, though some observers said he was actually in the building when the message came in. The Army sent a Western Union telegram rather that use a scrambler telephone that could have reached Hawaii in seconds.

The typists had all gone home when the final part of the message arrived at the Japanese Embassy. The diplomats themselves were horrified by the prospect of war, They had gotten so drunk the night before that they couldn't get the message typed in time to drop it off a half-hour before the bombs were scheduled to fall.

Kurusu and Nomura dropped Japan's declaration of war off after the attack. It read: 'It is a fact of history that the countries of East Asia for the past hundred years or more have been compelled to observe the status quo under the Anglo-American policy of imperialistic exploitation and to sacrifice themselves to the prosperity of the two nations.' Ulysses S. Grant had said the same thing during his tour of the world after his second term as president. 'I have never been so struck with the heartlessness of Nations as well as individuals since coming to the East. But the day of retribution it sure to come.'[5] When retribution came, Cordell Hull, a conservative Southerner and Spanish-American War veteran who probably hated Grant's memory for defeating the Confederacy and supporting Reconstruction, wasn't ready for that kind of talk from 'colored people.'

In all my fifty years of public service I have never seen a document that was more crowded with infamous falsehoods and distortions – infamous falsehoods and distortions on a scale so huge that I never imagined until today that any government on this planet was capable of uttering them,[6]

Roosevelt's family on his mother's side had made a huge fortune in the Chinese opium trade under British protection, and he was not present to be offended. FDR spoke before Congress on Monday, 8 December, asking for a declaration of war because of the 'unprovoked and dastardly attack by Japan.'

Despite the drunken farce at the Japanese Embassy, the Japanese had already declared war on paper and at Pearl Harbor. Newspapers had predicted a war starting on 1 December. *United States News* had shown all the best bomber lanes to Japan on 31 October. Roosevelt himself had known war was coming at least the night before the attack, and said so to Harry Hopkins and friends. His 'day of infamy' speech was an outrageous presumption that the US Congress and the American public were stupid, but since the war had already started neither the Congress nor the people saw any option except to fight. Congress voted unanimously to declare war, without being told Japan had already done so. Congresswoman Jeannette Rankin of Montana abstained, as she had rather more plausibly in 1917.

When the Japanese bombed Pearl Harbor, Daniel Inouye, future winner of the Congressional Medal of Honor and future US Senator, had shaken his fist and cursed the airplanes. Inouye had already taken some abuse from his Japanese-language teachers – the people Kilsoo Haan saw, perhaps plausibly, as fostering a dangerous dual loyalty.

'We think the Japanese Government is stupid and has embarked on a campaign it has absolutely no chance of winning, 'Kilsoo Haan's sometime adversary, Togo Tanaka, an American-born Phi Beta Kappa from UCLA, wrote in a newspaper editorial published on 8 December. Tanaka said that the Japanese-American community 'had not been in sympathy with Japan's expansion program.' Togo Tanaka himself had then been arrested, with no explanation, on the same day and was held for 11 days and then released without formal charges or an explanation. Officials from the War Department – more political than the FBI and less informed about legality – had interrogated Tanaka about dual loyalty when he asked if his bilingual newspaper could keep publishing in case of war with Japan. Togo Tanaka had estimated that about 5 per cent of the Japanese-born population might be suspect. He divided the suspects about evenly. Half were '*Aka*' (reds), people who tended to be well-educated but were discontented, he thought, because of their own shortcomings. The other half were said to be ultra-nationalists who tended to be thick-headed and unable to learn English. Within the three weeks following Pearl Harbor, the FBI, the Bureau of Naval Intelligence and the Bureau of Army Intelligence had arrested 2,192 Japanese within the continental United States and another 879 in Hawaii. Some of these people were actually dangerous – even under detention Japanese fanatics almost murdered a couple of Japanese-Americans, including Togo Tanaka himself, for their loyalty to the US. Most were simply victims of circumstance.

Arrests of people actually born in Japan were less than circumspect. Iwao and Hanae Matsushita, a husband and wife both born in Japan, had come to the US in 1919 as young married adults. They both loved America but they were legally ineligible for citizenship. Iwao worked for a Japanese corporation and he and his wife were intensely fond of nature – that most Japanese of obsessions. The Matsushitas made more than a hundred trips to Mount Rainier and shared their nature photographs with the Seattle Camera Club. They were so fond of the national parks – and also so unhappy with Japan's aggressive behaviour in Asia – that when Iwao Matsushita was transferred back to Japan, he quit his job. He was arrested immediately on the outbreak of war. Japanese birth, a fondness for cameras and quitting a solid job was all the circumstantial evidence needed to put him in jail.[7]

Pearl Harbor also spelled the doom of the US Asiatic Fleet that had patrolled the coast of China from its base in the Philippines. Unable to survive Japanese air attacks without American air cover, the Asiatic Fleet joined the Dutch, British, and Australian warships trying to stop the Japanese from seizing the Dutch East Indies and obtaining the oil they needed. In a series of battles culminating on 27 February, the Allied fleet clashed with a Japanese fleet of roughly the same size. The Japanese sank the cruiser USS *Houston* and two American destroyers, along with most of the Dutch, British, and Australian ships, for a combined Allied loss of 10 ships and 2,173 sailors. Japanese naval aircraft sank the venerable old USS *Langley*, the Navy's first aircraft carrier, while she was being used to transport aircraft to defend the Dutch East Indies. Allied morale plummeted as defeat after defeat convinced disheartened white soldiers that the Japanese were not monkeys but supermen. Fighting the Japanese in the jungle, Winston Churchill was to warn, was like jumping into the ocean to fight a shark.

Scapegoats were obviously needed to protect the administration from condemnation about the war warnings they ignored through bungling, sheer stupidity, or something more devious.

Roosevelt's first choice was the man he had unexpectedly appointed to replace Admiral James Otto Richardson, dumped for warning FDR and Knox that the Navy wasn't ready, Admiral Husband Kimmel had also tried to warn FDR – and hadn't been informed by FDR even when the White House received the decoded Japanese diplomatic message. Ten days after the attack, Kimmel and General Walter Short were both demoted and replaced.

General Walter Short took his demotion humbly. Kimmel – whom Roosevelt had appointed because he was a scrapper – fought for the rest of his life to win exoneration.

'The Pacific Fleet deserved a fighting chance,' Kimmel wrote in *Admiral Kimmel's Story*, published in 1954. 'Had we had as much as two hours of warning a full alert of planes and guns would have greatly reduced the damage. We could possibly have been able to locate the Jap carriers, and our own carriers *Lexington* and *Enterprise* already at sea to the westward of Oahu might have been brought into the picture instead of expending their efforts to the southward as a result of faulty information. The great intangible, the element of surprise, would have been denied the Japs.'

The easy way out was for people who had slept through the war warnings – and especially for those who helped trigger the attack – was to forget about seeking out dangerous fanatics and to blame the entire Japanese community for wholesale treason. A hate campaign would take the American peoples' minds off the search for traitors whose eyes were the same shape as their own.

Three days after the attack on Pearl Harbor, Henry Morgenthau Jr. asked J .Edgar Hoover for his opinion on rounding up the entire Japanese and Japanese-American population of the West Coast, Hoover was appalled and bluntly told Morgenthau that the Attorney General Nicholas Biddle would not approve any 'dragnet or round-up procedure.' Hoover told Morgenthau that many of the Japanese in question were American citizens and such an action would be illegal. The FBI Director also knew it would be absolutely unnecessary: informed by loyal Japanese-Americans including Togo Tanaka, by Korean dissidents including Kilsoo Haan, and by information the FBI had picked up during a burglary on the Japanese Consulate in Los Angeles and another burglary of the Black Dragon Society office, Hoover had a comprehensive list of people he wanted to arrest and had already started. Of the 879 soon detained in Hawaii, many were Japanese-Americans working as divers, welders and heavy equipment operators to salvage the sunken battleships of Pearl Harbor.

The FBI and Naval Intelligence were satisfied now that Togo Tanaka's potentially dangerous 5 per cent of Japanese were in custody, but the Roosevelt cabinet – especially Morgenthau, a front man for Harry Dexter White even if he didn't know it – was definitely not satisfied. Just as the Nazi Part had blamed the Jews for Germany's defeat in World War I, the people who were really responsible for Pearl Harbor, through utter bungling if not through active treason, fostered their own 'stab in the back' myth directed at the Japanese-Americans. Disregarding the provocation when FDR restricted the oil flow and Acheson cut it off completely, the Roosevelt administration, some of the newspapers, and eventually Hollywood made it appear that the Japanese had attacked a friendly nation without warning and that their only reason was an attempt to join Hitler in taking over the world. Theodore Geissel – 'Doctor Seuss' – worked for the leftist publisher Ralph Ingersoll. Geissel drew cartoons of Japanese saboteurs in California queuing up to receive TNT for sabotage.

Under protest, J. Edgar Hoover now sent the FBI to break into selected Japanese-American homes to confiscate weapons, cameras and radios needed for a fantasized uprising. The results were disappointing.

Kilsoo Haan had long argued that the Japanese militarists of Japan were recruiting Nisei – second-generation Japanese-Americans – as potential agents. He suggested investigation of individuals, but not a wholesale round-up, since he knew many Japanese-Americans were loyal to the US and resented attempts at recruitment.

After Pearl Harbor, KIlsoo Haan took a new stance with a letter to the Justice Department on 14 January: Koreans must be allowed to separate themselves from the Japanese-American community even though they were legally Japanese nationals based on the annexation of Korea in 1910. He agreed, however, that Koreans should be asked to carry identification badges as long as these identified them as Korean and not Japanese. On 23 January 1942, he received a letter from Earl G. Harrison, special assistant to the Attorney General Francis Biddle.

The regulations, just adopted, governing certificates of identification for aliens of enemy nationalities provide that Koreans, who under the Alien Registration Act of 1940, registered as Koreans, are not required to apply for Certificates of Identification, provided that such persons have not at any time voluntarily become German, Italian, or Japanese citizens of subjects.

On 25 January, the *Los Angeles Times*, crediting Kilsoo Haan, reported that Koreans would no longer be regarded as enemy aliens. 'The effect of the Justice Department's change of attitude will be to unfreeze the credit of Koreans in this country and release them from surveillance by government authorities. Korean nationals have resented their classification as Japanese.'

On 18 March 1942, Roosevelt signed Executive Order 9066 establishing the War Relocation Board, over the objections of J. Edgar Hoover and of Senator Robert Taft of Ohio, who called it the sloppiest criminal law he had ever heard of.

Japanese-Americans born and raised in the United States, many of them Christians, many of them graduates of American high schools and colleges, were given a few hours or days to pack and were put on buses or trains for ten concentration camps in isolated mountain and desert locations. Some collapsed of heat stroke before they arrived at the hastily constructed tar-paper and clapboard barracks where multiple families shared a single room. By 7 June, 112,000 American men, women, and children were behind barbed wire eating wretched food in harsh climates. About a dozen inmates were shot dead by guards and many others were savagely beaten up, sometimes in revenge for a brother or friend killed in battle with the 'Japs', sometimes because they wandered outside the safety zone, often trying to catch fish to supplement their rations. Many older Japanese succumbed to culture shock and simply lost the will to live.

Eleanor Roosevelt spoke out against the relocation – the relocated Japanese artist Chiura Obata sent her one of his paintings as a sign of gratitude – and Attorney General Francis Biddle moved around behind the scenes to liberalize a release program for Japanese-Americans who could prove their unquestioned loyalty. The average Japanese-American from California, Oregon or Washington State spent about 900 days in concentration camps during World War II. The fact that the Koreans living in America were exempt was perhaps Kilsoo Haan's greatest achievement – which could have been surpassed only if his war warnings about Pearl Harbor had been taken seriously.

MOUNTAIN HAZE OF DEATH

The Pearl Harbor attack that left half the firepower of the Pacific Fleet stuck in the mud on the bottom of Pearl Harbor and killed 2,400 Americans turned Kilsoo Haan into the only Korean most Americans of the 1940s had ever heard of.

Kilsoo Haan undoubtedly enjoyed the attention but he never wavered in throwing his phenomenal energy and the useful information from his Korean agents into the battle to free Korea from Japan – and to foster enough amity with the US to keep Russia or China from moving into Korea after the Japanese left. Both as a Christian and as a Korean nationalist, he was every bit as much an anti-Communist as he was anti-Japanese. Haan spoke at luncheons and dinners all over the US, often to Republicans or conservative Democrats who had qualms about FDR and some of the strange people around him.

'I don't remember my father very well,' his son Stan said some years after Kilsoo Haan's death. 'I spent most of my time with my mother.'[1]

Kilsoo Haan may have had enemies who were not Japanese. On 24 August 1942, *Time* magazine took a swat at Kilsoo Haan's credibility with a story entitled 'Straight To The Armpit.'[2]

Kilsoo K. Haan, US representative of both the admitted revolutionary Korean National Front Federation and the

Sino-Korean People's League, is Korea's most vocal Washington spokesman. He is short and 42; he wears rimless spectacles and is given to loud, figured ties. He is often heard, seldom heeded. But last week Kilsoo Haan came into his own.

Papers through the US featured his 'secret report' that a young Korean patriot had shot and slightly wounded Japanese Premier Hideki Tojo on 17 June. The would-be assassin's second shot went wild, but seriously wounded onetime Premier Koki Hirota. As Tojo was carried to the hospital with a wound 'under the left armpit', the patriot, whose name was Park Soowon, was shot full of holes by Japanese police, who in the process brought down the Japanese ace, Major Yuzo Fujita, and two Japanese photographers. Tokyo police succeeded in rounding up 50-odd members of a Korean terrorist group that had been operating in Yokohama, Tokyo, and Osaka but, said Kilsoo Haan, 'their number is legion, and they will continue to operate'.

Although his scoop has yet to be confirmed, Kilsoo Haan was serenely confident that it would be. As evidence of its plausibility, he drew up a list of Korean acts of terrorism. The list was more notable for length than for accuracy. Most impressive of the checkable acts was the 1932 bombing of a reviewing stand in Shanghai after a parade in honor of Japan's Emperor: General Yoshinori Shirakawa lost his life, Minister to China Mamoru Shigemitsu his leg and Admiral Kichisaburo Nomura his right eye. Author of that bombing was one in Hokichi. [?] As for most other Korean terrorists, their aim was no better than Park Soowon's.

Journalists often engaged in a sort of body-trading with politicians. Columnist Drew Pearson, for instance, won gratitude and some exclusive tips from the Roosevelt White House when he embarrassed General Douglas MacArthur, who had dumped his young Eurasian mistress for repeated infidelities. Pearson blackmailed MacArthur for a grubstake for the girl after one of Pearson's male acolytes joined her list of conquests.

Kilsoo Haan was a serious embarrassment to the Roosevelt camp – Haan's persistent, documented Pearl Harbor warning as confirmed by both Drew Pearson and by Eric Sevareid had shown that Washington was at least asleep on watch, assuming that the White House had not wanted the attack to happen. Somebody in power with favors to exchange for a little journalistic slander clearly wanted Kilsoo Haan discredited, and if possible silenced as a news source.

Time omitted Kilsoo Haan's accurate predictions – the date of the Pearl Harbor attack and the use of the midget submarines – and focused on the Tojo-Hirota shootings, which were fictional. Hideki Tojo had led the Japanese cabinet decision that voted to bomb Pearl Harbor. Koki Hirota had argued that the United States would never go to war for China. Hirota urged no Japanese military action. Both survived the war and were hanged a few moments apart after the Tokyo Trials.[1]

One element of the report that *Time* ridiculed may have been based not on outright fabrication but on faulty observation or faulty translation. Mitsuo Fuchida – not 'Yuzo Fujita' as in the *Time* article – had led the air attack against Pearl Harbor. Commander Mitsuo Fuchida later survived an emergency appendectomy while serving with the Japanese fleet just before the battle of Midway in early June. At Midway, Fuchida was aboard the Japanese aircraft carrier *Akagi* when it was hit by American dive-bombers and caught fire. Commander Fuchida was compelled to slide down a rope, weakened by his appendectomy operation. He broke both ankles and was evacuated back to Japan and hospitalized. Korean agents may have discovered that Mitsuo Fuchida, a big name in Japanese military aviation, had been seriously incapacitated and may have mistaken the appendectomy dressing for a gunshot wound. The actual Major Yuzo Fujita was a Japanese Army aviator, winner of the Harmon Trophy in 1938, and not involved at Pearl Harbor, which was a navy operation.

In October of 1942, after the Japanese defeat at Midway and while the Japanese and the Americans were battling for Guadalcanal in the Solomon Islands, Korean agents supplied Kilsoo Haan with informaton that could have led to an attack or attacks far deadlier than Pearl Harbor. On 28 October 1942, the *New York Times* reported:

> Japanese Submarines Said To Carry 300 Men.
> Special to the *New York Times*. Washington, October 27. – Japan has produced four 'super submarines' combining armaments with large passenger and cargo and has a large number scheduled for early completion, it was reported today by the Korean National Front Federation.
> The submarines were reported as of the 4,500 tons gross with a cruising range of 20,000 miles. One of them, according to the information, has made a trip to Europe and returned to Japan carrying 300 German airplane and shipbuilding experts. Each submarine is said to mount four six-inch guns and carry two 'collapsible' planes.
> The Federation statement added that that Japan planned to put twenty-four such additional submarines in service by June of next year.

The Special sounded like something out of the 19th-century novels of Jules Verne – but incredibly enough, the story was substantially accurate, in some aspects actually understating the menace to the United States. A little more than a month after the attack on Pearl Harbor, which he ordered with misgivings and the knowledge that he could not win an extended war, Admiral Isoroku Yamamoto submitted a proposal for a fleet of eighteen large submarines capable of making three round trips to the West Coast of America without re-fueling, and capable of carrying seaplanes that could attack the coastal cities of the United States.[5] Each submarine would also be able to circumnavigate the globe without re-fueling. The designs were approved on 17 March 1942 and construction of the first giant submarine, the I-400, began at the Kure Dock Yards on 18 January 1943.

Kilsoo Haan's agents were incredibly adept. They had a detailed plan, substantially accurate in almost every detail, published in the *New York Times* three months before the first of the giant submarines was even under construction. Four other giant submarines were under construction within the next year. Plans for the others were dropped due to war-time shortages.

The I-400 and the other giant submarine completed, the I-401, were the largest submarines ever built, and remained the largest prior to the US nuclear-powered submarines of the 1960s. The Japanese submarines were powered by four diesel engines and could travel at 34.6 kilometres per hour on the surface. The two electric motors of 2,100 horsepower each could drive the giant submarines at 22 kilometres per hour submerged – faster than most American submarines, especially in the underwater mode. The Korean agents had predicted a weight of 4,500 tons. The actual weight of the I-400 was 6,500 tons. The Korean agents reported a range of 20,000 miles. The actual range was more than 30,000 miles. The submarines featured eight torpedo tubes for the deadly 'long lance' torpedo, a better torpedo than Americans would have for the first three years of the war. Original plans had called for two seaplanes with collapsible wings stored in water-proof hangars. The actual submarines carried three two-seater seaplanes. The Aichi *Seiran* – 'Mountain Haze' – a streamlined torpedo plane with a top speed of 295 miles per hour, was far faster than the US *Devastator*, which had proved a slow-flying death trap for American pilots at Midway. The Torpedo Eight Squadron from the USS *Hornet* lost every one of fifteen Devastator torpedo planes and scored no hits on the Japanese fleet despite the great courage displayed by the flyers. One, Ensign George Gay, was recovered alive after two days in the ocean,

The faster and tougher *Seiran* planes, once taken from their waterproof deck hangers, would be lowered into the ocean by a huge crane, with their crankcases already pumped full of pre-heated oil to speed the warm-up before takeoff. Nobody expected these planes to return to the sub, except during drills – they were intended for one-way missions to bomb the coastal areas of the US.

Korean sources reported that the giant submarines would mount four 6-inch guns. The actual single 5.5-inch gun on the I-400 class submarines was effective to 15,000 yards and out-ranged anything on a sub-hunting American destroyer. The submarines also mounted three three-barreled 25-millimetre anti-aircraft guns and a single-barreled 25-millimetre gun, super-heavy machineguns far more powerful than the anti-aircraft batteries on the older American warships at Pearl Harbor and Midway. I-400 was coated with a special paint to reduce the effectiveness of radar and sonar. Design features were included to reduce electrical tension due to underwater travel. The test depth for dives by the I-400 class submarine was 100 metres – 330 feet, half again the safe dive of a 1942 American fleet submarine. So Japanese giant submarines were, in fact, even more formidable and dangerous than the prototypes described by the Korean agents who reported them to Kilsoo Haan in Washington before their keels had been laid at Kure.

The detailed data on the I-400 submarine program was one of the greatest home runs in the history of military intelligence. As with Kilsoo Haan's Pearl Harbor warning, the data was greeted with skepticism, if not ridicule. American naval and military intelligence slumbered through what ultimately could have been the worst US disaster of the war.

But on 26 August 1945, two weeks after the Japanese surrender following the atomic bombings, the I-401 suddenly popped up on the radar of the USS *Segundo*, a standard-sized submarine, and surrendered. The Japanese *Seiran* aircraft had been launched to crash at sea just after take-off two days before contact, and the torpedoes had been launched to sink into the ocean without detonating. The Japanese captain committed suicide rather than witness the US Navy boarding his ship. His subordinates handed over two *samurai* swords and the crew stayed aboard and explained how the ship worked. A second submarine, a modified semi-giant listed as I-14, 370 feet long, also surrendered. The I-14 carried two *Seiran* seaplanes rather than three and was 30 feet shorter than the I-400 series submarines.

The American naval officers and naval engineers who examined the I-401 were astounded at the level of proficiency the Japanese had reached in underwater design – so much so that when the Russians asked to tour the I-401, the crewless giant submarine was towed into deep water and sunk with an American torpedo on 31 May 1946, to prevent the Russians from learning anything from a design that was so far in advance of either the USSR or the US. The I-401 had been saling to launch a conventional bombing attack on the Pacific locks of the Panama Canal when the Japanese crew received a radio message to end hostilities on 15 April.[6]

The worst case scenario was only discovered after the war. An operation called 'Cherry Blossoms at Night' had been proposed and partially planned to drop plague-ridden fleas on San Diego in the hopes of starting an epidemic and crippling the largest naval base on the West Coast. The idea echoed a short story by Jack London, *The Unparalleled Invasion*, written in 1909 but more famously published in *The Strength of the Strong,* a book of short stories published in 1915.[7] Set in the future with a narrative supposedly starting in 1976, *The Unparalleled Invasion* describes a modernized China driving the Japanese from the Asian mainland and routing a French invasion bid. America drops glass containers of germs from airships – apparently German-style Zeppelins – and most of the population of China is wiped out in a pandemic. The German Army moves in to wipe out those Chinese whose natural resistance gets them through the man-made plague. Jack London was criticized for writing a story in which mass extermination by disease was even mooted. The Japanese may have read the story. Shortly after it appeared in 1915, a Japanese girl showed up, travelling entirely alone, at Jack London's farm in Sonoma, California, and was welcomed by Jack and his wife Charmian. No Japanese woman of those days travelled alone with one exception – the *bushijo*, or soldier girl, a sort of female *samurai* often employed as a spy in feudal times. The Japanese girl enjoyed a pleasant visit – Jack actualled loved the Japanese in private life – and she was fondly remembered by Jack and Charmian.

Shortly, Paul Nagata, Jack's Japanese houseboy, decided he wanted to complete his education and get married, and left the farm in Sonoma. Vacationing in Hawaii, Jack London met his next and last houseboy, Tomo Sekine. The new houseboy moved in at the farm and helped nurse Jack through what was obviously soon to become a fatal case of nephritis, a kidney disease probably brought on by Jack's heavy whiskey drinking and a diet of raw or rare meat. Charmian had fallen into a deep sleep on the night that Jack died, but Sekine was at his side. The next morning,

Sekine woke Charmian and told her that he was having trouble waking Jack, who had been taking opiates for his pain.

While the grieving entourage was preparing Jack London for burial, Sekine approached Charmian and told her that he had left a special note written on a piece of paper tucked into Jack's lapel before his cremation: 'His words were silver, but now his silence is golden.'[8] No Japanese who read this had a moment of doubt that Sekine was claiming credit for the death of Jack London. Whether Sekine killed Jack London acting under orders or simply helped Jack to die peacefully is unknown. Americans looked Tomo Sekine up after the end of World War II. Sekine's grainy newspaper photograph was that of a tough *samurai* from Kyushu, not a humble houseboy. Many Jack London scholars who have read about Sekine believe that Jack London's death was assisted suicide. Writing a story that seemed to endorse what Rafael Lemkin first named 'genocide' toward the end of World War II could have triggered a quiet assassination. Sekine, for all his affection for Jack as a 'regular guy,' never called him 'a good person' – in samurai lore, if you kill a 'good person' you yourself may win still glory by dying in battle but your descendants will suffer for the murder of the innocent.

Hideki Tojo – the stock villain of American propaganda films after the Americans decided to keep Hirohito around as a figurehead against Communism – was also a *samurai*.

'There was a fierce debate in Tokyo, and a document discovered recently suggests that at a crucial meeting in late July 1944 it was Hideki Tojo – whom the United States later hanged for war crimes – who rejected the proposal to use germ warfare against the United States,' an article by Nicholas D. Kristof reported in the *New York Times* on 17 March 1995.

Tojo, in fact, had just been ousted one step ahead of a proposed assassination, so that other diplomats could seek an immediate armistice with the United States 'but he retained enough authority to veto the proposal. He knew by then that Japan was sure to lose the war, and he feared that biological assaults on the United States would invite retaliation with germ or chemical weapons being developed by America.'[9]

Tojo, despite his rigid loyalty to the Emperor, had previously refused to hand over the thousands of terrified Jewish refugees that Japan was sheltering to Hitler, despite a Nazi request. The vast majority of Jews who found shelter with the Japanese survived the war. Tojo had also opposed the shooting of the Doolittle aviators who had bombed Japan in the surprise air raid of 18 April 1942. Tojo did not dispute that the Doolittle aviators had bombed a marked hospital and strafed a school. He argued bluntly that soldiers had to follow orders and could not be punished as criminals for acts of violence committed under those orders.

Tojo was more noted for his sharp memory than his imagination – his nickname was *kamisori*, the razor. He appears to have had a strong sense of his personal honor.[10] Whether he was pragmatic or chivalrous – or both – no bubonic plague fleas nor anthrax drops by seaplanes launched from the I-400 series giant submarines were approved Cancelling the plague attacks on San Diego could have saved thousands of lives and Kilsoo Haan, however reluctant he was to find a kind word for Hideki Tojo, would certainly have been glad that the plague and anthrax germs never reached California.

The secrecy that covered the whole I-400 submarine program, once the threat of plague and anthrax was eliminated, was a set-back to Kilsoo Haan's career. Kilsoo Haan and his agents had pulled off a far more impressive piece of espionage than the Pearl Harbor warnings. But because nobody was allowed to hear about the I-400 submarines, nobody heard about those second wave of warnings, which proved Kilsoo Han and his agents to be amazingly accurate.

14

THE DAWN BEFORE
THE DARKNESS

Kilsoo Haan's Pearl Harbor warning had put Korea back on the political map, especially after Drew Pearson's 'Washington Daily Merry-Go-Round' column had reinforced the Pearl Harbor warning and quite possibly kept Kilsoo Haan out of a deportation camp. The status of the Korean as the man who warned America about Pearl Harbor made a lot of newspapers.[1] On 22 December 1941, US Secretary of State Cordell Hull sent a telegram to Clarence Gauss, US Ambassador to China, asking him to make 'very discreet inquiries to the National Government in regard to the so-called provisional government of the Republic of Korea, claiming to have its seat in Chungking.' This was was the temporary and beleaguered capital of Chiang Kai-shek's China.[2]

Clarence Gauss – a career diplomat stationed in China since 1912, a US-born German-American and a Republican – telegrammed Cordell Hull from Chungking on 3 January 1942. Gauss was concerned about Communist infiltration – still taken seriously in parts of the State Department while being taken for granted in Morgenthau's Treasury Department, which was full of Communists and sympathizers.

I gather the present attitude [of Chiang's government] is not enthusiastic. There are reportedly no more than 200 Koreans in this area. There is a small corps of Korean volunteers in the Chinese Army... The Provisional Government [of Korea] is understood to be dominated by the moderate Korean Independence Party, the strength of which is not known. I am told that the left wing National Revolutionary Party has a large following among Koreans in Manchuria, but that it is not accorded a place in the so-called Provisional Government.[3]

Syngman Rhee got wind of Cordell Hull's interest and on 7 February 1942, Rhee contacted the State Department to remind them of a letter to President Roosevelt of 6 June 1941 that he had forwarded from Ku Kim, the anti-Japanese leader most respected by most Koreans. The letter from Ku Kim read:

Sir: I have the honor to remind Your Excellency of that fact that, although the diplomatic intercourse opened between the United States and Korea in 1882 was forcibly suspended in 1905, the cordial, friendly spirit and good will existing between our two peoples has never been interrupted. Now the changed situation in the Far East warrants the restoration of that friendly relationship for mutual benefit.

The Provisional Government of the Republic of Korean, temporarily situated in Chungking, China, earnestly wishes to re-open that friendly intercourse and it is hoped that their desire may be reciprocated by the Government and people of the United States.

At a recent meeting of the Cabinet Ministers of the Korean Provisional Government, Dr. Syngman Rhee, Chairman of the Korean Commission in Washington, was appointed as the official representative of his Government, invested with full power and authority which he may exercise at his own discretion in all diplomatic dealings with the Government of the United States.

By virtue of this authority vested in me as Executive Chief of the Korean Provisional Government, I beseech Your Excellency to receive him and the message he is instructed to present in behalf of the 23,000,000 Korean people suffering under an alien domination.

I take this opportunity to assure Your Excellency of my highest consideration and best wishes for your great Republic;

Yours very respectfully,

Kim Ku[4]

Ambassador Clarence Gauss then reported a 'vague and unsatisfactory' interview with a representative of the Korean Provisional Government whose name he was unable to transliterate, (Chinese ideographic writing and the Korean *hangul* phonetic alphabet are completely different, as are the spoken languages.) The Korean admitted reluctantly that the Nationalist Chinese had not yet recognized the Korean Provisional Government and that he felt the Chinese might be planning to annex Korea once Japan was defeated, just as the Japanese had annexed Korea in 1910. Gauss was still worried about the Korean resistance members in Manchuria being Communist or pro-Communist.[5]

Adolf Berle, the Assistant Secretary of State and Sumner Welles, the Acting Secretary of State during the tempoary absence by Cordell Hull, then informed the Koreans that they were encouraged to keep supplying the US with information but that the US did not intend to recognize any particular Korean government, The State Department did not want to offend the Koreans. Neither did it want to support them, particularly since their movement was seen as small and diffuse and the Chinese Nationalists controlled the largest Asia force opposed to Japan.

Syngman Rhee replied on 24 March with restrained indignation that 'the Provisional Government of the Republic of Korea is the sole presentative of the Korean people' and that ignoring Korean independence 'would seem to further countenance the act of wanton aggression perpetrated by the Japanese Government upon the people of Korea.'[6] Neither side had all its cards on the table. The Koreans had learned to their horror in the 1920s that Theodore Roosevelt had endorsed Japan's take-over of Korea by the Japanese. They also knew that there were far more Koreans in the Japanese Imperial Army than there were in the Korean resistance movement – some of them ranked as high as colonel.

Ambassador Gauss reported into the Secretary of States the next day. 'The official Chinese attitude toward the Korean question ... was one of sympathy but hesitation to accord formal recognition to any particular group in the face of obvious disunity among the Korean expatriates and the inability of any one of their organizations to show that it has a real following among the Koreans in the homeland.[7] Gauss added that the Chinese seemed to be sympathetic toward the agitation for the independence of India by Gandhi and Nehru – not something that the pro-British State Department wanted to sponsor at that time without Britain's approval.

Gauss dug deeper. He discovered that there were two divisions of Koreans serving with the Soviet Red Army in Siberia and that these troops could be used for any invasion of Korea in case Russia and Japan went to war – with the obvious implication that Korea would then be a Soviet client state rather than an independent nation. Ambassador Gauss reported from Chungking on 18 April that Chiang had decided to propose recognition of the Korean Provisional Government.[8] Cordell Hull replied on 29 April that the FDR administration was in basic agreement with Chiang's proposal.[9] He also urged the FDR administration to endorse the Korean Provisional Government before the Soviets endorsed some other group. Hull, a veteran of the Spanish-American War in Cuba, was a southern progressive but he was not in any way a fan of Marxism, more particularly of Stalinism. Cordell Hull's uneasy attitude towards having Henry Morgenthau Jr. reportedly function as 'the second secretary of state' was not based entirely on jealousy.

Cordell Hull may not have been entirely prepared for the man who cropped up next – Kilsoo Haan. Haan wrote to Hull to propose cooperation between the groups he claimed to represent and the Korean Provisional Government represented by Ku Kim in China and Syngman Rhee in Washington:

> Mr Haan expresses the belief that, if the [State] Department were to arrange to have Mr. Rhee and Mr. Haan meet with an officer of the Department, a unity of Korean groups in Hawaii and the continental United States could be effected,

and he suggests formation of a committee on which both groups would be equally represented for the purpose of making this unity effective. He also recommends early reorganization of the 'Korean Provisional Government' at Chungking with a view of achieving unification with the so-called radical Korea groups and suggests that the Provisional Government be limited to 12 Korean officials with 2 Chinese advisors, 6 of the 12 to be named by Dr. Rhee and Kim Koo [Ku Kim] and 6 by Commander Kim Yak-san and Dr. Kimm Kin-sik.

As Mr Haan in his letter is extremely critical of the Chungking group and charges that it has since 1919 been branding as communists all other patriotic groups of Koreans, using highhanded methods toward those groups, and employing misleading propaganda in order to maintain a dominant position in the Korean independence movement, it would be prima facie doubtful whether any practicable benefit would result at this time from Mr. Haan's suggestions. However, in an endeavor to be helpful and in line with this Government's policy of giving, where practicable and appropriate, sympathetic assistance to the national aspirations of subject peoples who desire to contribute to the war effort, the Department contemplates sounding out Dr. Rhee as to his willingness to meet with Mr. Haan informally and unofficially in the presence of one of two officers of the Department. If this meeting takes place, The Department will inform you of its character and results. Meanwhile you may in your discretion discuss with the appropriate Chinese officials the subject matter of Mr. Haan's letter and communicate with the Department their comments together with such comment as you may care to make. Such discussions, if held, should, of course, be in strict confidence and without mentioning Mr. Kilsoo Haan by name.[10]

Ambassador Gauss reported back in a telegram on 13 May that both sides had rejected the offer 'due to petty intransigence on both sides.' The Chinese told Gauss that the two groups were feuding among themselves.[11] Kilsoo Haan was quoted as saying that his group could field 15,000 men, but Gauss called these figures 'fanciful'.

KIlsoo Haan had been rebuffed by Ku Kim – more likely, by Syngman Rhee, who remembered him as a newspaper boy from Hawaii – but he got off a letter trying to establish a role in the reorganization of Korea exactly a year before the whole thing became official. On 30 November 1942, he asked the State Department to give written assurance 'that after the war has ended the United States Government will assist Koreans in the setting up of an independent government in Korea. As stated in the letter and explained orally by Mr Haan, the purposes of obtaining such written assurance is to enable Mr Haan to convey that information confidentially to Korean agents in Japan proper and in Korea who are in need of encouragement.'[12]

George Atcheson, assistant chief of the Division for Far Eastern Affairs of the State Department was mystified as to why the letter was so important to Kilsoo Haan:

> Haan indicated that only written assurance would satisfy the Korean agents to whom he referred... Mr. Haan indicated that primarily the advantage would be that of strengthening morale but that there was also a military aspect as receipt of information that that written assurance had been obtained might be expected to encourage the agents to greater activity... Mr. Haan was unable to clarify his reasons as to why such assurance should be addressed to him and finally stated that the addressee would be immaterial provided he were supplied with a copy of the desired statement.[13]

Kilsoo Haan never got the letter. He had probably wanted it for his extensive files and to build his own credibility as an important leader in the Korean independence moment – and to make sure that the events of 1905 did not recur with China replacing Japan as the new ruler of Korea.

Ambassador Gauss reported from China that Kilsoo Haan was now the odd man out in the proposed new government of the independent nation of Korea.

Kim Yak San reputed formally accepted 5 December post Vice Commander Independence Army under authority Provisional Government. Dr. Kimm Kiu-sik, another important Korean revolutionary figure heretofore dissident now said to be joining government group. Kilsoo Haan expected consequently to be under heavy pressure [to] abandon independent stand'[14]

15

RIGHT ABOUT FACE

General Charles De Gaulle, beleaguered leader of the Free French, heard about Pearl Harbor on the radio on the night of the attack at his home in exile in England. He pondered the implication and spoke briefly to his aide, Colonel Passy:

> Now the war is certainly won! And the future has two phases for us: the first will be the salvage of Germany by the Allies; as for the second, I am afraid it may turn out to be war between the Russians and Americans and the Americans run a great risk of losing the war if they do not succeed in taking the necessary steps in time.[1]

Winston Churchill, wrote on hearing of the Pearl Harbor attack: 'So we have won after all.' Churchill said he took to his bed that night 'and slept the sleep of the saved and the thankful.'[2] Churchill, like his ally and sometime adversary, Charles De Gaulle, saw no future in a long alliance with Russia after Hitler was destroyed. Churchill had written in 1919, when the Russian Bolsheviks had attempted armed Communist take-overs in Germany, Hungary, and Poland: 'I have not conquered the Huns, the tigers of the world, to be defeated by the baboons.' He too probably considered a final showdown with Russia, Britain's rival for control of India and the markets of China, as inevitable.

Kilsoo Haan saw his own war against Japan as very likely to be followed by a struggle to keep Russia out of Korea. Keeping Russia out of Korea had been the reason that Theodore Roosevelt had handed over control of Korea and development rights over Manchuria in the first place. But Franklin Roosevelt appears to have skipped a few classes in history. FDR believed that he was fighting the Prussian generals – the same people who had backed two attempts to kill Hitler, one that drew blood in 1934 and one that flopped in 1938 when Britain – to Winston Churchill's anger and disgust – failed to back the Czechs at Munich. FDR let his advisers do most of the thinking about matters outside the US. And FDR's advisers were the people De Gaulle and Churchill were leery of.

Kilsoo Haan tried to maintain and expand his popularity after the Pearl Harbor warning. He offered to assist the FBI in seeking out those Japanese who might actually be dangerous – especially Togo Tanaka, who had insulted him personally – in a letter to FBI Director J. Edgar Hoover, who sent him a thank-you note on 4 February 1942, on personal stationery:

I have requested Mr. S.K. McKee, Special Agent in Charge of the Field Division of this Bureau located in the District iof Columbia, to arrange to contact you immediately for the purpose of securing from you the additional information you indicated to the Attorney General you possessed that would be of value in guarding the internal security of this country...
Sincerely yours,
John Edgar Hoover
Director[3]

Hoover had in fact opposed the wholesale round-up of Japanese nationals and Japanese-Americans on the West Coast. Kilsoo Haan himself had some trusted sources among the Japanese-American community who opposed Japanese nationalism and he might have provided useful intel about individuals, but the FDR administration's wholesale evacuation of the Japanese-Americans to concentration camps made any such expertise worthless.

On 3 September 1942 Kilsoo Haan provided another useful piece of information, which proved accurate: Japan had refused to invade Siberia as an ally of Nazi Germany even after Hitler had declared war on the United States after the attack on Pearl Harbor. The information was sent to FDR at the White House.

My dear Mr. President,

On August 24, 1942, I received word from reliable sources that there would be a 'Cabinet crisis' in Japan.

Our informants reported that there was a definite rift between Ambassador [Eugen] Ott of Germany and Premier Tojo of Japan over the question of an invasion of Siberia.

We were informed that the Japanese had promised the Germans that they would invade Siberia in June if the Nazis had succeeded in taking Stalingrad and the Caucasus. The German Embassy in Tokyo has continually pressed the Japanese to invade Siberia, and the Kwantung Army has ardently supported the thesis of the German Embassy,

The Tojo Cabinet, we are informed, has steadfastly refused to invade Siberia, excusing itself by stating that the Germans had not yet taken Stalingrad. Now that the Germans are at the gates of Stalingrad, they have again refused the German Ambassador's demand, stating that it is too late in the season. In other words, weather conditions in Siberia make an invasion unfavorable.

Last week, as associate editor of 'Affairs Week By Week,' I published the above information in a news release.

In view of the above information we believe that the reported 'Cabinet Crisis' which did take place was caused by the pressure of Ambassador Ott, the Kwantung Army group and Foreign Minister Togo for an immediate Siberia campaign. And in view of Ambassador Ott's failure to force the Japanese Cabinet to attack Siberia we also believe that the Siberian campaign has been temporarily abandoned in favor of increased military movement toward the Southwestern Pacific.

According to the published Japanese naval war plans, the key to the control of Australia is Port Moresby. Hence, it is our belief that Premier Tojo is now following the 'naval school' of thought which favors the consolidation of the occupied areas in the Southwest Pacific and aid to Hitler by consolidating the radical elements in India to bring about internal disorders for an eventual attack on India.

As head of the Pacific War Council, we hope this information will be taken into consideration.

Very respectfully yours,

Kilsoo K. Haan

Washington Representative, Sino-Korean People's League[4]

Kilsoo Haan's information was accurate: the Japanese never attacked Siberia and in 1944 they attacked northern India. The Japanese had mobilized a force estimated at 100,000 soldiers from India as part of their army and Japan was seen as a liberator in Indian public opinion, and often still is today. Hitler never conquered Stalingrad: the German Sixth Army took most of the city later in 1942 but was surrounded inside when the Russians cut through the Romanian forces covering the Axis supply lines. Hitler obtusely refused approval for a break-out from the Stalingrad pocket while there might still have been time. The destruction of the Sixth Army signaled the beginning of the end of Nazi Germany in the early winter of 1943.

Kilsoo Haan kept getting sideswiped by jealous Korean nationalists who understood that his Pearl Harbor warning had made him the most visible Korean nationalist in America, and envied him to the point of invidious slander. Senator Guy Gillette fired back at these Korean detractors with a letter to the United Korean Committee, a rival group, on 10 December 1942, a year after the Pearl Harbor attack. Senator Gillette had met with Kyuan Dunn, public relations officer of the United Korean Committee who appear to have defamed Kilsoo Haan to Senator. Gillette did not specify the charges but Robert Oliver Tarbell, a hired American publicist for Syngman Rhee, sometimes circulated rumors that Kilsoo Haan was a Communist born and raised in Soviet Siberia and that his California real estate license had been revoked for improper behaviour.

'There have been particularly virulent attacks made on Mr Kilsoo Haan of whom we spoke yesterday,' Senator Gillette wrote to J. Kyuang Dunn.

I hold no brief for Mr. Haan and have no means of knowing the truth or falsity, merit or lack of merit, of many of the charges made. But I do know from my personal knowledge that Mr. Haan and those associated with him here in Washington have frequently called at my office, and I have at all times found them showing evidence of the deepest possible interest in Korea and Koreans and their welfare. If there are private feuds among the Koreans, whether just or unjust they should by wholly subordinated to the interest of this whole people and not allowed to interfere with or jeopardize the work of Koreans and their friends in their efforts to secure the future for Korea. Referring again to Mr. Haan, may I say that I have known him since 1937 when I first observed him as a witness before the Congressional Committee on Statehood which was holding studies of Hawaiian statehood at that time. During this time and the years following, I have had no occasion to observe anything in his conduct or work which caused me to doubt in any way his sincerity and responsibility.

Be that as it may, it behooves all of us interested in Korean future independence, and especially the Koreans themselves, to lay aside their conflicting personal interests in forwarding the great work to which they are devoted.

Sincerely.

Guy M. Gillette[5]

On 1 March 1943, Kilsoo Haan sent out a report to the Korean Underground that got him into some trouble. 'Beware of the pro-Soviet-Pro-Red-China blocks operating in the State Department, also in General Stilwell's Command in Burma,' Kilsoo Haan wrote to his Korean agents. 'In particular beware of the political advisor, Dean Rusk, to General Stilwell.' The federal government did not appreciate this report when it fell into their hands.

'Early in March 1943 I called on Dr. George McCune, the head of Korean Affairs in the State Department and candidly discussed this report,' KIlsoo Haan wrote.

The State Department expressed anger at our own 3-1 1943 report. On 8-16, 1943, I was ordered to appear before the hearing by Board Officers 'to determine the issuance of an order excluding me from the military areas or parts or zones of the United States.'

'You are hereby notified that an inquiry is in progress to consider the question whether military necessity requires the issuance of an order excluding you from the Eastern Military Area or certain parts of Zones thereof and similar areas in other parts of the United States proscribed pursuant to Presidential Executive Order No. 9066, dated February 19, 1942 [Japanese-American Relocation order].

'You are further notified that you will be given the opportunity of a hearing before a Board of Officers convened for the purpose and that this board will meet at Room 105, 2145 – C Street, Northwest on the 19th day of August, 1943 at the hour of 2:30 p.m. You may, if you so elect, appear before the Board at that time and be afforded the opportunity to produce witnesses and to provide evidence in your own behalf.

'3. It is requested that you advise the Board in writing in the enclosed self-addressed envelope, at least 24 hours in advance of the hearing, whether you will appear.

'4. For your information and guidance, the following are pertinent regulations concerning the conduct of the hearing before the Board:

'a. All matters pertaining to the hearing are confidential and no publicity will be given them by the Board.

'b. You may, if you so desire, be accompanied by an advisor to assist you before the Board. This advisor may be any relative or friend in whom you repose confidence. His sole function will be to advise you. He will not be permitted to examine witnesses.'

Possibly with the influence of Senator Guy Gillette, Kilsoo Haan was able to satisfy the board as to his loyalty to America's interests without undue trouble. 'I was cleared and was at liberty to travel throughout America,' he wrote after the hearing.[6]

Kilsoo Haan kept supplying information to the Office of Strategic Services – precursor to the Central Intelligence Agency – through the remainder of 1943 and into 1944, which were rated as of considerable importance by OSS officers. On 2 September 1943, Charles V. Crittenden, chief of the Map Information Section of the OSS, sent a courier to pick up a map that Kilsoo Haan had offered him.

'The bearer of this letter, Corporal Melvin San Win, is a member of our organization,' Crittenden wrote. 'Since you indicated a willingness to lend us the map of the Pacific area in your possession, he has been delegated to bring it to us. We are very grateful for the loan of this map and will return it in a very short time.'

On 21 September 1943 Crittenden thanked Kilsoo Haan for his cooperation. 'We wish to express our appreciation for the loan of the enclosed maps, which we have found very useful indeed. If you would be so kind as to sign the two enclosed cards so that our records will be complete, we will be further indebted to you.' The letter was counter-signed by Arthur Robinson, chief of the OSS Map Division.[7]

But on 11 January 1944, Kilsoo Haan once again heard from the Justice Department, according to Haan himself, on behalf of the indignant State Department.

'When the State Department failed to prohibit my traveling in USA, it made another attempt, this time to put me away for the duration of US–Japan War,' he later wrote.[8] Once again, as with the threats of incarceration just after the Pearl Harbor warning, an American journalist came to his rescue. Ray Richards wrote in an article in the *New York Journal-American*:

KIlsoo K. Haan, noted Korean independence agent, brought himself into frontal collision with the Department of Justice today by refusing to register with the department the identity of Secret Service operatives

'To register the spies according to the Justice Department's terms would reveal their names to the public,' Haan wrote, '[this] would mean their death.'

Haan has been the center of recurrent official disturbances in Washington for several years. His frequently accurate forecasts of Far Eastern developments have proved embarrassing to many Administration officials who had laughed them aside, but a large number of Congressmen, critical of lack of American preparation against the Japanese menace, have defended him vigorously.

The next day, Ray Richards wrote in the *News-Post* Washington Bureau: 'Standing fast in its demand that the Sino-Korean People's League register the names of purported Korean secret agents in Japan, the Department of Justice today refused to guarantee the names would not be made public.'[9] Haan's contention that making the names of Korean agents available to the general public – and eventually to the Japanese – would be a death sentence to the agents and the end of an intelligence operation that had made a number of useful predictions.'

Another reporter also came to Kilsoo Haan's aid. Raymond Z. Henle, writing the 'Washington Wire' column for the *Post-Gazette*, paraphrased Kilsoo Haan's comments on the agents in fuller detail. 'Mr Haan says that not even he knows all the key people who are doing Korean espionage. He says the Korean system is to divide agents into groups so that if one group is completely wiped out by the Japanese, the other group will carry on. Members of the "A" group do not know the membership of the "B" group.'

The system as described to Raymond Z. Henle was sensible, the use of 'cells' was a staple of Communist infiltration and was also used by groups including the Irish Republican Army during 'The Troubles' and the German Nationalist Organization Consul which specialised in assassinating Communist leaders and others at about the same time. The fact that Kilsoo Haan claimed not to know the names himself also made it more difficult for the Justice Department to pressure him. The Justice

Department case, vindictive or otherwise, faded away, probably with some embarrassment.

And new developments in China shortly proved that Kilsoo Haan had once again predicted a disaster in the making that was ignored by some of the same US officials who forgot to 'Remember Pearl Harbor.'

OPERATION ICHI-GO

Kilsoo Haan's Pearl Harbor warning was still famous in war-time Washington over two years after the bombs fell, as he learned when he appeared before the House Committee on Immigration and Naturalization in testimony about H.R. 1882, a bill to repeal the Chinese Exclusion Act of 1882. His warning to the group had nothing to do with Chinese immigration but it could have been as important as the Pearl Harbor warning if anyone had listened to him.

Even as Japanese-American citizens and Japanese-born aliens alike were being sequestered in concentration camps, both Chinese-Americans and Japanese propagandists – despite their intense mutual hostility – were asking why the Chinese had once been forbidden to enter the United States and were restricted, even in 1943, to the quota of 100 immigrants per year established in 1924, and why they were not allowed to become US citizens. In the late spring of 1943, the House of Representatives convened hearings in Washington to discuss repeal of the Chinese Exclusion Act of 1882 under the chairmanship of Representative Samuel Dickstein of New York.

The hearing, which started on 19 May and lasted until 3 June, featured a number of speakers with some knowledge of China and the Chinese. Congressman Dickstein, himself born in Lithuania and raised in New York City, had been elected to the House of Representatives in 1922 and was to serve until the end of 1945.

Kilsoo Haan, born in Korea, represented the Sino-Korean People's League and the Korean National Front Federation. The irony was that while both Korean groups were anti-Communist to an even greater extent than they were anti-Japanese, Samuel Dickstein turned out, after his death, to have been the only member of Congress to be a paid Soviet spy. Dickstein's Soviet handlers referred to him in their internal communications as '*crook*' and pointed out that his fiscal demands usually exceeded the value of his information.

Dickstein had started his investigations into disloyalty by examining anti-Semitic and pro-Nazi propaganda and showing far less interest in anti-British and pro-Communist propaganda. Hitler's maniacal declaration of war on the United States had made Dickstein virtually bullet-proof, like a great many other Soviet sympathizers and about 360 Soviet agents in the federal government. The Venona transcripts long after his death revealed his role in obtaining visas for Soviet agents. As far as the other Congressmen at the hearing were concerned – most were from the South or the Middle West – he was just another liberal from New York City.

What Kilsoo Haan had to say, however, was overlooked just as his Pearl Harbor warnings were overlooked – though in this case, Haan himself was somewhat at fault. The reportage of what happened may or may not have been skewed.

STATEMENT OF KILSOO K. HAAN, WASHINGTON REPRESENTATIVE, KOREAN NATIONAL FRONT FEDERATION AND SINO-KOREA PEOPLES' LEAGUE

Mr. Haan. I represent the Korean National Front Federation, as well as the Sino-Korean People's League.

The Chairman. [Samuel Dickstein] Are you the same Kilsoo Haan who came before this committee 2 years or 3 years ago and gave us some information on Japan and their activities?

Mr. Haan. Yes; I am the same Haan, sir.

The Chairman. I wish we had listened to you then,

Mr. Haan. Thank you.

The Chairman. Go on. Now be brief, will you, Mr. Haan.

Mr. Haan. Yes.

Mr. Leniski. Mr. Haan, again, before you proceed, are you the man who tipped us off on Pearl Harbor before it was actually in effect?

Mr. Haan. Yes, sir.

Mr. Lesinski. And nobody believed you. [Rep. John Lesinski, a Polish-American Democrat from Michigan, had a son on active during with the U.S, Navy at the time of the hearing who survived the war and later replaced him in Congress.]

Mr. Haan. Of course, at that time the situation was quite different. As a preface to my talk, I would like to present comments of various officials and public comments of American leaders regarding our work and also a memo giving some of the factual things that have developed, based upon some of our previous reports, based on time before and since Pearl Harbor, which might clarify certain issues that I am prepared to enter into.

I believe this H.R. 1882 primarily should be considered purely as a war measure and not a domestic immigration question as if the war had already been won.

I am not here pleading for Korea or for the Koreans. I am pleading for China as a means to effect victory, and also to set up an orderly collaboration between China and the other Asian nations in that particular area, basically, to save as many lives of Americans as possible in that particular area of the war with Japan.

I thank you for this generous gesture of good will, permitting me to testify before your committee once again today.

In behalf of the Koreans, permit me to express my humble opinion in favor of the House Resolution 1882. 'To grant Chinese rights of entry to the United States and rights to citizenship.'

As representative to the Korean National Front Federation and Sino-Korean People's League, I believe our record in getting advance information of the Japanese anti-American activities before and since the Jap attack on Pearl Harbor and the information which I am about to submit to the committee will help the committee in some degree in its consideration of the subject in question.

The Chairman. You must be very friendly with Japan.

Mr. Haan. Well, we get along pretty well. On January 24, 1943, Premier Hideki Tojo of Japan is said to have submitted a bold and revolutionary separate-peace plan with China to the Japanese Supreme War Council last November 1942 for their approval. This separate-peace proposal with China will be launched not later than September 1943.

I have submitted this information to the United States Government. This information was received through our agents in the Orient. The informers gave this significant data, as well as information of a nature which will help us to generalize the coming events in the Far East.

The Chairman. What informants are you talked about?

Mr. Haan. Our agents.

The Chairman. Your agents?

Mr. Haan. Yes, sir.

The Chairman. All right. Go on.

Mr. Haan. According to the information. Tojo has already requested Wang Ching-Wei, the head of the Nanking government [Japanese puppet government] to pave the way among his former associates and close friends who are now in the Chungking Government and the Kuomintang Party.

Tojo is said to have told the supreme war council that he believes that Japan's major objective to crush the Anglo-Americans can be best achieved if China can be made to see the benefits of a separate peace with Japan.

Liberal conditions for a separate peace: In order to achieve Tojo's aim, it is said he will propose a revolutionary, bold, but liberal considerations for separate peace – said to be that:

1. China to break and withdraw from the United Nations and to remain neutral for the duration

2. Japan to restore to China all of the occupied territories, status quo as of 1937, however, Japan reserving the right to control and use for the duration all the railroads and harbors now under the control of the Japanese military.
3. Japan and China to name equal number of delegates to set up an International Commission, creating the machinery to reorganize Manchuria for joint ownership of Manchuria between Japan and China after the war.
4. Japan to grant China 1,000,000,000 yen credit...

The Chairman. How much is 1,000,000.000 yen?

Mr. Haan: One billion yen will be approximately...

The Chairman. $10?

Mr. Haan. No, Four yen make $1 in American money.

Mr. Lesinski. $250,000. [sic]

Mr. Haan. Japan to grant China 1,000,000,000 yen credit in the form of lend-lease patterned after the U.S. lend-lease principle, to aid in her reconstruction work and to finance China's participation in all the industrial enterprises now in Manchuria, under joint ownership under the present Japanese management.

Those who are close to Premier Tojo proclaimed that his separate peace proposal with China will be a 'master stroke' in winning over the people of China and India toward Japan 'for an early victory.'

I may perhaps recall the incident in which Premier Tojo had already visited Nanking last March, and we are told, has already proposed his 'separate peace with China' plan and is now working feverishly with China toward that end.

Premier Hideki Tojo February 7, 1943 p.m., gave a party at his Tokyo residence in honor of the aged Mitsuru Toyama, head of the Black Dragon Society. At this party Premier Tojo disclosed that:

Rear Admiral Katsutaro Miyazaki had been chosen to head the invasion force against America, and Gen. Shunroku Hata to head the invasion army.

Rear Admiral Katsutaro Miyzaki is the head of the Naval Affairs Department of the Kure Naval Station, and Gen. Hata was, until recently, head of the Japanese Army in China stationed in Nanking, China. Premier Tojo 'under great emotional strain' declared: Until America is whipped into submission, Japan's daily life is war. 1943 is Japan's year of victory.'[1]

Kilsoo Haan had outlined plans for Operation Ichi-Go – a joint offensive against the Chinese Nationalist armies in eastern China by elite Japanese troops – including some of the 200,000 Koreans voluntarily serving in the Japanese Army, augmented by those Chinese under Wang Ching-wei who supported temporary Japanese rule for China as opposed to the rampant corruption of the Nationalists. The Congressmen in questioning other witnesses in other interviews revealed themselves to be skeptical of the fighting qualities of Chinese soldiers. But one of the best-kept secrets was that there were at least a half-million Chinese serving in Japanese-led units, including field-grade officers as high as colonel, and that some of them provided to be excellent soldiers under good leadership.

Kilsoo Haan seems to have deliberately misinterpreted some Japanese statements – 'In January 1943 Col. Nakao Yahagi declared it would ne necessary to land on the American continent.' Haan never explained why a mere colonel was important enough to cite alongside General Hata and Admiral Miyazaki, but the context made it plain that Colonel Yahagi was talking about reinforced the Aleutian Islands, not taking over Los Angeles. Fighting had already taken place, and the Japanese had taken and lost Attu, shown as a base for the bombing of Japan in the Halloween 1941 pictogram in the Halloween issue of *United States News* along with Guam and the Philippines, captured by Japan during the first few months after Pearl Harbor to forestall air strikes on the home islands. The Japanese, as a matter of record, saw no hope of invaded the continental United States.

The rest of Kilsoo Haan's information, however, was accurate and extremely plausible to anyone who knew Japanese internal politics. Mitsuro Toyama and the Black Dragon Society had always been anti-colonial and anti-European rather than anti-Chinese. The name 'Miyazaki' was magical in China: the giant samurai Torazo Myazaki, also called Toten Miyazaki, was the right-hand man and enforcer for Dr. Sun Yat-sen, the man who freed China from the Manchu Dynasty. Their adventures together – against white colonialists as well as Manchu oligarchs – were legendary. Torazo Miyazaki's son was the perfect man to foster renewed friendship between China and Japan. The father was considered a hero of Chinese liberation: his statue today is next to Sun Yat-sen's statue at the Nanking Museum of (Japanese) Atrocities as perhaps the One Good Japanese, just as Princess Nashimoto is Korea's One Good Japanese. Katsutaro Miyazaki, son of the giant samurai, had himself tried to intervene to prevent further fighting after the Marco Polo Bridge Incident that started the Second Sino-Japanese War in 1937. Miyazaki was recalled at the last minute by hot-headed Japanese nationalists who thought the Chinese could be defeated with ease – which proved not to be the case. Even the toughest Japanese militarists were willing to listen in 1943 when Toyama and Miyazaki told them that China was not Japan's real enemy and the real goal of China and Japan was to join hands and expel the 'red beards' – the Russians – and the 'white faces' – the English – from all of Asia west of the Amur River, and then to foster peace and prosperity among themselves.

Cooperative Chinese-Japanese development of Manchuria had been proposed by Hirobumi Ito and had been endorsed by Theodore Roosevelt in the Root-Takahira Agreement. Since America had no colonial outposts in China, the US was not on the Japanese hit list, as Russia and Britain were, until Pearl Harbor drew America into a war that the Japanese had started trying to end after the defeat at Midway and the capture of Guadalcanal through diplomatic negotiations. But nobody at the Dickstein hearing appeared to take Kilsoo Haan seriously – despite the statements by Congressman Dickstein and Congressman Lesinki, it was a replay of the Pearl Harbor warnings because once again the warning was shrugged off.

On 1 December 1943 – after his warnings to the House Committee but before the Japanese tank and infantry avalanche of

Operation Ichi-Go – Kilsoo Haan issued a statement on behalf of the two Korean nationalist groups he represented in Washington.

> Twenty-six million Koreans will rejoice and be ever grateful to the Three Powers for this timely and effective Roosevelt-Churchill-Chiang promise, when the millions of Koreans in Korea, Japan, Manchuria and China learn of this solemn, sacred promise, there will be plenty of fireworks behind Japan and strategic areas. We are sincerely thankful for this opportunity to participate in this war against Japan, our common enemy. We do not desire freedom and independence on a silver platter. We are more than willing to give our lives and share death and heart-sick to win this war. In reality, the Roosevelt-Churchill-Chiang promise to free Korea means the fulfillment of the long-awaited treaty obligation of the three powers toward Korea.

Kilsoo Haan was responding to a joint statement made by FDR, Churchill, and Chiang Kai-shek at the Cairo Conference, where the three leaders had met to plot final victory against the Axis:

> The several military missions have agreed upon future military operations against Japan. The Three Great Allies expressed their resolve to bring unrelenting pressure against their brutal enemies by sea, land, and air. This pressure is already rising.
> The Three Great Allies are fighting this war to restrain and punish the aggression of Japan. They covet no gain for themselves and have no thought of territorial expansion. It is their purpose that Japan shall be stripped of all the islands of the Pacific which she has seized or occupied since the beginning of the First World War in 1914, and that all the territories Japan has stolen from the Chinese, such as Manchuria, Formosa, and the Pescadores, shall be restored to the Republic of China. Japan will also be expelled from all other territories which she has taken by violence and greed. The aforesaid three powers are mindful of the enslavement of the people of Korea and are determined that in due course Korea shall be free and independent.[2]

The Cairo Conference had not included Stalin. The Soviet dictator boycotted the conference because Chiang Kai-shek was at war with Japan but not active against Germany, and Stalin wanted no part of a war with Japan in 1943. Vitalii Pavlov of the NKVD, with the covert assistance of Harry Dexter White and his dupe, Henry Morgenthau Jr., had managed to get a war started between the United States and Japan. Stalin wanted no part of that war with Japan until the Soviets and the other allies had defeated Germany and the other Axis nations in Europe – Hungary, Bulgaria, Rumania, Finland and the Baltic states, along with anti-Communists from the Scandinavian countries and even anti-Communist legions from Belgium, the Netherlands, France, and Spain (Italy had declared war on Germany one month earlier).

Kilsoo Haan had to get his statement on record as quickly as possible: his rival for power over the independent Korea to be, Syngman Rhee, had been lobbying for two years to be taken seriously as the real leader of the Koreans opposed to Japan, just as Kilsoo Haan had himself. Rhee, once a house guest of Woodrow Wilson at Princeton, had a better inside track to diplomatic circles than Kilsoo Haan did. But as Congressman Dickstein and Congressman Lesinki had noted six months before, Kilsoo Haan was recognized as the man who had warned America about Pearl Harbor. Ku Kim, the leader most Koreans recognized as the hero of the anti-Japanese resistance in Korea and in China, was represented in the US by Syngman Rhee, but Koreans saw Ku Kim, not Syngman Rhee, as the actual leader. Cynical Koreans observed that all Syngman Rhee seemed to do was write letters, A few more of Syngman Rhee's letters, the Koreans said, and the Japanese might all die of fright...

Kilsoo Haan also knew that some of the statement was balderdash. Britain and the United States had consistently backed 'Japanese aggression' as far as Korea and Manchuria were concerned because they had wanted help in the previous war with Germany andwith possible future trouble with Russia. Most Asians were more anti-Russian than they were anti-Japanese and the situation could go out of kilter very quickly if Kilsoo Haan could not prove that Korea was more valuable to the Allies than the goodwill of Soviet Russia.

On 19 April 1944 – a few months later than in the schedule Kilsoo Haan revealed at the Congressional hearing the year before – the Japanese actually struck, and all bets for Korean independence backed primarily by Chiang Kai-shek were off. The Japanese tank avalanche caught both Chiang Kai-shek and Washington completely by surprise, despite Kilsoo Haan's detailed forecast.[3] The Japanese troops had been heavily indoctrinated, as Kilsoo Haan's warning had suggested, to think of the Chinese as friends and to avoid the sort of rape, wanton brutality and looting that had broken out spontaneously at Nanking and elsewhere. The emperor's troops had received propaganda leaflets telling them that the real enemy was not the somewhat baffled Chinese but the 'white-faced demons.' The Japanese soldiers marched singing songs about the kindness of their hearts. They also marched behind 800 Japanese tanks. The late-production Chi-Ha Tank was equipped with 57-mm cannon in an off-set revolving turret, with one machinegun in the bow and an extra machinegun mounted in the back of the turret to keep boarders armed with Molotov cocktails or hand grenades away from the engine deck. The Chi-Ha and other tanks and 400,000 infantrymen were supported by 1,500 artillery pieces, 12,000 trucks, and 70,000 horses for rough terrain.[3]

General Joseph Stilwell had engaged the Japanese in a grudge match in the malarial mountains of Burma using both American and American-trained Chinese soldiers. While Stilwell was recapturing Burma and wearing out his men with tropical diseases and hunger, the Japanese marched south from their bases around Shanghai and Nanking over open terrain and began systematically to cut China in half.

The first phase of Operation Ichi-Go began with a Japanese drive down the Yellow River against the gap in the Peking-Hankow Railroad. The fourteen Chinese divisions in the path of the Japanese offensive, said to be some of the best divisions in the Nationalist Chinese Army, collapsed.[4]

The second phase was the attack on American air bases from which the 14th Air Force was targeting Japan, just as *United States News* had warned on 31 October 1941, five weeks before Pearl Harbor. The American 14th Air Force bases had opened in June.⁵ Major General Claire.Chennault, the commander of the American Volunteer Group, known as the Flying Tigers, now absorbed into the 14th Air Force, tried to stop the Japanese tank and infantry assaults with strafing by fighter planes and light bomber attacks. He failed. The Japanese had decided to overrun the American air bases and block plans for American air raids on Japanese industry.

On 18 June 1944, the city of Changsha fell without a fight and the Japanese began attacking Hengyang, the first of the American air bases built to bomb Japan. General Stilwell was called back from Burma where his exhausted troops, having fought with enormous courage in malaria country on short rations, were one vast sick list and had to be 'taken out of the line.'

'Stilwell stood beside the road and shook hands with every man that passed,' one US veteran of the Burma invasion remembered. 'He was a real soldier and a soldier's soldier and everybody hated him.' Many of the American-trained Chinese, some of them teenagers, were simply abandoned to die when they collapsed in the jungles.

Back in China, Stilwell and Chennault argued about air support: Chennault, whose wife Anna was Chinese, wanted to maintain joint US-Chinese plans to bomb Japan. Stilwell wanted Chennault to fly strafing missions against the advancing Japanese and to supply those Chinese soldiers who were still fighting. Chinese peasants, some of whom thought Japan was actually a part of China⁶ turned against the retreating Nationalists with crude weapons and reportedly buried some of their own countrymen alive as punishment for looting and rape.⁷ With the help of Chinese peasant insurgents and Chinese and Koreans in Japanese uniform,, the kill ratio of the Japanese Army's Ichi-Go campaign showed 40 Chinese killed for every Japanese soldier killed – even though the Japanese were the ones who were attacking.⁸

One group of Chinese heroes emerged from the chaos and disgrace: General Xue Yue and his men. Trying to hold Hengyang despite complete lack of logistical support, Xue Yue and his men were written off by Chiang Kai-shek – jealousy may have been a factor, since Xue Yue had the courage and charisma that the older Chiang generally lacked.

General Xue Yue's support system became tangled in the arguments between Stilwell and Chennault. Stilwell, in particular, took a brutal attitude: When Xue Yue's men asked urgently for supplies, Stilwell reportedly said: 'Let them stew.' He also refused an urgent request from Xue Yue to have the Chinese soldiers under Stilwell's command make an attack on the Japanese troops outside his perimeter who were about to overrun Hengsha.[9]

On 7 August, General Xue Yue's Tenth Army sent out a final urgent message: the Japanese were in the city but the Chinese would fight to the last. In the end, 300 Chinese soldiers were able to break out or slip though and most of the others were killed fighting to the death along with Xue Yue. Jack London had pointed out in 1905 in 'The Yellow Peril' that 'The Chinese is not a coward.' He also predicted that once the 'Brown Men' from Japan organized 'The Yellow Men' from China, the colonial era in Asia would be forcibly brought to a close. Operation Ichi-Go proved at least temporarily just how right Jack London was.

The Japanese attacked the next American air base at Guilin. Nationalist Chinese soldiers forced Chinese civilians off overloaded trains at gunpoint to make good their own escape, despite Chiang's orders that fugitives should be shot.[10]

President Roosevelt, influenced by Stilwell, urged Chiang to allow Stilwell to take over complete control of the Chinese Nationalist forces. General Stilwell flew over Guilin and pronounced it a rat trap. Stilwell himself ordered the Americans to pull out. The Chinese prostitutes in the city hung up signs bidding the American airmen farewell: 'So long, buddies, and good luck.'[11] The girls themselves were in no mood to escape – word of mouth had it that Japanese brutality wasn't what it used to be owing to the Black Dragon Society propaganda to help the Chinese expel the white enemies.

To Stillwell's amazement, he himself was relieved at Chiang's angry request and replaced by General Albert Wedemeyer, former US Army Chief of Plans. Japan's top Chinese advocate or collaborator, Wang Ching-wei, long in failing health, died of complications of pneumonia on 10 November. After the Japanese tanks captured Nanning, the capital of Guanshi Province on 24 November[12], Operation Ichi-Go slowed down and stopped. The Japanese had lost 23,000 soldiers and had cut China in half from north to south from above the Yangzte River at Shanghai down to the border of French Indo-China, also under Japanese control. The Chinese Nationalists had lost 750,000 soldiers.[13] The Japanese may have seen their tanks as less adaptable to the mountains of Sichuan Province, but rumor had it that Chiang Kai-shek had ultimately offered the Japanese a secret deal: both Chiang and the Japanese generals were anti-Communist and anti-Russian to a far greater degree than they were opposed to each other. The death of Wang Ching-wei, a devoted friend of Dr, Sun Yat-sen, also cost Japan a lot of credibility as a possible friend of China. But the Japanese had captured all the American air bases in eastern China and the American bombing of Japan ceased until airfields could be completed at Saipan and Tinian in the Marianas.

The Japanese had also destroyed Chiang's credibility as a leader of the democracies. When Madame Chiang toured the United States at the end of 1944 she was so reviled that she suffered a convenient nervous breakdown and cut short her unpopular speaking tour. Roosevelt, who had once found her fascinating, was said to be delighted to get her out of the country. Treasury Secretary Henry Morgenthau – the talking head for the Soviet agent Harry Dexter White – had backed Nationalist China against anti-Communist Japan with a $25 million loan in 1938. After China's German military advisers left, Chiang also obtained some support from the Soviet Union.[14]

In 1943, with Japan clearly losing the war in the Pacific and Chiang Kai-shek facing defeat before the Ichi-Go catastrophe, Morgenthau – advised by Harry Dexter White – refused a billion-dollar loan that Chiang's government had wanted to stabilize inflation.

Continental Asia – including Korea – was now ripe for a Soviet landslide. Ichi-Go had shown that the Nationalists could not stop a determined Japanese offensive, and the Soviets had far better tanks than the Japanese. A large number of rural Chinese had fought for Japan. Americans like Theodore White and Edgar Snow extolled the Chinese Communists and excoriated Chiang Kai-shek's Chinese Nationalists – once seen by State Department expert Stanley Hornbeck as the hope of Asia – as barbarians very much on a level with Hornbeck's view of the Japanese, but without the fanatical courage or mechanical ability. Nationalist China lost much of its American support. Korea lost its principal backer for independence.

Kilsoo Haan's warning about the federation of Chinese and Japanese soldiers had been accurate up to a point. He would have known that throwing in a possible invasion of American territory was implausible: Kinoaki's book, published in his own translation, *How Japan Plans To Win,* had pointed out just the year before that Japan lacked adequate tanks, armored vehicles and trucks and that the relatively high quality of American infantrymen made a boots-on-the-ground invasion of the continental United States an absurdity. Haan probably added the possible invasion of the US Aleutian Islands and Alaska – borrowed from a long-outdated 1911 book by the Virginia-born Chinese General Homer Lea, *The Valor of Ignorance* – to try to jolt the Congressmen awake and get them over their obvious indifference to all things Asia (such as the value of the yen). But the Chinese catastrophe that was Operation Ichi-Go soon developed into the worst catastrophe in Korea's tragic history.

17

SINKING SPHERES OF INFLUENCE

The virtual collapse of Chiang Kai-shek's Nationalist Army in the face of Operation Ichi-Go may have astounded Stanley Hornbeck, the State Department expert who bet five-to-one in later November of 1941 that Japan would never dare to attack Pearl Harbor. Hornbeck appeared to have never heard of the Japanese words *bushido* and *sepukku*. Unlike Hornbeck, Owen Lattimore, Chiang's special political advisor, read Chinese, and in Chinese ideographs, the character for 'crisis' consists of two pictographs meaning 'disaster' and 'opportunity.' Lattimore may not have caused the disaster but he saw the opportunity. Chiang Kai-shek through his mismanagement and the greed of his in-laws, and Chennault and Stilwell, through their personal feuding, were all culprits in the Nationalist Chinese downfall. But Lattimore – who owed his political career to Harry Dexter White, the Soviet sympathizer and Pearl Harbor provocateur – made the most of their bungling.[1]

Syngman Rhee, among others, had seen Owen Lattimore as a probable traitor and said so, according to his American publicist, Robert Oliver Tarbёll, long before Lattimore became the focal point of two investigations brought on by defecting Soviet agents. Syngman Rhee, of course, had also called Kilsoo Haan a Communist born and raised in Siberia and an accusation is not proof. 'Doctor' Lattimore, who taught at Johns Hopkins University without a college degree of his own, came up blank when the Soviet NKVD messages were decoded, but he never seems to have made a decision that would have cost Stalin any sleep.

Advised by Owen Lattimore – never proved to be a Communist agent, through several Communist defectors swore than he had been one – and by other ultra-liberals, FDR appointed a special emissary, former Major General Patrick Hurley, a World War I combat veteran with the Silver Star and the Purple Heart. Hurley became the new ambassador to China when Clarence Gauss retired. Patrick Hurley had successfully smuggled three loads of food and supplies through the Japanese blockade to the American defenders of Bataan in the Philippines in early 1942, But his hostile critics described Hurley as 'senile' and said he had trouble remembering the names of people he was talking to. Hurley admittedly mangled Chinese names, referring to the Chinese Communist leader Mao Tse-tung as 'Moose Dung.' Hurley once attended a banquet with the Communist leaders where he punctuated the dinner with Choctaw Indian war cries – 'Ya-HOO!' and even demonstrated a war dance. He first liked Mao, then distrusted Mao, and later befriended Mao again for purely diplomatic purposes – but with strong reservations. Hurley, a former Republican Secretary of War and Oklahoma oil man, also referred to Chiang Kai-shek as 'Mister Shek' – he didn't know enough about Chinese to understand that 'Chiang' was the family name.[2]

On Hurley's watch the career State Department people, whom both Kilsoo Haan and Syngman Rhee had tried to warn Washington about, tried to craft a deal to take the Chinese Communists into the war for the unconditional surrender of Japan –which ignored the Japanese offer of a conditional surrender that would have evacuated China and left Chiang free to fight the Chinese Communists. Hurley became disenchanted with the same people Haan and Rhee had distrusted and warned against. Eventually, Hurley – an anti-Communist to the core – strongly supported Chiang against Mao, if only by default.[3] He was appalled when he learned that at Yalta a dying FDR, supervised by Alger Hiss, had granted Russia concessions of Chinese territory that the Russians had lost when Theodore Roosevelt – Eleanor Roosevelt's uncle – had negotiated for China at the end of the Russo-Japanese War in 1905. Ultimately, Patrick Hurley embarrassed the Truman administration by dramatically resigning as ambassador to China, citing an undue Communist influence among some members of the US State Department.[4]

> I requested the relief of the career men who were opposing the American policy in the Chinese Theatre of war, These professional diplomats were returned to Washington and placed in the Chinese and Far Eastern Divisions of the State Department as my supervisors. Some of these same career men whom I relieved have been assigned as supervisors to the Supreme Command in Asia. In such positions most of them have continued to side with the Communist armed party.[5]

Neither Kilsoo Haan nor Syngman Rhee had been able to convince Washington that heavy Communist influence in the US State Department was a danger to the eventual freedom of Korea. Patrick Hurley, an American with a chest full of decorations and service ribbons, had similar problems convincing the Truman administration that these same people were a danger to a free China. But Kilsoo Haan continued to work for friendship between the future free Korea and the US in every way he could.

In March of 1945, in response to his own initiative, Kilsoo Haan received a letter from Senator Claude Pepper, a Florida Democrat, about Senate Bill 730, an effort to provide a specific immigration quota for Koreans, since the Cairo Conference had promised them their freedom from the Japanese Empire when the now-obvious defeat of Japan set Korea free – or so it was hoped. Pepper was an odd ally for Kilsoo Haan – he was at that time an avid admirer of Stalin and the Soviet Union. But Senator Pepper also hated Japanese militarism, and in that opinion he and Kilsoo Haan were temporary allies.

March 14, 1945

Dear Mr. Haan

It was my pleasure to introduce into the Senate yesterday the bill relative to the immigration quota of Koreans, which we have discussed several times in the past.

You people have suffered longer than any other under the Japanese yoke. I strongly feel that you are fully deserving of the recognition which would be accorded to you by the passage of this bill. The Koreans, insofar as possible, have cooperated with the Allies in their magnificent fight against Japanese militarism. I hope that we can push the bill through to a successful early conclusion.

I will be glad to confer with you about this at any time.

Best wishes to you, and
Always sincerely,
Claude Pepper.[6]

Two weeks later, on 30 March, after patching things up with Kyung Dunn Kilsoo Haan received a letter from Earle R. Dickover, Chief of Japanese Affairs at the US State Department.

My Dear Mr. Haan:

In reply to the letter of March 9, 1945 signed by you and Mr. [*Kyung*] Dunn offering the services of the Sino-Korean People's League and the United Korean Committee in giving 'technical aid or points of view' to the San Francisco conference, and requesting that the Department of State provide for some form of Korean attendance at the conference,. I have to inform you that only United Nations, that is, the states party to the Declaration of January 1, 1942, are eligible to receive invitations to the San Francisco conference.

The Department appreciates the cooperative spirit manifested in your letter and is glad to note your statement that the Koreans will take an active interest in the efforts made by the United Nations at the San Francisco conference for the formation of an effective international organization.

I am sending a similar letter to Mr. Dunn.

Sincerely yours,.
For the Secretary of State:
Earle R. Dickover,
Chief, Division of Japanese Affairs[7]

KIlsoo Haan attended the events related to the founding of the United Nations in San Francisco without credentials, essentially as a gate-crasher. He fudged just a bit and describe himself and Sang R. Park as 'press correspondents' for the Korean independence movement. Kilsoo Haan spoke of 'What Korea Wants' in a radio interview of 24 April, spoke at the Lake Merritt Breakfast Club and the San Francisco Sequoia Club on 26 April, at the Alameda Kiwanis on 2 May, and at the San Francisco Businessman's League at the St Francis Hotel and the Yerba Buena Masonic Lodge in Oakland on 3 May. He made some useful contacts. He was photographed with Ruth Bryan Owens, the first woman ambassador in US history, daughter of William Jennings Bryan, Woodrow Wilson's Secretary of State and three-time candidate for the Presidency.[8]

On 11 June 1945, Joseph C. Grew, then the acting Secretary of State and former ambassador to Japan, contacted Senator Pepper to express the State Department's support for S. 730, the Korean immigration quota bill, 'to authorize the admission into the United States, under a quota for Koreans, Persons of Korean race, to make them racially eligible for naturalization, and for other purposes.'

State statutes in California at the time forbade interracial marriages between whites and Asians and would continue to do so until the State Supreme Court of California ruled the ban unconstitutional in 1950 – a year that Koreans would remember for another reason entirely.

18

RUSSIA

The Japanese had approached the Vatican and the Swiss in the hopes of a negotiated peace shortly after Premier Hideki Tojo resigned from the government in 1944. The Japanese had also – foolishly – approached Stalin, who had signed a non-aggression pact with them after clashes along the Mongolian–Manchurian frontier in 1939. The Japanese got their response from Stalin two days after the first atomic bomb fell on Hiroshima.

Russian armored forces invaded Japanese-held Manchuria and headed south into Korea. The invasion was a walk-over slowed up only by looting and rape of Japanese settlers and Chinese and Korean women alike. No Japanese tank could stand up to the heavy Russian tanks and self-propelled guns that had finally defeated the Tigers and Panthers of the *Wehrmacht*. The Kwantung Army was so demoralized that they handed over their own 'comfort women' to the Russians.

Stalin had known more about the atomic bomb than President Harry Truman had at Potsdam, through the espionage of Julius and Ethel Rosenberg, but Russia didn't yet know how to make one. The Americans still had a strategic edge over the Russians because the US was the only nuclear power and this edge, rather than any innate goodwill on Russia's part, forced Stalin to listen to reason when negotiating for territory that the Russians never much cared about. The Russians wanted Poland, Hungary and Czechoslovakia and they wanted as much of Germany as possible.

Korea was less than an afterthought. Stalin had blandly told the Americans and the British at Tehran a month after the Cairo Conference that it was right that Korea should be independent.[1]

At the Yalta Conference with the dying FDR and the brilliant young Alger Hiss, Stalin had agreed to a boots-on-the-ground invasion of Japanese territory three months after the war with Nazi Germany ended. The dismal flop of the Nationalist Chinese forces during Operation Ichi-Go through most of 1944 started to make this look like a military necessity: Nationalist China was clearly not up to conquering Japan. The results were catastrophic for Korean independence.

The US War Navy Committee in Washington, primarily influenced by the State Department, agreed that the Russians should accept the surrender of the Japanese north of the 38th Parallel of latitude and that the Americans should accept the surrender of the Japanese south of the 38th Parallel.[2] The American official who drew a line across Korea on a National Geographic map at the 38th Parallel was none other than Dean Rusk – the man Kilsoo Haan had told his agents never to trust in 1943, when he was warning them about the Soviet-Red-Chinese Block in the US State Department.

Killsoo Haan had picked up on Dean Rusk when Rusk was a US Army major, promoted four grades on graduation from Officer Candidates School without military training or experience and appointed as General Joseph Stilwell's chief of planning. Rusk was a gifted former Rhodes Scholar from a very poor Southern family. His father, a country preacher, had called in in a veterinarian to deliver him on the kitchen table when his mother had a difficult time giving birth. Rusk was noted for his diffidence and modesty. He was a boy or a man who did what he was told, and sometimes used devious means to get things done for his superiors. When the local Hindu people in India objected to the slaughter of cattle, Rush had only older cattle slaughtered, and where the slaughter could not be observed. 'Our forces ate a great deal of hamburger.'[3] Upper-class Koreans like the traditional Japanese, who also traditionally disdained to kill cattle or eat beef. They relegated butchers to the lowest social class, so much so that Koreans with 'butcher's names' are sometimes looked down on even today. Korean reports back to Kilsoo Haan about Rusk may have reflected this.

'The Indian nationalists also demanded that we give our soldiers permission to marry Indian girls,' Rusk wrote in his memoir. 'We compromised by agreeing that soldiers under orders to go home would be given permission to marry within thirty days of departure. We did this even though American troops in Europe and the Pacific were not allowed to marry local people. Our reasoning was rather simple. We figured that most soldiers within thirty days of the girl back home would lose their interest in marrying a local woman.'[4]

Kilsoo Haan may have simply decided, based on the information he picked up from his Korean agents and their Chinese Nationalist friends, that Rusk was just an accommodating racist and would have the same contempt for Koreans that he did for the race and customs of the Hindu people. But Kilsoo Haan's 1943 warning took on a strange aura of predictive power when Dean Rusk literally drew the line that cut Korea in half in 1945.

Rusk understood and acknowledged that the Cairo Conference had agreed Korea would emerge as an independent nation, but he admitted he knew nothing about Korea. The Japanese surrender after the second atomic bomb and during the Russian invasion caught him by surprise. Rusk admitted that many US military officers did not want to send troops onto the Asian mainland.

Colonel Charles Bonesteel and I retired to an adjacent room late at night and studied intently a map of the Korean Peninsula [at the Operations Division of the War Department in Washington]. Working in haste and under great pressure, we had a formidable task: to pick a zone for American occupation. Neither Tic [Bonesteel] nor I was a Korea expert, but it seemed to us that Seoul, the capital, should be in the American sector. We also knew that the US Army opposed an extensive area of occupation. Using a *National Geographic* map, we looked just north of Seoul for a conventional dividing line but could not find a natural geographic line. We saw instead the 38th parallel and decided to recommend that.[5]

The American military arrived at the southern port of Pusan to a scene of utter chaos. When General John Hodges landed in Korea he asked how many political parties there were in the country.

He was told there were 54. He retreated up the gangplank of his ship and sensibly poured himself a very large drink. The Koreans had been telling one another that Korea had always been a paradise before the Japanese took overfor so long that some of them came to believe it. Some Koreans ran riot. The bemused Americans relied on Japanese troops to maintain some kind of order.

Kilsoo Haan was livid: 'On the heels of shooting by Japanese police of peaceful Koreans who tried to welcome the American occupation forces, Lieutenant-General John R. Hodges announced that all Jap officials in Korea will be retained to rule the zone of occupation,' he wrote under his own by-line on 16 September 1945, for the New Bedford *Standard-Times*.

'One cannot lightheartedly dismiss General MacArthur's decree as merely a policy of expedience. Past events in Japan and Korea raise many pertinent questions which demand careful examination of American policy in Korea.'⁶

What Kilsoo Haan did not say was that about half of the 'Japanese' police in Korea were ethnic Koreans, widely hated by most other Koreans for their brutality and corruption. Koreans said among themselves that you could always spot a Korean in Japanese police uniform – the turncoat gave the hardest beatings but was the easiest to bribe. The Korean mob may not have been at all friendly to people they saw as outside oppressors or domestic traitors. Or the 'Japanese' police may have been trying to send the Korean demonstrators a message that they were still able to defend themselves.

MacArthur had come down hard on his own American forces in Japan, where the early occupation was characterized by the rape of Japanese women – more than 1,000 rapes were reported to police within the first weeks – and the beating of Japanese men who objected. MacArthur issued highly publicized orders that any American who raped a Japanese woman would hang. Any GI who slugged a Japanese civilian without provocation would get 10 years in military prison. The rapes and beatings diminished. MacArthur's humane and constructive occupation of Japan was remembered as his finest hour even by people who considered him pompous and arrogant and saw his military decisions as fluctuating between genius and blundering. MacArthur, as an anti-Communist, later proved to be the best American friend Korea ever had. But as long as the chaos continued, the Americans relied on the 'Japanese' police to keep order and on the surrendered Japanese soldiers to keep the infrastructure operating.

Less than a month after he denounced the shootings, Kilsoo Haan issued another statement in the New Bedford *Standard-Times* on 11 October, urging an interim provisional government of Koreans, Americans, and Russians. He warned that the present situation might lead to war. He suggested that the interim commission hold office for one year, starting on 1 January 1946. The Commission's duties would be to eliminate the zones of occupation and unite Korea – which had historically been a unified country even under Mongol, Manchu Chinese or Japanese control –under a temporary joint US-Soviet Command, and to prepare for a general election the following May to elect thirteen officials for a national Korean government. Thirteen and a united Korea; they should be so lucky.

After the election, Kilsoo Haan said, a constitutional convention would form a provisional representative government not later than 14 August, on the anniversary of the pre-war Atlantic Charter. He also suggested that the convention should create a system 'to weed out collaborators – Koreans, Americans, and other foreign agents – who [had] acquired land and other properties in Korea with the aid of the Japanese [and] form a provisional Land Holding Cooperative to take over all Japanese-owned land and wealth and to hold in escrow the properties of all Koreans and foreigners found guilty of collaborating with the Japanese... Property held in escrow later to be returned to the rightful owners.'[7]

Haan's proposal showed that he had been away from Korea since his childhood. The Japanese had long since worked out a program in which land seized for debt from Korean peasants by Korean *yangban* or by money-lenders had largely been returned to the original owners. Even those Koreans who hated Japanese arrogance and police brutality admitted these programs had been beneficial, as had the hydro-electric plants. Herbert Hoover noted that the Japanese-founded fertilizer plants that had made Korean agriculture more than self-sufficient and the hydro-electric plants were located north of the 38th Parallel.[8] The Russians stole the key parts and shipped them back to Russia, just as they did in eastern Germany.

While General Hodge, Dean Rusk and Kilsoo Haan all moved with a certain hesitation, and not all in the same direction, one man seemed to know exactly what he was doing: Owen Lattimore, former State Department consultant to Chiang Kai-shek. Despite newspaper articles that described his group as 'Soviet sympathizers,' Lattimore was sent to advise General MacArthur on the occupation of Japan. His purported mission was to break up the Japanese cartels seen by liberals and Leftists as responsible for 'Japanese militarism.' What Lattimore actually did was to strip post-war Japan of all production facilities for aluminum and magnesium and half of all machine tools – which meant that in case of future trouble with the Communists, the Japanese would be unable to maintain their own aircraft or rebuild aircraft for the Americans.[9] *Readers Digest* reporter Dennis McEvoy noted that Lattimore seemed extremely friendly with Edgar Snow, whose reportage emphasized Japanese and Nationalist atrocities but saw Mao's Communists as universally beloved.[10] He was also friendly with Japanese Communists such as Seiji Yoshida, who 'confessed' to kidnapping Korean women from Jeju Island for 'comfort women,' a lie he recanted after both Japanese historians and South Korean journalists discovered that the 'comfort women' were real but the kidnapping was fictitious.

As soon as the American presence was established in southern Korea, Kilsoo Haan helped expedite much-needed medical supplies to the Korean people and received thank-you notes from the Korean Bible Society, which distributed them.

On 1 March 1946. He wrote a letter to General Hodge about a matter of concern after Hiroshima and Nagasaki:

I have received word from our agent, Northern Korea, that the Soviet occupation authorities have discovered [a] large deposit of uranium and have already carted away quantities of uranium.

Whether this information may be of value, I do not know.

However, under the cloudy international situation pregnant with grave possibilities, our agents are apprehensive.

Will you please do what you can to check this information and do what is best to protect the security and interest of the U.S.A. Wise and meaningful preventive measure(s) can and will bring peace.[11]

Haan recorded that on 29 March 1946, General Hodge replied: 'Your information is interesting and I assure you that it will be carefully checked. I will treat it and its sources confidentially.'

Once again, Kilsoo Haan's information was accurate. The Soviets were indeed processing uranium and would test their first effective atomic bomb in August of 1949, to the astonishment of the US State Department. A year later, in the course of the Korean War, South Korean troops allied with the American forces found the actual uranium ore plant the Korean Underground had identified through Kilsoo Haan.

On 14 December 1946, less than a year after Owen Lattimore had stripped Japan of aluminum and magnesium capacity and half of its machine tools, Kilsoo Haan continued to lift his sights beyond revenge on Japan and pointed out the greater danger he had been watching for some years – a Russian-Red Chinese coalition to dominate the entire Eurasian continent, the land mass and population center that the German Geo-Politicians called 'the world island', as described in one of Frank Capra's 'Why We Fight' propaganda films. Haan wrote in a Korean Underground report later circulated to the US press that Soviet General Nicholai Bulganin had declared 'It is the ultimate aim of the Soviet Union to keep America out of Europe and Asia... Russia is to build a strong political and military cordon across the heart of Eurasian, from Berlin to Canton, China.'

Haan said that in a secret agreement in March 1946, Mao Tse-tung had accepted Russia's leadership in international affairs. The Russians and the Chinese also agreed to a mutual acceptance of the image of America: 'American is the center of world reaction... America is the sworn enemy of oppressed people... America is the soil of future aggressive wars.' He said that Russia and China had agreed to have Chiang Kai-shek defeated 'by 1950.'[12]

Winston Churchill, himself an anti-Communist since 1919, if not before (and you can't get much earlier than that) had said the same thing in his famous 'Iron Curtain' speech in Fulton, Missouri in March of 1946. But Stalin had supported Chiang rather than Mao Tse-tung all through the war, probably to tie up as many Japanese troops as possible and keep them out of Siberia and Mongolia, The US State Department learned about the Stalin-Mao alliance only in 1950 – four years after Kilsoo Haan broke the story.

At the beginning of 1948, Owen Lattimore was advising Congress not to waste any more money either on Nationalist China or on Korea, though he supported Congressional aide to Israel, which had broad popular support. Lattimore said that Korea did not have 'an even social texture and the large measure of social equality' of Israel and that Korea was 'incompetent to use intelligently either economic or military forms of aid ... it will waste American aid even more incompetently and corruptly than the Kuomintang in China.'[13]

After heavy fighting with Mao's Communists through the second half of 1949. Chiang Kai-Shek lost control of the Chinese mainland and evacuated his forces to Taiwan. President Harry Truman signed a Mutual Defense Act that pledged $75 million for the 'general area of China.' Dean Acheson, advised by Lattimore and Robert Service of the State Department, made sure that none of the money got to Chiang. 'Mao is not a true [Soviet] satellite in that he came to power by his own efforts and was not installed in officer by the Soviet army,' Acheson reported.[14]

'There is no evidence that the furnishing of additional military material would alter would alter the pattern of current developments in China,' Acheson wrote to the Senate Foreign Relations Committee on 12 March 1949 'There is, however, ample evidence that the Chinese people are weary of hostilities and that there is an overwhelming desire for peace.' A bill to provide $1.5 billion for the defense of Chiang's China against Mao's Communists was rejected.[15] The State Department also reported that Chiang lacked support from the Chinese people and most of his own soldiers.

Owen Lattimore lobbied for Chinese Communists and parried Hanson W. Baldwin's comment that China would not soon become unified: 'The Communists have done well enough in the territory they control to stand comparison with the Kuomintang...

There is a case for negotiating a political compromise with the Communists before pressing the question of military control.'[16]

US General Albert Wedemeyer, former Army Chief of Plans who had actual military experience in China after taking over for Joseph Stilwell, disagreed Wedemeyer wrote in 1958:

> Dean Acheson was either misinformed or is deliberately misleading Congress when he cited 'our military advisors on the spot' as the authority for his statement that the Chinese Nationalist forced had lost no battles against the Communists for lack of arms or ammunition. Thanks to the State Department, American military observers had not been permitted to enter combat areas and therefore could not render first-hand reports of that nature. A civilian engineer representing the J.C. White Company of New York was present in the Soochow area during the fighting and told me personally that the Nationalists fought tenaciously against the Communists. He saw thousands of wounded and dead, both Communists and Nationalists. The latter withdrew only as the ammunition supply was exhausted.[17]

The constituent assembly that the Korean patriots including Kilsoo Haan had asked for was established on 10 May and on 31 May Syngman Rhee was elected as Korea's first president. Owen Lattimore – a man Syngman Rhee distrusted even more than Kilsoo Haan had distrusted Dean Rusk – began to ramp up his anti-Korean stance now that South Korea had a government that was strongly anti-Communist.

On 26 June 1949 Ku Kim was sitting at home reading Chinese poetry when a South Korean officer walked in and shot him four times. Ku Kim had been feuding with Syngman Rhee over Korea's future since the end of 1946. Rhee had argued that founding a separate South Korean state would be a necessity if the Russian-controlled northern half of Korea could not be convinced to allow free and honest elections. Rhee offered to take charge of the new state. After serving as the war-time president of Koreans affiliated with Chiang Kai-shek, Ku Kim had shown his habitual modesty and stepped aside after the Japanese surrender to allow Syngman

Rhee, who was better educated and had better contacts with the Americans, to run for president. But Ku Kim himself enjoyed a respect for his daring assassinations and ability to stand up to Japanese torture that Syngman Rhee could only envy – and did envy.

Ku Kim was also unalterably opposed to any permanent partition of Korea and insisted on maintaining negotiations with Kim Il Sung. Rumors began to percolate that Syngman Rhee, rather than the Soviets or the North Korean Communists, had ordered the assassination of Ku Kim, 'the assassin' behind the Shanghai Bomb Plot that put the Korean resistance on the map in 1932. The officer who shot Ku Kim was given a life sentence and set free in a very short time.

Ku Kim's defiant courage had convinced Chiang Kai-shek, not otherwise a very imaginative statesman, that the Koreans were an impressive people. Americans whose traditional view of assassination was shaped by the murder of Abraham Lincoln were less than impressed with South Korean politics and more than a little tired of the querulous Syngman Rhee. When Kilsoo Haan heard that Ku Kim had been murdered, he looked his son Stan in the eye and said: 'If I go back to Korea, I'm dead!'

Owen Latimore, whose 1945 book *Solution in Asia* came out in February 1945, suggested among other things that the Emperor of Japan and his entire male line be interned or perhaps interred in China, a suggestion which, once it reached Japan, turned the demand of 'Unconditional Surrender' into a probable death sentence for a very scared emperor and his son. Hirohito chose to support a Japanese fight to the death – other people's death. Lattimore also had a suggestion for the future of Korea:

> It is as nearly certain as anything in politics can be that when the lid is taken off, the long-repressed political instincts of the Korea people will boil over in many factional movements. They will undoubtedly quarrel with each other, but undoubtedly the major tendency will be both fiercely nationalistic and radical... Our own habits of political thinking will expose us to the danger of throwing our weight against Korean movements which we think 'too radical' ... It is to our interest that the

Russians, and therefore Communism, should be associated with us, the Chinese, and the British in joint responsibility for a moderate but clearly progressive policy which will return responsibility to the Koreans as fast as possible.[18]

Ku Kim had been the only Korean with the willingness to negotiate and the perceived strength to make negotiations plausible; Syngman Rhee and Kilsoo Haan hated one another but they were both recognized anti-Communists – to Lattimore's apparent dismay.

On 17 July 1949, Lattimore wrote bluntly in a State Department publication: 'The thing to do, therefore, is to let South Korea fall – but not to let it look as though we pushed it.'[19]

Shortly, this was made to happen. Only the actual intent is debatable The Russians had pulled their troops out of North Korea in in January of 1949, after having trained a North Korean Army indoctrinated with Communism and equipped with T-34/85 Russian tanks and medium and light artillery. The North Korean leader Kim Il Sung was a former major in the Soviet Red Army with a record of service against the Japanese – Kim had taken one village and held it for several days before the Japanese took it back. Kim Il Sung, however, had a full-time campaign biography ready: born in a log cabin (like Abraham Lincoln) on the slope of a sacred Korean mountain, he was the grandson of the Presbyterian minister of the sect that had showed the strongest support for Korean rights during the Japanese occupation – or so he said. This was a man whose imaginary past predicted a great future,

The US, meanwhile, had withdrawn its 50,000 troops from South Korea and left behind only 500 advisors with light equipment adequate for police work or guerilla fighting. Of the $10,500,000 specifically earmarked for Korea by the Military Assistance Bill signed by President Truman on 29 October 1949, exactly $200 in signal wire had been dropped off at Pusan by June of 1950.[20]

On 12 January 1950 the new Secretary of State, Dean Acheson, made a speech at the Washington Press Club in which he drew the line of American's defense perimeter in the Pacific: the United States would defend Japan, but not Korea or the Nationalist Chinese of Taiwan.[21] Acheson later tried to justify this statement by pointing out that he was simply re-stating the position of the US Joint Chiefs of Staff at the end of 1947. Acheson waffled on about whether the US had any responsibility to defend South Korea: 'South Korea could take care of any trouble started by North Korea,' he said at one point, but added that an actual Soviet Russian invasion might be a different matter.[22]

The day after Acheson spoke, Kilsoo Haan's nemesis Dean Rusk, now the Under Secretary of State, declared in San Francisco that the Chinese Communist revolution was not Russian in essence and did not aim at a dictatorship.[23] Alger Hiss of the State Department had been FDR's principal State Department aide at Yalta, and a few months later was appointed Secretary-General of the United Nations Charter Conference at San Francisco, where Kilsoo Haan couldn't get his ticket punched and attended as a gate-crasher representing a future independent Korea.

Dean Acheson talked out of both sides of his mouth about the future of Korea on 12 January 1950, but he never equivocated on a different issue when his young friend Alger Hiss, who had advised FDR at Yalta, was found guilty of perjury two weeks later. Hiss had lied about passing state secrets to a Soviet agent since 1938 and the defector, later *Time* magazine senior editor Whittaker Chambers, had copies of Hiss's memos by way of proof, some of them hidden inside a hollowed-out pumpkin on his farm. The memos also disclosed Harry Dexter White's obsessive interest with Japan's oil supply long before 1941. Alger Hiss was sentenced to five years in prison. Dean Acheson rushed to his friend's defense. 'I should like to make it clear to you that whatever the outcome of any appeal ... I do not intend to turn my back on Alger Hiss.'[24]

At Yalta, FDR had famously agreed to let Stalin take over the eastern half of Poland and had allowed Poland to annex a large piece of eastern Germany – including Silesia, where 60 per cent of the ethnic German and ethnic Polish electorate had voted to stay German in a plebiscite in 1921 supervised by neutral international observers.

The Yalta Conference had also decided to demand that the Chinese Nationalists and the Chinese Communists be required to cooperate, and that Russia be given Chinese territory in Manchuria and pre-War Japanese territory on Sakhalin Island and control of the Kurile Islands, which had been Japanese since before Commodore Perry called by. A top secret decision was made that Korea, which had been publicly promised its independence at the Cairo Conference by FDR, Churchill, and Chiang, would be handed over to a joint a joint US–USSR trusteeship *for the next 40 years.*[25] This decision came just a few weeks before Owen Lattimore's *Solution in Asia* stated that Russia should take a role in Korea that those Koreans who were not Communists didn't want. Once the word got out that the Russians would be coming, Kilsoo Haan would no doubt have agreed that Alger Hiss was a good man not to turn your back on.

Kim Il Sung, the North Korean mystic of the magic mountain and the self-proclaimed Lincoln log cabin baby, knew more about America than most Americans knew about Korea. In Korean folk culture, numbers and dates have a powerful importance. Kim, or perhaps his Russian advisors, appears to have picked an auspicious date for what he had in mind – 25 June 1950 was the anniversary of Custer's Last Stand.

19

THE SKY FALLS IN

On 25 June, the T-34/85 Russian tanks rumbled over the border of South Korea and encountered confused South Korean troops armed with a World War II bazooka that would not pierce Soviet armor. Some South Koreans who had been trained by the fearsome Japanese actually disabled the T-34-85 tanks by jamming the treads and then setting fire to the engine – the tactic that convinced the Japanese to mount a rear-firing machine gun in their own late-war tank turrets. Those South Koreans who had been trained by the peacetime US soldiers of 'the baseball army' – volunteers who joined up after the World War II draft ended – usually joined their instructors in the general rout. Tragically, some Americans captured by the North Korean troops were shot in the head or beaten to death with rocks. When their buddies found the mangled bodies and the newspapers and radio picked up the murder stories, no quick withdrawal from South Korean was politically acceptable. Five years after the end of the war with Japan, the United States was involved in a 'police action' inside the former Japanese Empire that became the Korean War.

Dean Rusk – the man to beware of in Kilsoo Haan's 1943 Korean Underground memo – appears to have tried to draft a speech for Dean Acheson that might have been less of an invitation to aggression: 'The day before, I helped prepare

several drafts of that speech, and Acheson disliked them all,'
Rusk wrote in his memoir

> Finally he told us 'We have wasted enough time on this. I'll
> just go home and jot down some notes and go down there
> tomorrow and make a speech' True to form, Acheson spoke
> extemporaneous; we had no chance to flyspeck the text...
> Unfortunately the Soviets and everyone else overlooked
> Acheson's UN reference. He didn't intend to brush aside
> everything beyond our so-called defense perimeter but his
> remarks were nevertheless subject to misinterpretation. We at
> the Department decided that issuing clarifiers after the speech
> would simply make matters worse, I advised Acheson to sit
> tight and let the matter blow over. But it didn't.[1]

Dean Acheson's statement that South Korea was outside the US
defense perimeter was his most far-reaching contribution to US
diplomacy since the meddling that turned the oil embargo to Japan
from an oil cut-back to an oil shut-down. Acheson had hardened
Roosevelt's stance on the export of oil. What FDR intended as
a catalyst for negotiations to get Japan out of China became
the catalyst for Pearl Harbor.[2,3] The Acheson statement about
Korea being outside the US defense perimeter was widely if not
universally blamed for encouraging the North Korean attack by
a trained army against an under-manned police force armed with
useless bazookas.

'Well, we don't know what to think about you Americans,' the
Soviet diplomat Andrei Vyshinsky told an American businessman
over dinner after the Korean War started. 'Look at Korea. You did
everything you could to tell us you were not interested in Korea,
and when the North Koreans went in there, you put your troops
in... We can't trust you Americans.'[4]

The Russians were not the only ones. On 22 May 1947, Kilsoo
Haan had reluctantly sent a letter to the CIA complaining that
the policies which had been secretly established at Yalta and
implemented by the joint Soviet and United States occupation and
the US State Department had seriously undermined the Korean

Underground and his own ability to deliver information to the US. The covering letter to the CIA was written by Representative Willis W. Bradly of California, a US Navy officer in World War I and World War II and winner of the Congressional Medal of Honor. Congressman Bradly vouched for the integrity and loyalty of Kilsoo Haan.

...The faith of the Korean underground workers in the United States has, all through the years, been strong and unwavering. They have believed that, in spite of many failures and compromises, the United States was Korea's friend. The underground organization has repeatedly offers its services to the U.S. Army and Navy, though the Army and Navy never saw fit to accept. The Koreans have always believed that cooperation been the U.S. and Korea would be of mutual advantage.

Post-war occupation polices have, however, placed doubts in the minds of many Koreans who worked so long and at such great sacrifice for the defeat of the Japanese and for the liberation of their country. The Sino-Korea People's League recently received from Korea a report, dated September 10, 1946, that the Korean underground organization from which the League reports originated had disbanded as a result of dissatisfaction and dissention over occupation policies, The report states that sixty per cent of the former members are now actively opposed to present U.S. occupation policies, while the other forty per cent either accept and agree with the policies, or take a neutral position.

The work of the League will continue, to Dec, 31, 1946, but henceforth our link with what was formerly the Korean liberation underground no longer exists, unless and until the underground workers have again organized on a basis sympathetic to America.

In the interest of Korea's independence and the security of America,

Sincerely,
Kilsoo K. Haan,[5]

At the bottom of Kilsoo Haan's formal typed letter was a hand-written note:

> Attention: Confidential May 12, 1947
> Those agents who still believe in America have reorganized. Hence their report of what the Soviets are doing regards war preparation under the name of national security.
> To me this is very – yes highly, important undertaking for us and we need American official sympathy.[6]

After the shake-up in the Korean underground was restored, Kilsoo Haan supplied information – observed as early as the end of 1946 – that the Soviets had attempted to test an atomic bomb in Siberia but the test was ultimately a failure.

> We have just received information from Korean agents in Vladivostock, dated September 10, 1946, to the effect that shortly before that time three Soviet scientists conferred with local Vladivostok officials. These scientists were on their way from Northern Korea to the industrial cities of the Ural region.
> Two Koreans overheard the scientists discuss the success of the first atom bomb test held on August 15, 1946. One of the scientists said 'By July we shall have one hundred bombs. 'July' is obviously meant to be July 1947.
> According to the information we received from the Koreans there are three atom bomb plants in Russia today. The largest is at Magnitogorsk; the second largest is at Nisha Tagil and the third at Komsomolsk. Twelve Koreans are reported to be employed at the Komsomolsk plant which is underground and is known as Plant 52.
> We are fully aware of the difficulty of verifying this report, but are sending it along for what it may be worth. We are making no other uses of this information, but are sending it to you exclusively.[7]
> On November 2, 1946, six of the 18 Korean workers from Plant 52 at Komomolsk were moved to Magnitogorsk.
> One of the six Koreans who witnessed the Soviet A-bomb test, August 1946, one hundred miles north of Nisno Kolmak

in Siberia, was informed by friends that it was the belief of his superiors that the Soviet A-Bomb failed to meet the quality and standard of the U.S. A-Bomb.

The Soviet officials showed much disappointment.[8]

My friends from Komsomolsk. Siberia, informed me that at Nishno Kolymak [there was] the completion of a rigid test, Jan. 3 to 10, guiding a small submarine by remote control as well as launching an airplane from this small submarine.

It is said as soon as the plane was in the air, the radio control guided the plane over to its target 250 miles from the mother submarine.

Some of the Soviet officials believe this feat can be successful 360 miles away before the end of 1947.

Super Submarines

The Russian Navy is now in the blue print stage, working on super-submarine of 5,000 tons.

The Koreans believe Soviet Russia will eventually have a 'formidable fleet of super submarines' as part of her growing Pacific Fleet.

These submarines will each carry one 'radio controlled pocket submarine' and devices to launch 'Rocket Bombs.' It is also said the super submarines will have other devices which will revolutionize naval warfare.

My friends cautioned that utmost discretion be observed for reason which you know best.[9]

KIlsoo Han's warnings this time around aroused such little interest that on 13 May he scribbled a hand-written note to Colonel E.K. Wright, his previous contact in the Central Intelligence Group in Washington to find out if they had been received, since the radio-controlled airplane report, unlike the atomic bomb tests reports, were never acknowledged. His spelling suggests that he may have had a few drinks or at least written in great haste:

On the 4th of March 1947 the undersigned person made certain report on the Soviet 'radio control remote test' and her super submarine building naval program.

Although I have made an inquiry since the above report made to you on the 4th if [sic] March – I have to date have not receive any acknowledgment whether you receive [sic] the above mention report, Could you inform me if you di or did nor recieve [sic] the report?

Sincerely,
Kilsoo Haan[10]

The next note Kilsoo Haan received from the State Department may have been embarrassing since he never filed it. His letter from Congressman Bradly was included with almost everything he wrote, and he also had a form letter listing some of the achievements of the Sino-Korean People's League.[11]

For many years, for the purpose of expelling the Japanese enemy from their homeland, an underground organization of Korean patriots systematically supplied the Sino-Korea People's League, with headquarters in Hawaii, with highly important reports pertaining to the plans and activities of the Japanese. This information was invariably passed on to the United States Government, by the Washington Representative of the League, for whatever use could be made of it. Typical of the information forward are the following items:

1. Sending agents at the request of the U.S. Navy to the Japanese Mandated Islands and the report of its findings to the Navy 1936.
2. Report to the U.S. Department of State, March 25, 1941, that Japan and Russia to sign a non-aggression Pact before April 29, 1941. The pact was signed on April 13, 1941.
3. Report to U.S. Navy, May 1940 that Jap Navy was building 'Midget submarines' for the purpose of it [an] attack against Hawaii.
4. Submit to the War and State Departments the Japanese war plan book – 'Three Power Alliance and a U.S. Japan War' Feb. and March 1941. The Jap war plan Oct. 1941 to House Immigration Committee.

5. Dec. 5, 1941, report to Department of State, the Japanese sneak attack n Hawaii. Dec. 7th, the first Sunday of December 1941.
6. Report to U.S. Navy the Japanese Navy building of 'Super-Subs' of 4,500 tonners, etc.

The reply from the U.S. State Department this time may not have been prompt but was definitely explicit.

Oct 10, 1947

Dear Mr. Haan

Your letter of September 17, 1947 addressed to Colonel William Eddy in which you request 'at least $6,000 per year' to support certain activities in which you are presently engaged has been received.

There are available to the Office of Intelligence Research no funds for securing the services of persons other than those regularly carried on Department of State rolls. The several documents appended to your letter are returned herewith.

Sincerely yours.
W. Park Armstrong Jr.
Acting Special Assistant[13]

On 7 September 1949, Kilsoo Haan wrote in a Korean Underground Report sent to various US agencies that the Soviet Regional War Plan called for the liberation of South Korea, followed by the liberation of French Indo-China. He noted that seasoned Korean veterans who had fought the Japanese in Manchuria and China were being moved to North Korea from China. On 1 June 1950, he reported joint North Korean and Russian Army maneuvers in North Korea to test the new North Korean Army.

He received the usual response.

20

BLAMING THE MESSENGER

Nobody in Washington had been allowed to take Kilsoo Haan seriously by the time the Korean War actually broke out and turned into a Korean national tragedy – a tragedy in the truest Greek sense since some Koreans had admittedly helped bring the disaster on themselves, though most of the blame could also be fixed on Russia, on Japan, on China, on France and Germany; and on the United States. Kimm Kiu-sik, the gentle old scholar who had once mentored a young Syngman Rhee and had actually attended the League of Nations founding, was a favorite of General John Hodge because he was a moderate conservative who was willing to talk to Communists about unification, though he was not himself a Communist. Syngman Rhee edged Kim out as vice-president in 1949, about the same time that Ku Kim was assassinated. When the North Koreans invaded South Korea, Kimm Kyu-sik was abducted by the North Koreans and died in custody within a few months.[1]

Douglas MacArthur was 70 years old when the North Koreans invaded South Korea but his aides said the news made him look and act ten years younger. MacArthur stopped the North Korean advance with air power and the stiffened resistance of South Korean forces, joined by US troops rushed from Japan. The US developed a solid perimeter around the southern seaport of Pusan, Then, in a daring attack further north at Inchon, MacArthur outflanked the North Koreans, cut off their supply lines and drove them out of Seoul, out of the North Korean capital at Pyongyang, and into China.

'No one, including myself, foresaw Chinese intervention,' Dean Rusk wrote. 'We didn't detect any massing of major Chinese forces in Manchuria. Our intelligence did detect some movement of Chinese troops in the North, but we didn't think they were posed for a major assault...We believed that since Mao Zedong had just seized power one year before and his regime was trying to consolidate its hold on the mainland, the chances were good that the Chinese would not come in.'[2]

Rusk recalled that Dean Acheson told Truman the Chinese should not be allowed to drive US forces out of Korea,[3] This statement came a year after Owen Lattimore that decided that South Korea must be allowed to collapse with no hint of blame falling on the Americans. The North Korean attacked turned Kilsoo Haan's would-be benefactor, Claude Pepper, from a Stalin admirer to an anti-Communist. Former Vice President Henry Wallace – dumped from Roosevelt's 1944 presidential ticket because he was such an eccentric and such an obvious Leftist sympathizer that conservative Democrats as well as Republicans found him unacceptable – also became an anti-Communist after the invasion of South Korea.

Political observers, including Allen Weinstein in *The Haunted Wood*, have noted that if Henry Wallace had been vice president when FDR died in 1945, his candidate for Secretary of State would have been Alger Hiss and his candidate for Secretary of the Treasury would have been Harry Dexter White, both Soviet agents. Wallace had taken a tour of the Siberian gold mining area at Magadan and Kolyma with the ever-reliable Owen Lattimore as his interpreter. A whole issue of *National Geographic* by Wallace and Lattimore became a heart-warming endorsement of the Soviet system. Lattimore took a photograph of happy, hunky Russian prospectors who told him they would rather be fighting Nazis in Europe than mining gold, but wanted to do their duty. Wallace spoke no Russian. Lattimore's photograph showed ethnic European Russian police guards dressed in prisoners' work clothes. The actual Kolyma workers included Polish POWs, German POWs,

Orthodox Russian clergy, Orthodox Jews who refused to recant, and disillusioned Japanese and Korean Communists. None of these looked like the men in the photograph, especially after they began to die of starvation. The deaths from starvation and exposure at Magadan and Kolyma were once estimated at three million, but recent Russian figures suggest an actual total of about 135.000 deaths, and another 50,000 prisonerst shot while trying to escape. Most of the 850,000 survivors were sent home as chronic invalids after they were worked half to death and died some few months or years later. Vice President Henry Wallace, with Lattimore translating, told *National Geographic* that the people he saw were all happy and healthy, eating fresh melons raised for them in greenhouses.

Owen Lattimore was first described as a Soviet agent by a Russian defector named Alexander Barmine in December of 1948, a few months after his mentor, Harry Dexter White, took an overdose of digitalis following his questioning about the number of Communists he had placed in the Treasury Department without consulting the FBI or internal security. Louis Budenz, a US Communist defector, also accused Lattimore of being a Communist, though not an actual spy. Lattimore beat a perjury charge on a technicality but was finished in government by the end of the Korean War. He took off to teach in Mongolia.

The Russians were not present at the United States Security Council meeting where North Korea was declared the aggressor and the Korean conflict became the first war fought under the banner of the United Nations.

'The United States contributed to the Korean War 450,000 men at a given time, but more than a million men were rotated through Korea,' Herbert Hoover wrote in retrospect, 'Fifteen nations of the sixty members of the United Nations contributed less than 45,000 men.'[4]

'In blunt language the United Nations numerical contribution to the war in Korea was piddling in light of the strength of the free world,' General Mark Clark said, as quoted by Herbert Hoover. 'Of the fifty-three nations who endorsed the decision for the United States action against the aggressor in Korea, only fifteen other than the United States provided ground, air, or sea combat forces.'[5]

Many of the regular soldiers from France, Greece and Turkey proved to be redoubtable fighters, but their numbers were almost inconsequential against the vast forces of the Chinese. The British Commonwealth provided a responsible number: three infantry brigades, a tank brigade and half an artillery regiment with combat engineers from the UK, two infantry battalions and a fighter squadron from Australia, a regiment of artillery from New Zealand, and a reinforced infantry brigade with tanks and artillery from Canada. The French, also facing a Communist-sponsored uprising in Indo-China, sent a reinforced infantry battalion; the Turks sent an infantry brigade; the Greeks send an infantry battalion. The other United Nations participants sent one infantry battalion each, or ambulance corpsmen.[6] The United Nations turned out to be a poor wellspring of fighting men.

The State Department tacitly wrote off Chiang Kai-shek as almost a comic figure, after his forces had worn down the Japanese since 1937 and had lost to the Communists only after American advisors and aid was withdrawn.

'As for Taiwan's offer to send troops to Korea, the whole thing was a fraud,' Dean Rusk wrote. 'Just after the North Korean invasion I received a telegram from Chiang Kai-shek that Taiwan had earmarked two divisions – thirty-three thousand [men] – for service in Korea, but Chiang also said these divisions needed outfitting from boots to helmets, the most modern weapons and two years of intensive training before they would be ready. From an operational point of view, this offer was virtually worthless.'[7]

The same might be said of Rusk's intelligence operation after the US refused Kilsoo Haan a salary and angered most of his agents by supporting a continued Japanese presence in occupied Korea and negotiations with the North Koreans. To his credit, Kilsoo Haan had tried to warn various US agencies that the attack was coming six months before it happened, despite US refusal of his request for a salary and the lack of respect he received from most Washington officialdom. He was ignored, as he always was. Rusk failed to understand that many of the Chinese soldiers funneled into the first year of the Korean War has served as soldiers in Chiang Kai-shek's army or were otherwise regarded as expendable by the Communist government: Christians. landlords, sons of fathers with more than one wife – the kind of people who never would be missed in Mao's New China.

The majority of Chinese soldiers were passive prisoners. When the Korean War ended in June of 1953, only 83,000 of the 135,000 Communist prisoners in UN hands – predominantly the heavily indoctrinated North Koreans, who had remained troublesome behind barbed wire – would accept repatriation. Most of the actual Chinese asked to go to the United States or, failing that, to Chiang's Taiwan.[7] MacArthur, who had grown up in the Old Army of the frontier with proud 'Colored' regiments and Indian scouts, had employed a Chinese nursemaid for his son. He was not a racist like Dean Rusk. And MacArthur thought that using Chinese forces was a great idea. He was overruled and, when the gentleman protested too much, he was sacked, to the vast disgust of the American people and a large part of Congress, and to the horror of the South Koreans and most of the Japanese. The State Department had let slip another opportunity. The former Chinese Nationalist troops and land-owners' sons being funneled into Korea in the Red Army would have fought very badly against Chiang's Chinese Nationalists and might even have revolted, as so many Chinese had revolted against the Nationalists during Operation Ichi-Go, the campaign that had cost Chiang his credibility.

MacArthur had taken part in another protest unknown until the 21st century. Even the US State Department, now minus Owen Lattimore, realized that there was one anti-Communist nation in Asia that produced reliable –if intimidating – soldiers. Dean Rusk reported how he and John Foster Dulles had 'become heavily involved in negotiating the Japanese Peace Treaty. John Foster Dulles and I worked closely on this project, with Dulles taking charge of the negotiations… Although Dulles and Acheson later had many personal difficulties, they were a beautiful team in negotiating the Japanese Peace Treaty.'[8]

The Japanese version of what actually happened before the 'beautiful' treaty was signed in San Francisco came from Kazuko Aso, the younger daughter and confidential secretary of Japanese Prime Minister Shigeru Yoshida, a pacifist and a secret Catholic who was to accept the Last Rites on his deathbed some years later. Kazuko Aso was openly Catholic and instinctively a pacifist, like most Japanese women. In her biography *My Father, Shigeru Yoshida*, published in Japan in 1993 and never translated into English, she described John Foster Dulles' idea of negotiations. Dulles called for a conference with Prime Minister Yoshida in Tokyo and, in her presence, told Yoshida that the Japanese Army would be immediately re-armed and sent back to fight the Chinese in Korea.

'We cannot do that,' Yoshida said. 'All the ghosts of Manchuria would draw their swords against us!' Yoshida knew that the last years of Japanese rule in Manchuria had broken down into a series of unspeakable atrocities, including about 3,000 documented lethal medical experiments on Communist prisoners – the Chinese claimed 250,000 – and that Japanese physicians had performed gruesome invasive procedures on live prisoners and allowed victims to die of plague, anthrax, and venereal diseases. Yoshida had not approved the experiments, but he understood that the Japanese were widely feared and hated in that part of Asia.

'I'm not going to take any nonsense from a barbarian who eats raw fish!' Dulles said sharply. 'You're going to do as you're told.'[9]

Yoshida, however, did not do as he was told. He ran to get help from Douglas MacArthur. General MacArthur approved Yoshida's concept of a 100,000-man Japanese Self Defense Force that would never be sent overseas but would defend the Japanese home islands in case of invasion. MacArthur was so popular in Japan and in most of the US that the idea of re-arming the Japanese for a fresh invasion of Korea was allowed quietly to slip away into the diplomatic mist.[10]

Separately and together, the arrogant General MacArthur and the enigmatic Prime Minister Yoshida had a better grip on reality than the Acheson-Rusk-Dulles State Department team. Landing Japanese troops in Korea after 35 years of often brutal rule could have backfired into a full-fledged Second Korean War that united North Koreans and South Koreans against the Japanese invaders – and against their American sponsors.

The use of Japanese forces in Korea represented a lost opportunity only to those who knew nothing of Korean history.

When the French asked the British to help them recapture Indo-China in 1945–1946, the British authorities had re-armed their Japanese military prisoners. The Japanese soldiers had re-taken Indo-China from Ho Chi Minh in five weeks. The second Japanese invasion of Indo-China under British leadership was to remain The Last Banzai. The Japanese themselves had blustered when they were asked to help the Dutch subdue the Indonesians, and in Indonesia in the 21st century the Japanese remain less hated than the Dutch. Japanese soldiers who had survived the war returned to rebuild what was left of Japan.

The Americans tried to stem the tide of Communism without Japanese troops. Japanese industry, in fact, got a jump-start by re-building and repairing damaged American military equipment despite the fact that Owen Lattimore, who was never convicted of being a Communist, had carried off the aluminum, the magnesium, and half of the machine tools.

In the end, the American and South Korean soldiers did most did most of the fighting and the Korean people did most of the dying. The U.S lost over 33,500 men killed in action during the Korean War and and a significant number due to illness and accident. The US-equipped South Korean Army lost somewhere between 20,000 and 40,000 soldiers killed in action. Korean civilian deaths have been informally estimated at two to three million.[11] The British lost 1,078 killed and 2,674 wounded, with 1,060 lost or taken prisoner.[12] The war was so exceptionally unpopular with the American soldiers who fought, especially the draftees, that one out of three American POWs is said to have collaborated with the Chinese Communists. The figure was one out of 10 for the British, who were mostly professional soldiers, and zero for the Turks.[13] This figure must be examined against the figure that 58 per cent of all US POWs died in Communist custody – a far worse figure than the death rate of prisoners of the Japanese in World War II. Every US chaplain died in Communist custody. So did most of the Army doctors.

As the war wore on, Americans started to get angry. In the last battles before the 1953 Armistice, in trench and bunker fights like Pork Chop Hill and Outpost Harry, American soldiers including draftees fought to the death alongside South Koreans and Greek regulars rather than give ground, The Americans killed huge numbers of Chinese at close quarters and with massive artillery.[14]

Americans were impressed by the Korean people who gave up their homes and jobs and risked their lives to escape from Communism, in the wake of US forces retreating during the Chinese counter-attack in 1951. Liberals who had tilted leftward during the Hitler years changed their minds when, five years after Lend Lease, Russian Mig-15s sometimes flown by Russian pilots were killing Americans over Korea, while the Chinese accused those US pilots who survived of practising germ warfare when they were captured.

The Korean War shattered Dean Acheson's astounding arrogance. Dwight D. Eisenhower was elected president on the vow to go to Korea if the war had not ended when he took office. Eisenhower snubbed Truman at the inauguration for wasting American lives and let the Chinese know he intended to use the new atomic cannon if the war was still going on when he assumed control. John Foster Dulles, late of the beautiful negotiation with Japan, took over as Eisenhower's secretary of state. John Foster Dulles may have been gruff and no fan of raw fish, but nobody ever suspected him of being a Communist sympathizer, and after the Korean War the vast majority of Americans agreed with his position.

On 17 June 1953, the armistice was signed at Panmunjom and Korea – a unified country under rule by the medieval Mongols and the modern Japanese – was cut in half.

Kilsoo Haan's instinctive reaction to the murder of Ku Kim and the kidnapping of Kimm Kyu-sik was to get his wife Stella and his son Stan and daughter Cynthia as far away from Korea and the large Hawaiian Korean community as possible. He still had enough influence to bring the family through immigration to California, where they would re-united and spend the rest of their lives together.

The rest of Kilsoo Haan's life was divided between helping to support his family and trying to remind the world that Ruusian-Chinese Communism was a far greater threat than the Japanese had ever been. The unofficial government policy seems to have been to marginalize Kilsoo Hann to the greatest possible degree so that the number of his warnings that had been ignored – at a huge cost to both American and Asian lives – would not come back to haunt the officials who shrugged them off. Under this kind of pressure, a few of his sparse later communications seemed to verge into paranoia. He saw the early Civil Rights movement as sheltering Soviet plans for a separate African nation in America, an idea that US Communists had pushed until they found out that African-Americans were not interested. He also predicted a battle for Outer Space – several years before the Russians launched Sputnik and shook up the US scientific community. But Kilsoo Haan also received fan mail from Vice President Hubert Humphrey and Vice President Richard Nixon, who both at least considered his contributions.

Ironically, one tactic used by the people who wanted to diminish his Pearl Harbor and Korean War warnings was to categorize Kilsoo Haan – the man who had warned of the Soviet-sponsored attack on South Korea – as a Soviet agent. On 3 August 1942, Kilsoo Haan had in fact contacted the Military Attache of the Soviet Embassy in Washington, Captain P.N. Asseev by letter, and had lunch with him. Shortly afterwards he attempted to penetrate the Soviet consulate in San Francisco as he had once penetrated the Japanese consulate in Honolulu – as a double agent.

The NKVD official in San Francisco contacted NKVD headquarters in Moscow when they received Kilsoo Haan's application. As soon as NKVD headquarters in Moscow heard his name, NKVD headquarters in San Francisco received a coded telegram laced with expletives that the female American VENONA code-breakers, now able to read Soviet coded messages, could not translate. NKVD Moscow asked NKVD San Francisco if they were such (expletives not translated) that they did not know that Kilsoo Haan was a dedicated anti-Communist. His employment was not authorised by Moscow.[15]

An even more unlikely paper trail existed to declare that the man who had warned of the Pearl Harbor attack, the giant submarines, and Operation Ichi-Go was actually a *Japanese* spy. In the Henry Clausen Report, intended to uncover the cover-up about Pearl Harbor, Kilsoo Haan was cited as having received money from the Japanese consulate in Hawaii on three occasions in 1936. Kilsoo Haan had gone public with his infiltration of the

Japanese consulate in Hawaii – a nest of spies if ever there was one – in 1937. Korean agents Kilsoo Haan had left behind kept an eye on the charts of Pearl Harbor and contributed anonymously to his accurate warnings in the last quarter of 1941.[16]

Conversely, Dillon S. Myer, who had served as the director of the War Relocation Authority that placed 110,000 Japanese and Japanese-Americans in concentration camps, tried to place some of the blame on Kilsoo Haan for that relocation. Myers wrote that 'Kilsoo Haan, a Korean who claimed support from certain non-existent organizations' was one of those who 'urged action, ranging from surveillance by the army to complete evacuation or internment of all Japanese.'[17] Kilsoo Haan's organizations were entirely factual and he himself had urged specific investigations of individuals but had never urged wholesale evacuation. Some of his informants were loyal Japanese-Americans and he understood that only a minority of the Japanese community were legitimate suspects. He had simply asked that Koreans not be classified as Japanese nationals and this was perhaps his most resounding success.

During World War II, the Japanese-American soldiers in the US Army amassed the greatest combat record of any unit of similar size in American history: 52 Distinguished Service Crosses, 560 Silver Stars, 4,000 Bronze Stars, and 9,486 Purple Hearts for wounds sustained in combat. The 14,000 men who served in the 442nd Regimental Combat Team in Italy and Southern France sustained 93 per cent casualties, killed or wounded.[18] The record of Japanese-American war-time sabotage back in the US, on the other hand, was zero. Most decent Americans realized by the time Dillon Myer wrote his book *Uprooted Americans* in 1971 that relocation was intensely racist and intensely stupid. The American Civil Liberties Union – which had supported the removal at the time – later referred to relocation as the greatest violation of civil rights in American history, except for slavery. Myer himself actually tried to help Japanese-Americans return to civilian life despite racist objections from their former neighbors. But Myer had some tracks to cover, so he threw some of the blame on Kilsoo Haan. Most Asians – including Korean-Americans – wanted no part of relocation because they knew that it could have happened to them. Kilsoo Haan never made the list of Asian-American Heroes even in the Korean community, simply because he was described – wrongly – as a proponent of relocation.

Dillon Myer also took a swat at J. Parnell Thomas, a Congressman from New Jersey who had come to California and made a speech criticizing the camps without ever seeing them.[19] Even Togo Tanaka had agreed that a few of the Japanese-American were actually disloyal. So too had Kilsoo Haan, probably the source of Parnell Thomas's fact sheet. Rep. Thomas, a Republican, had told his constituents in New Jersey in June of 1941 that the United States could expect a war with Japan later that year, shortly after Harry Dexter White started to work on Vitalii Pavlov's NKVD orders to start one. Perhaps more to the point, J. Parnell Thomas, a World War I veteran and the father of two World War II veterans, had chaired the House UnAmerican Activities Committee at which he himself, Congressman Richard Nixon and Congressman Karl Mundt had commented caustically on the number of Communists that Harry Dexter White had placed in the Treasury Department. The New Dealer Dillon Myer's dislike of J. Parnell Thomas may have had the same motivation as his dislike of Kilsoo Haan. Richard Nixon said afterwards that the New Dealers seemed eager to destroy J. Parnell Thomas after Harry Dexter White died of an overdose of digitalis following the hearing in August of 1948. The Harry Dexter White case offered an unwanted look inside the Roosevelt Administration.

Gordon Prange, an official Navy historian and Pearl Harbor expert, was another who helped marginalize Kilsoon Haan. On 20 May 1955, in a letter to Kilsoo Haan from the University of Maryland where he was a professor, Prange wrote:

It so happens that I am doing a volume on that fateful year [1941] and I shall be going to Japan this summer to complete my writing and research. Senator Gillette will figure in several of my chapters and you will be a part of them as well – a good part too, I believe, if everything works out the way I think it will. Upon the advice of Senator Gillette I am writing to you to ask whether it would be possible for me to talk to you about this subject on my way to Japan either in June or July...

As I told Senator Gillette, I feel certain that that with a little more evidence I can score a telling bull's eye for both of you in my volume.²⁰

Gordon Prange, in fact, wrote nothing about Kilsoo Haan in *At Dawn We Slept* (1981). When John Toland actually credited Kilsoo Haan for delivering a credible warning in his own book *Infamy* (1982) and later mentioned that Haan was told to keep quiet or face detention, Gordon Prange's continuators, Donald M. Goldstein and Katherine Dillon, writing after Prange's death, said in *Pearl Harbor: The Verdict Of History*, 'Prange was well aware of most of the incidents Toland took up ... such as those involving Kilsoo Haan. On the basis of interviews and other research, Prange concluded that no solid evidence existed to support them.'²¹

Within two weeks of Kilsoo Haan's 1941 warning, Drew Pearson had written a nationally syndicated column that rendered Kilsoo Haan arrest-proof unless and until something new could be trumped up. The Kilsoo Haan files contained letters on letterhead stationary mentioning some of Kilsoo Haan's warnings dated before the attack. Eric Sevareid, a CBS newsman famous for his honesty, repeated the whole warning story – minus Kilsoo Haan's name – on camera in *Between the Wars* in 1998. When the Korean Broadcasting System got a look at his files, the documentary listed eight separate Kilsoo Haan warnings about Pearl Harbor delivered before the attack, with copies of some of the notes and letters shown on camera.

Kilsoo Haan became a naturalized American citizen in 1956 – perhaps ironically, the heroism of the Japanese-Americans in the US Army may have helped convince Congress to vote a bill allowing non-whites of proven loyalty to qualify for naturalization. The naturalization of non-whites had been forbidden before 1952. Haan was working for Chun King Corporation in Santa Cruz, California, by the time he was naturalized, marketing American-style Chinese food that was probably more palatable to Americans than the truth about Pearl Harbor. He retired in 1969 and sometimes picked fruit for exercise and pocket money. He kept making speeches about the dangers of Communism. He was locally applauded and nationally ignored.

Kilsoo Haan died in July of 1976. His wife Stella, who had supported his work to rescue Korea from Japan and his later attempt to save Korea from Russia, lived until the last years of the 20th century. The neighbors remembered her fondly. The Haan children do not encourage interviews.

A 2004 Korean feature film depicted Kilsoo Haan as a sort of Korean James Bond, with lots of gunplay, swordplay, and auto crashes. Kilsoo Haan's actual life was less exciting, but far more fascinating in what it tells Americans about the real history behind World War II and the Korean War. Kilsoo Haan, the man who warned of the Pearl Harbor attack, also predicted the Japanese submarine aircraft carriers – but it took an incongruous act of decency or common sense by Hideki Tojo, the American media's stock Japanese villain, to head off an airborne plague attack on San Diego because nobody in Washington was interested in the factual submarine aircraft carriers of the I-400 series. The US Navy appears to have copied some of the I-400 series technology when the crews unexpectedly handed them over at the end of the war, and then made sure the Russians never got the chance to do likewise.

Kilsoo Haan predicted Operation Ichi-Go in some detail. Operation Ichi-Go caught the Americans and the Chinese completely by surprise, after Kilsoo Haan had described most of the pre-planning at a public hearing by a committee of Congressmen almost a year before the Japanese tanks and Chinese renegades he predicted rolled over the Chinese troops. The undermining of Chiang Kai-shek as a plausible ally by the catastrophe of Operation Ichi-Go had a drastic effect on the fight for Korean independence, because Chiang Kai-shek was the only one of the leaders at the Cairo Conference who was actually interested in it.

Kilsoo Haan had also warned about the coalition of the Soviet Union and Communist China years before anybody in Washington believed it would happen. During World War II, Stalin had actually supported Chiang Kai-shek, rather than Mao Tes-tung, because Chiang's army actually tied down a million Japanese troops the Soviets didn't want to face in Siberia or Mongolia – the reason the NKVD urged Harry Dexter White to instigate Pearl Harbor.

Kilsoo Haan had predicted that the Soviets were working on atomic bombs as early as 1946, that the first atomic bomb tests were failures, and that the program seemed to be functional by 1949 – the year the Soviets detonated their first known atomic bomb. The Soviet atomic bomb made the Korean War possible because the United States was no longer the only nuclear power. Had the Russians had the atomic bomb during the Berlin Airlift of 1948–1949, all bets might have been off for keeping Germany, the industrial dynamo of Western Europe, out of the Soviet bloc.

Kilsoo Haan had most tragically of all predicted the Korean War five months before 137 Soviet T-34/85 tanks rumbled over the 38th Parallel and started a war that killed many thousands of Americans and two to three million Koreans. That he said all these things is beyond any doubt. Some clippings from national newspapers and many official responses on letterhead stationery prove that he actually made these statements to some very important people. The only question that remains is why almost no one listened to the man who wasn't crying wolf.

ENDNOTES

Chapter 1

1. Kilsoo Haan, papers on file at the American Heritage Center, University of Wyoming at Laramie. The papers are not numbered and in some cases the only possible chronology comes from the dates of mailing.
2. Ibid.
3. Carden, Eric, *Pearl Harbor Extra*. Castle Press, New Jersey, 2001. A collection of newspaper front pages. Newspapers around the US were predicting a war with Japan for five days before the bombs fell on Pearl Harbor.
4. Toland, John, *Infamy: Pearl Harbor And Its Aftermath*, Doubleday and Company, Garden City, New York, 1982, pp 289–290
5. Kilsoo Haan papers. The Marshall Islands is the group of islands nearest to Hawaii.
6. Ibid
7. Toland, *Infamy*, pp 260–261
8. Kilsoo Haan papers
9. Gillette, Guy, *Current Biography*, 1946, pp 207–210
10. Kilsoo Haan papers
11. Ibid.
12. Toland, *Infamy*, page 311
13. Pearson, Drew, and Robert S. Allen, 'Washington Daily Merry-Go-Round', Monday, 15 December 1941

Chapter 2

1. Online Archive of California Collection Guide: Guide to the Kilsoo Haan Papers, 1933–1973
2. The account of Korean history is compiled from Korean-language books not available in English. The overview is largely substantiated by English language sources including *Japan's Imperial Comspiracy* by David Bergamini, *Rising Sun And Tumbling Bear* by Richard Connaughton, *Korea's Place In The Sun*, by Bruce Cumings, *Giving Up The Gun* by Noel Perrin, *Syngman Rhee* by Robert Oliver Tarbell, and *The Tide at Sunrise* by Dennis and Peggy Warner. The Korean language books are intensely patriotic. Bergamini liked the Japanese people but depicted Hirohito as an evil genius trying to take over the world single-handed and his theory is widely dismissed by modern scholars. Connaught's book is straightforward military history. Cumings is an expert on Korea but widely criticized for certain internal biases. Perrin, who won the Bronze Star serving with the US Army in World War II, was extremely pro-Japanese and wrote Korean history off as nonsense. Tarbell was a virtual propagandist for Syngman Rhee. The Warners are somewhat pro-Japanese but reasonably objective.
3. Brand, Gregor, *Jacob Merkel: Reformer Der Japanischen Armee Und Militaertheoretiker Aus Eifler Familie*, Biography article in German of Jacob Merkel, the German military advisor to the Japanese Army.
4. Konrad, Ruediger, *Waldemar Pabst: Noskes Bluthund Oder Patriot*. Waldemar Pabst, a Prussian staff officer who ordered the execution of the Bolshevik insurrectionist Rosa Luxemburg in 1919, was pursued by the notoriety of it for the rest of his life. In 1962, when he finally admitted to having approved her death, he looked at the Berlin Wall and remarked: 'If you like what you see over there, then call me a murderer.'
5. During the World War II era, the Andrews Sisters had a song called 'Coca Roca Roca Ree' – *Kokuryukai?* An insider joke; nobody was supposed to know what the top-secret name meant. Hugh Byas, among other white journalists, frequently attended Black Dragon Society drinking parties and found them a lot of fun.

Chapter 3

1. The account of the assassination of Durham White Stevens comes from the contemporary newspapers mentioned in the text. An article by the author on the subject appeared in *American History Magazine*.

2. Smith, Jean Edward, *Grant*, Simon & Schuster, New York, 2001, page 612

3. Scribner's *Dictionary of American Biography* provides background on Heard, Martin, and Stevens, and their families. (Most libraries have discarded this very useful reference work.)

4. Charles LeGendre's horrific medical reports and other papers are in the US National Archives in Washington DC.

5. London, Jack, *Jack London Reports*, Doubleday and Company, Garden City, New York, 1970, collected dispatches from Korea and other writings including his essay 'The Yellow Peril' where he predicted in 1905 that the Japanese and Chinese would join forces to drive the whites out of Asia. Kilsoo Haan tried to warn America that this would happen in 1944 – his warning was deliberately misconstrued.

6. *The 1905 Secret Taft-Katsura Agreement: America's Betrayal of Korea,* dokdo research, Korean website in English.

Chapter 4

1. The details of the Ito assassination are from the Korean DO-SAN books, supplemented by Japanese newspapers of the era. The actual last quote comes from a Japanese newspaper. The idea that Ito's last words were 'What a fool!' appears to have been invented by an expatriate American author.

2. T. R. Fehrenbach, *This Kind of War*, MacMillan, New York, 1963 first edition, describes this confrontation in some detail. Fehrenbach, a U.S. Army officer in World War II and Korea, tends to see the Japanese as uniformly barbaric but effective and the Koreans in general as mean-spirited buffoons. He also uses hyperbolic Korean numbers for all Japanese outrages and has the Japanese banning the Korean language in schools right after annexation: in fact, the Japanese taught science, mathematics and Japanese in the Japanese language but taught Korean and Korean cultural courses in the Korean language

for about 20 years. Extending the Korean language ban to Korean history and cultural courses didn't take place until the 1930s, in retribution for the Shanghai Bomb incident.

3. The dialogue between Do-San and Ito is from a Korean language source.
4. Ibid.
5. London, Jack, *Jack London Reports*.
6. Ibid.
7. *American National Biography*, Oxford, New York, Volume 18, Page 833. See also *Mayor James Phelan* from FoundSF website by Robert Cherny.
8. Wikipedia, *The Yellow Peril*.
9. Hirobumi Ito is portrayed, without using his name, as an unexplained Japanese guest at the Roosevelt White House in the John Milius film *The Wind and the Lion*, played by Japanese-American actor Clyde Kusata. He talks mostly in grunts but when asked to make a speech, he offers one in perfect English.
10. The Japanese author Michinori Saito in his book *The Man Who Shot Ito* dismissed the idea that Ahn was a hired gun and said he was a pure-hearted idealist. Ahn Jong Gun, however, expressed an admiration of the Emperor Meiji for stopping "The White Peril" – Tsarist Russia – from taking over Korea. Ahn seems not to have realized that Ito provided much of the foresight and force behind the Meiji throne.

Chapter 5

1. Stan Haan quoted on camera in the Korean Broadcasting System documentary on Kilsoo Haan, 2001. The documentary used the Kilsoo Haan files and comments from Japanese as well as Korean experts and Haan's son Stan.
2. Tarbell, Robert Oliver, *Syngman Rhee*. Tarbell is a great source of document quotes and anecdotes but his book is a work of political propaganda not only against Japan but against anyone who disagreed with Syngman Rhee.
3. Princess Nashimoto's name in Korean was Yi-Bangja. See 'The Japanese Princess Who Could Have Been The Empress Of Korea', http://gondoljvelem.blogspot.com/2012/11/

the-japanese-princess-of-korea.html, a translation of a Korean article. Koreans doted on her because she respected them.

4. Fehrenbach, T.R., *This Kind of War*, pp 22–34. Fehrenbach quotes witnesses to the Sam-il outrage who are palpably honest but the number of victims he cites is wildly inflated. The truth was bad enough.
5. Tarbell, Robert Oliver, *Syngman Rhee*. Oliver's indignation led to padded numbers in describing what were genuine outrages. According to Japanese civilians who were themselves horrified, the Korean people burned alive in the church at Suwon were fleeing rioters, not members of the congregation. The burning of the church with people inside was entirely factual.

Chapter 6
1. Korean Broadcasting System documentary, *Kilsoo Haan*, interview with Stan Haan
2. Ibid.
3. Background from Scribner's *Dictionary of American Biography*.
4. Ibid.

Chapter 7
1. Mitter, Rana, *Forgotten Ally, China's World War II, 1937–1945*, page 54
2. Sergeant, Harriet, *Shanghai*, pages 184–190
3. Korean DoSan Book. *Yun Bong-Gil*
4. *The Illustrated London News*, 28 May 1932
5. Controversy was caused by an exhibition held in Shanghai in early 2019 where Yun Bong-Gil was referred to as an 'assassin,' rather than the more usual martyr or patriot.
6. Transliterating Japanese *Katakana* or Korean *Hangul* into the Roman alphabet can lead to disparate spellings of Korean or Japanese names.
7. Kilsoo Haan files, letter of 21 July 1933
8. Ibid, letter of 6 March 1934
9. Ibid, letter of 21 January 1935. Oren Long was later elected to the US Senate after Hawaii achieved statehood and was succeeded in 1962 by Daniel Inouye, who served until his death in 1912.

10. Ibid, letter of 29 March 1935
11. Clausen Committee note #118
12. HawaiiHistory.Org, 1937
13. Kilsoo Haan file, hand-written letter of 5 December 1937

Chapter 8

1. Iris Chang in *The Rape of Nanking*, signs off on the contemporary Chinese Communist figure of 300,000 dead and 20,000 to 80,000 rapes. Chang, a Chinese-American, was not born at the time of the massacre. The Nanking census showed that Nanking had about 200,000 residents before the Japanese capture. The vast majority survived the takeover. Several of the photographs in her book are demonstrably faked or taken elsewhere during the war between Chinese Nationalist and Chinese Communists. Some of the tortures – suspending someone by their tongue – are impossible. Lois Wheeler Snow in *Edgar Snow's China*, says 42,000 Chinese dead and every female from 10 to 70 raped. Snow was not present at Nanking, where Minnie Vautrin, John Rabe, and Georg Rosen prevented hundreds of Chinese girls from being raped and became heroic figures to the Chinese. Vautrin, Rabe and Rosen all reported that rape was frequent but not in those numbers. John Rabe in *The Good Man of Nanking*, initially estimated 50,000 to 60,000 Chinese dead from all causes and more than 1,000 rapes. John Rabe was actually in Nanking and accompanied Japanese officers who slapped and kicked the rapists and rescued a number of Chinese women and girls. Rabe later signed off on the Safety Zone Committee figure of 360 rapes and 41 murders of obvious civilians. Georg Rosen, the German Jewish diplomat and World War I veteran who hated the Japanese military, described many executions of Chinese caught out of uniform but also estimated the number of rape in the hundreds, not the tens of thousands. Rana Mitter in *Forgotten Ally*, quoting the Tokyo Trials of Japanese military leaders, says that 30,000 Chinese combatants were killed and '20,000 Chinese civilian men were killed on the false grounds that they were ex-combatants. The Japanese spared those Chinese whose families would vouch for them. Judge

Radhadbinod Pal of India confirmed that a number of murders and rapes took place but that the death toll and rape figures were seriously inflated to cover deliberate US provocation of the war with Japan and the mass killing of Japanese civilians by American air raids. No historian outside China or not on the Chinese payroll appears to take the Communist Chinese figure of 300,000 dead as binding. Japanese school textbooks all cover Nanking and mention about 100.000 Chinese dead. Right-wing contemporary Japanese statements that there were few if any murders or rapes are seen as ridiculous even in Japan.

2. Japanese historians claim that Timperley was not asked to testify at the Tokyo Trials because he had been on Chiang Kai-shek's payroll and his numbers were so obviously inflated.

3. Snow, *Edgar Snow's China*, page 164. Snow never seems to have witnessed a single Communist atrocity during his tenure with Mao but reported many Nationalist atrocities and many Japanese atrocities. R. J. Rummel, an expert on genocide affiliated with Rutgers University, reports that Mao killed several times more Chinese than Chiang Kai-shek and Hirohito put together, and that Chiang killed twice as many as Hirohito.

4. Mitter, Rana, *Forgotten Ally*, pp 133-141. Minnie Vautrin later committed suicide due at least in part to the horrors of Nankin, though the death of her aged father may have been the key factor.

5. Rabe, John, *The Good Man of Nanking*

6. Durdin, Frank Tillman, *New York Times*, 18 December 1937

7. Donald Ritchie discusses Yamanaka's films in his histories of Japanese cinema.

8. Koster, John *Operation Snow*, page 211, Fumiko Hayashi, a 'woman's writer,' had a very low opinion of Japanese men. She changed lovers about as often as she changed her clothes, yet was never a prostitute or a geisha. Hayashi was allowed to travel as a sort of female correspondent because Japanese women in particular respected her blunt honesty. American occupation authorities hounded her because her accounts of real Japanese atrocities with inflated numbers displeased them.

9. Ibid, page 103

10. The executions depicted in grainy black-and-white newsreel films both in Frank Capra's *Why We Fight* documentary and *The Battle Of China* and in Bernardo Bertolucci's feature film *The Last Emperor* are actually films of Chinese protestors being executed by Chiang Kai-shek's Nationalist Chinese soldiers in 1926, rather than executions by Hirohito's Japanese soldiers in 1937. Capra cropped in close to show the men jolting as they were shot in the head, but Bertolucci's long crop also clearly shows Chinese Nationalist soldiers in full uniform pulling the triggers. Soldiers in the same Nationalist uniforms marching to a flat Prussian-style drum are shown earlier in the same film. About 5,000 Chinese women and girls related to trade-union members were forced into brothels in 1926 to punish their families, which suggests that, based on the Safety Zone Committee figures, the 1926 Nationalist Chinese rapes in Nanking may have exceeded the Japanese outrages of 1937, though the Japanese certainly killed more Chinese captured out of uniform. When the Manchu Chinese Imperial Army led by the British General Charles Gordon recaptured Nanking during the Taiping War 80 years before, they reportedly executed everyone in the city, much to Gordon's dismay. Gordon saved whoever he could. The internal Chinese Taiping Revolt is said to have been the bloodiest war in world history between the Thirty Years' War and World War II.
11. Bergamini, David, *Japan's Imperial Conspiracy*
12. Koster, John, *Operation Snow*, pages 88–100

Chapter 9

1. Kilsoo Haan Files, letter from Senator Guy M. Gillette to Secretary of State Cordell Hull dated 6 April 1939. Gillette's biography is from *Current Biography* and unpublished notes written by an AP reporter in Iowa.
2. Ibid, 4 July 1939
3. Ibid, 25 January 1940
4. Ibid, 5 February 1940
5. Ibid, 19 February 1940
6. Ibid, 20 December 1939
7. Ibid, 13 May 1940

8. Ibid, 5 September 1940

9. Ibid, 3 September 1940, article by Henry H. Douglas, *Washington Post*, 3 September 1940.

10. Kilsoo Haan Files, letter dated 3 September 1940.

11. Ibid, hand-written statement appended to copy of letter dated 17 June 1940.

12. *The Three Power Alliance and the United States-Japanese War*, by Matsuo Kinoaki, Tokyo, Japan, 1940.

13. Koster, John, *Operation Snow*, translation of Kinoaki on page 57.

14. Ibid, pages 57–58

15. Ibid.

Chapter 10

1. Richardson, James Otto, *On the Treadmill to Pearl Harbor*, page 308. Admiral Richardson dealt with his role in Hawaii and his warnings of a probable attack in great detail. He includes full texts of telegrams and letters. He considered that Admiral Husband Kimmel and General Walter Short were made the scapegoats after considerable provocation of Japan.

2. Ibid, page 308

3. Ibid, pp 319–320

4. Ibid, page 320

5. Ibid, pp 327–328

6. Shizhang Hu, in *Stanley Hornbeck and the Open Door Policy*, provided a wealth of biographic information on Hornbeck and noted that Hornbeck seemed to have understood neither China nor Japan.

7. Hornbeck, Stanley, *Contemporary Politics In The Far East*, page vii

8. Shizhang Hu. *Stanley Hornbeck And The Open Door Policy*

9. Ibid, pp 26–29

10. Koster, John, *Operation Snow*, page 68

11. Ibid, page 73

12. Ibid, page 74. See also Richardson, *On the Treadmill to Pearl Harbor*, page 420

13. Kilsoo Haan File, 10 May 1941

14. Ibid, 10 May 1941

15. Ibid, letter from Frank Knox
16. Ibid, letter, 7 February 1941
17. Ibid, letter, US War Department
18. Ibid, letter to General George Marshal
19. Ibid, comments on Stephen Early
20. Ibid, Comments on Togo Tanaka
21. Rees. Laurence, *Behind Closed Doors*, documentary, BBC-PBS
22. Koster John, *Operation Snow*, pp 1–8. See also *The Venona Secrets* by Herbert Romerstein and Eric Breindel, 'An Agent of Influence Makes History.'
23. Dutch-language Wikipedia, Gerardus Johannes Berenschot
24. Letter in the Harry Dexter White state papers at the Seeley G. Mudd Library at Princeton, NJ.

Chapter 12
1. *Across The Pacific*, Warner Brothers, 1942
2. Carden, Eric, editor *Pearl Harbor Extra*, pp 6–12
3. Koster, John, *Operation Snow*, pp 153–156
4. Ibid, pp 213–214
5. Smith, Jean Edward, *Grant*, page 613
6. Koster, John, *Operation Snow*, pp 134–155
7. Burns, Ken, *The National Parks* (PBS)

Chapter 13
1. Stan Haan, speaking in the KBS documentary about his father Kilsoo Haan, 2001
2. *Time* magazine, article 'Straight To The Armpit', 24 August 1942
3. Koster, John, *Operation Snow*, pp 139–140 and 211–214
4. *New York Times*, 28 October 1942
5. Secrets of the Dead, *Japanese Super Sub*
6. *The Strength of The Strong* by Jack London, Little. Brown and Company, Boston, 1915.
7. Kingman, Russ, *Jack London*
8. Kristof, Nicholas D. 'Unmasking Horror – A Special Report', *New York Times*, 17 March 1995.
9. *The Oxford Companion To World War II*, Page 309. British sources support the Japanese contention that a school was

machine-gunned. American sources generally do not comment. The Doolittle Raiders denied this. Three Americans aviators who were over the age of 21 were shot and another died of disease in Japanese custody. The other four men captured were released after the war. By 1945, strafing of Japanese civilians by US aircraft became routine. No American aviators appear to have been charged.

10. *Military History* magazine, 15 September 2015, reported that the hull of the I-400, the other giant submarine that was actually launched, was discovered off Oahu in 2013. I-400 had also been secretly scuttled in 1946 by the US Navy to prevent inspection by the Soviets.

Chapter 14

1. Press release from the Kilsoo Haan file, American Heritage Center, University of Wyoming at Laramie.
2. Document 320: State Department papers under heading 'Korea: Interest of The United States in the Future Status of Korea and the Question of Recognition of a Provisional Korean Government.'
3. Ibid, response to Document 320
4. Ibid, Rhee to Hull
5. Ibid, Document 297, Gauss to Hull
6. Ibid, Rhee letter of March 24
7. Ibid, Document 335
8. Ibid, Document 432
9. Ibid, Document 342
10. Ibid, Document 370
11. Ibid, Document 554
12. Ibid, Document 473
13. Ibid, US State Department Memorandum from George Atcheson
14. Ibid.

Chapter 15

1. Lacouture, Jean, *De Gaulle, The Rebel, 1890–1944*, W.W. Norton & Sons, 1990, translated by Patrick O'Brian. Page 330. Colonel Passy was the nom de guerre of Captain André

Dewavrin, one of De Gaulle's top aides. De Gaulle, wounded by a German bayonet during trench fighting in World War I, read German, and was a life-long Catholic and anti-Communist French patriot. FDR hated De Gaulle and saw him as a would-be dictator.

2. Manchester, William, with Paul Reid, *The Last Lion: Winston Churchill, Defender of The Realm, 1940–1965*, page 423.
3. Kilsoo Haan File, letter to J. Edgar Hoover
4. Ibid, letter dated 3 September 1942, to President Franklin D. Roosevelt.
5. Ibid, letter from Guy Gillette dated 10 December 1942.
6. Ibid, two letters dated 1 March 1943 and 16 August 1943.
7. Ibid, one sheet with two letters from September 1943. Haan claimed in a hand-written note some years afterwards that these had been city maps for Hiroshima and Nagasaki and that he had helped save 'half a million American lives.' The claim is dubious because in 1943 the atomic bomb had not yet been tested and Nagasaki, in any case, had been a secondary target selected at the last minute due to cloud cover. Nagasaki was the center of Japanese Catholicism and a better knowledge of the city might in fact have removed it from the target list. At the time he collated his files, Kilsoo Haan was apparently attempting to use every method he could think of to reinforce his own importance in the face of constant official disregard and disparagement.
8. Ibid, letter with date of 1 May, text from newspaper articles by Ray Richards.
9. Ibid.

Chapter 16
1. Official Transcript, Congressional Hearing On The Repeal of the Chinese Exclusion Act, Testimony of Kilsoo K. Haan, pp 13–135
2. Copy of US State Department Press Release with Kilsoo Haan's own press release. Kilsoo Haan File, American Heritage Center.
3. Fenby, Jonathan, *Chiang Kai-Shek*, page 410
4. Ibid. Page 419

5. Tuchman, Barbara, *Stilwell And The American Experience In China, 1911–45*, page 457
6. Ibid.
7. Terasaki, Gwen, *Bridge to the Sun*, pp 28–30. Gwen Terasaki, a white Southern girl married to a Japanese diplomat, found the Chinese peasants to be lovable and often intelligent but was astounded by their ignorance. Her *amah* (housemaid) Ah Mei thought Japan was bigger than China and that Chiang Kai-shek was the emperor of Japan. Asked about the difference between Japanese and Chinese soldiers, Ah Mei said: 'Chinese soldier, he wantee first chicken, second pig, third woman, fourth rice. Japanese soldier first he wantee woman, then he wantee chicken, then he wantee rice.' Most Chinese peasants hated the Japanese and the Nationalist Chinese about equally. The peasants saw Icho-Go as a chance to settle up personally with Nationalists who had wronged them in the past.
8. Fenby, Jonathan, *Chiang Kai-Shek*, Page 417.
9. Ibid, page 417
10. Ibid, page 421
11. Ibid, page 422
12. Ibid, page 425
13. Mitter, Rana, *Forgotten Ally*, page 350
14. Ibid, page 214

Chapter 17

1. Newman, Robert P. *Owen Lattimore and the Loss of China*, University of California Press, Berkeley, 1992. See also Lattimore, Owen, *Ordeal by Slander*, Little, Brown, Boston 1950
2. Fenby, Jonathan, *Chiang Kai-Shek*, pp 424, 426, 428, 437–439, 443–445
3. Mitter, Rana, *Forgotten Ally*, pp 353–354
4. Tuchman, Barbara, *Stilwell*, pp 508, 513–514, 523–525. Barbara Tuchman savaged Hurley in her biography: 'Hurley opened the journey toward the tawdry reign of terror soon to be imposed with such astonishing ease by Senator Joseph McCarthy. The era of hysterics had arrived.' Tuchman seldom

mentioned that she was the niece of Henry Morgenthau Jr. and had early career support both from Harry Dexter White, exposed by the FBI as a Soviet agent in 1950, and of Owen Lattimore, denounced by Communist defectors but never formally convicted.

5. Don Lohbeck, *Patrick J. Hurley,* Henry Regnery Company, Chicago, 1956, page 430
6. Kilsoo Haan File, letter on US Senate stationery, dated 14 March 1945
7. Ibid, letter on US State Department stationery, dated March 30
8. Ibid, photograph in the file

Chapter 18

1. Hoover, Herbert, *Freedom Betrayed,* pp 741–742
2. Ibid.
3. Rusk, Dean, *As I Saw it,* page 116
4. Ibid, page 116
5. Ibid, page 124
6. KIlsoo Haan File, one sheet under headline 'Korean Nightmare'
7. Ibid.
8. Hoover, Herbert, *Freedom Betrayed,* page 742
9. Newman, Robert P., *Owen Lattimore And The Loss Of China,* pp 146–149
10. Ibid, page 149
11. Kilsoo Haan File, one-page letter headed by hand 'Korean Underground Report, 1 March 1946'
12. Kilsoo Haan File, one-page leaflet, Korean Underground Report
13. Newman, Robert P. *Owen Lattimore,* page 176
14. Chace, James, *Acheson,* page 220
15. Hoover, Herbert, *Freedom Betrayed,* page 730
16. Lattimore, Owen, *Solution In Asia,* pp 122–124
17. Wedemeyer, *Wedemeyer Reports,* page 410
18. Lattimore, *Solution In Asia,* pp 176–178
19. Lattimore, Owen, *Solution In Asia,* pp 176–177
20. Hoover, Herbert, *Freedom Betrayed,* page 749
21. Ibid, page 750

22. Ibid.
23. Kilsoo Haan File. AP press clipping from 13 January 1950
24. Chace, James *Acheson*, page 223
25. Shelton, Christina, *Alger Hiss: Why He Chose Treason*, pp 150–151

Chapter 19

1. Rusk, Dean, *As I Saw It*, page 164
2. Koster, *Operation Snow*, page 112
3. Smith. Jean Edward, *FDR*, pp 517–518, Smith, a reliable biographer who admires Roosevelt, blamed Dean Acheson's 'breathtaking arrogance' for essentially triggering the Pearl Harbor attack while Franklin Roosevelt and Cordell Hull were both out of town. Harry Dexter White, identified as a Soviet agent by the FBI in 1950, did everything he could to prevent a stand-down after Acheson tightened the oil cut-back into an oil cut-off.
4. Rusk, Dean, *As I Saw It*, page 164
5. Kilsoo Haan File, letter dated 22 May 1947
6. Ibid.
7. Ibid, Sino-Korean People's League letterhead, dated 14 October 1946
8. Ibid, dated 11 December, 1946
9. Ibid, dated 4 March 1947
10. Ibid, dated 9 May 13, 1947
11. Ibid, Sino-Korean People's League letterhead, 22 May, 1947
12. Ibid.
13. Ibid, postcard, 10 October 1947
14. Ibid, On document topped by letterhead Department of State with heading THE KOREAN WAR 1950

Chapter 20

1. Kimm Kyu-Sik reportedly died near Manpo on 10 December.
2. Rusk, Dean, *As I Saw It*, pp 168–169
3. Ibid, page 171
4. Hoover, Herbert, *Freedom Betrayed,* page 753
5. Ibid, page 753, quote taken from Clark's *From The Danube To Yalu*

6. Ibid, page 754
7. Rusk, Dean. *As I Saw It,* pp 175–176
8. Ibid, pp 175–176
9. Aso, Kazuko, *My Father, Shigeru Yoshida,* Yoshida was an enigmatic man. He had fudged on getting Britain into the Anti-Comintern Pact advocated in the later 1930s by Koki Hirota, an anti-Communist who later opposed the attack on Pearl Harbor. With France also out, the Anti-Comintern Pact shortly became the Axis. Kazuko also related that Shigeru Yoshida, an adopted royal, had inherited a great deal of money and by the time he died it had all disappeared. Whatever one thinks of her father, Kazuko Aso gives the impression of extreme personal honesty and the conversation she described probably took place very much as she said it did.
10. Eventually the Treaty of San Francisco, 8 September 1951, restored Japan's position as a sovereign state, opposed by the Soviet Union and the People's Republic of China.
11. Oliver, Robert T., *A History of The Korean People*
12. Roll Of Honour, British Memorial website
13. Fehrenbach, T.R. *This Kind Of War,* pp 539–555
14. Palermo-Smith, Glenn, *Hold At All Costs: The Story of the Battle of Outpost Harry,* documentary
15. Kilsoo Haan File, letterhead of Military Attaché, Union of Soviet Socialist Republics. *Venona* translation under 'Kilsso Haan.'
16. Congressional Investigation Pearl Harbor Attack, page 370
17. Myer, Dillon, *Uprooted Americans,* page 15
18. Ibid, page 96
19. Review of the citations for the Distinguished Service Cross in the 1980s later resulted in 21 awards of the Medal of Honor, which had almost routinely been denied to African-Americans, Jews, and Mexicans by some prejudiced unit commanders writing citations during the war.
20. Kilsoo Haan file, letterhead from University of Maryland, dated 20 May 1955
21. Prange, Gordon, *Pearl Harbor, the Verdict of History,* page 52

BIBLIOGRAPHY

Andrew, Christopher and Oleg Gordievsky, *KGB: The Inside Story*, HarperCollins Publishers, 1990

Andrew, Christopher, and Vasili Mitrokhin, *The Sword and The Shield: The Mitrokhin Archive and the Secret History of the KGB*, Basic Books, New York, 1999

Arimoto, Takashi, *History Wars*, Sankei Shimbun, Tokyo, 2015

Armor, John, and Peter Wright, *Manzanar*, Times Books, New York, 1988

Bacque, James, *Other Losses*, Prima Publishing, New York, 1991

Behr, Edward, *Hirohito: Behind the Myth*, Random House, New York, 1989

Berg, A. Scott, *Lindbergh*, Putnam Publishing Group, New York, 1998

Bergamini, David, *Japan's Imperial Conspiracy*, William Morrow and Company, New York, 1971

Bix, Herbert P., *Hirohito and The Making Of Modern Japan*, Harper Collins, New York, 2000

Blackbeard, Bill, and Martin Williams, *The Smithsonian Collection of Newspaper Comics*, Smithsonian Institution, 1977

Brimner, Larry Dane, *Voices from The Camps: Internment Of Japanese Americans During World War II*, Franklin Watts, New York, 1994

Buchanan, Patrick J., *Churchill, Hitler, and the Unnecessary War: How Britain Lost Its Empire and the West Lost the World*, Crown Publishers, New York, 2008

Caidin, Martin, *Air Force*, Bramhall House, New York, 1957

Caren, Eric C, editor, *Pearl Harbor Extra: A Newspaper Account of the United States' Entry into World War II*, Castle Books, Edison, New Jersey, 2001

Chambers, Whittaker, *Witness*, Random House, New York, 1952

Chase, James, *Acheson; The Secretary of State who Created the American World*, Simon & Schuster, New York, 1998

Chang, Iris, *The Rape of Nanking*, Basic Books, New York, 1997

Choe, Wanne J., *Traditional Korea: A Cultural History*, Hollym Publishing, Seoul, 1997

Cones, John W, *A Study in Motion Picture Propaganda: Hollywood's Preferred Movie Messages*, Rivas Canyon Press, 2005

Cook, Fred J., *The Nightmare Decade: The Life And Times of Senator Joe McCarthy*, Random House, New York, 1971

Courtois, Stephane, et al, *The Black Book of Communism: Crimes, Terror, Repression*, Harvard University Press, Cambridge, 1999

Costello, John, *Days of Infamy*, Simon & Schuster, New York, 1994

Connaughton, Richard, *Rising Sun and Tumbling Bear*, Cassell, London, 2004

Craig, R. Bruce, *Treasonable Doubt: The Harry Dexter White Spy Case*, University of Kansas Press, Lawrence, Kansas, 2004

Cumings, Bruce, *Korea's Place in the Sun: A Modern History*, W.W. Norton & Company Inc., 1997, New York

Cumings, Bruce, *The Korean War*, Modern Library, 2010, New York

Davis, Kenneth S., *FDR, Into the Storm, 1937-1940*, Random House, New York 1993

Davis, Kenneth S., *FDR, The War President, 1940-1945*, Random House, New York, 2000

Dower, John W., *Embracing Defeat: Japan in the Wake of World War II*, W.W. Norton, New York, 1999

Dray, Philip, *At the Hands of Persons Unknown: The Lynching of Black America*, Random House, New York, 2002

Farr, Finis, *FDR, Arlington House*, New Rochelle, New York, 1972

Fehrenbach, T. R., *This Kind of War*, MacMillan, New York, 1963

Feifer, George, *Breaking Open Japan*, Smithsonian Books, Harper Collins, New York, 2006

Fenby, Jonathan, *Chiang Kai Shek: China's Generalissimo and the Nation he Lost*, Carroll & Graf, New York, 2003

Fish, Hamilton, *FDR: The Other Side of the Coin*, Vantage Press, 1976

Fish, Hamilton, *Tragic Deception: FDR & America's Involvement in World War II*, Devin Adair Publishers, Old Greenwich, Connecticut, 1983

Fischer, Louis, *The Road to Yalta: Soviet Foreign Relations 1940-1945*, Harper & Row, New York, 1972

Fleming, Thomas, *The New Dealers' War: F.D.R. and the War Within World War II*, Basic Books, New York, 2001

Gannon, Michael, *Pearl Harbor Betrayed*, Henry Holt and Company, New York, 2001

Goodman, James, *Stories of Scottsboro*, Pantheon Books, New York, 1994

Gluck, Carol and Stephen R, Graubard, editors, *Showa: The Japan of Hirohito*, W.W. Norton, New York, London, 1990

Goldstein, Donald M., with Katherine V. Dillon and J. Michael Wenger, *The Way it Was: Pearl Harbor*, Brassey's US Inc., New York, 1991

Hack, Richard, *Puppetmaster: The Secret Life of J. Edgar Hoover*, New Millenium Press, Beverly Hills, 2004

Harries, Merion and Susie Harries, *Soldiers of the Sun*, Random House, New York, 1991

Hata, Ikuhiko, *The Nanking Atrocities*, Chisu Kuransha, Tokyo, Japan, 1986 (in Japanese)

Haynes, John Earl, and Harvey Klehr, *Venona: Decoding Soviet Espionage in America*, Yale University Press, New Haven, 1999

Herman, Arthur, *Joseph McCarthy: Examining The Life And Legacy Of America's Most Hated Senator*, The Free Press, New York, 2000

Hillier, J., *Japanese Color Prints*, Phaidon, London, 1966

Hitler, Adolf, *Mein Kampf*, translation by Ralph Manheim, Houghton Mifflin, Boston, 1942

Hoover, Herbert, with George H. Nash, *Freedom Betrayed: Herbert Hoover's Secret History of the Second World War and its Aftermath*, Hoover Institution Press, Stanford, California, 2011

Hornbeck, Stanley, *Contemporary Politics in the Far East*, D. Appleton and Company, New York 1916

Houston, Jeanne Wakatsuki and James D. Houston, *Farewell to Manzanar*, Houghton Mifflin, Boston 1973

Hu, Shizhang, *Stanley K. Hornbeck and the Open Door Policy*, Greenwood Press, New York, 1995

Jacobs, Benjamin, and Eugene Pool, *The 100-Year Secret: Britain's Hidden World War II Massacre*, Lyons Press, Guilford, CT, 2004

Johnston, Stanley, *Queen of the Flat-Tops: The USS Lexington and the Coral Sea Battle*, E. P. Dutton, New York, 1942

Jowett, Philip S., *The Bitter Peace: Conflict in China 1928–37*, Amberley Publishing, 2017

Kawahara, Toshiaki, *Hirohito and His Times: A Japanese Perspective*, Kodansha International, Tokyo and New York, 1990

Kawai, Kazuo, *Japan's American Interlude*, University of Chicago, Chicago, 1960

Kimmel, Husband E., *Admiral Kimmel's Story*, Henry Regnery Company, Chicago, 1955

Kingman, Russ, *A Pictorial Life of Jack London*, Crown Publishers, New York, 1979

Kinoaki, Matsuo, *How Japan Plans to Win*. English translation of *The Three-Power Alliance and The United States-Japanese War*, with Kilsoo Haan as official translator. Little, Brown and Company, Boston, 1942

Koster, John, *Operation Snow*, Regnery, Washington DC, 2012

Koster, Shizuko Obo, *Hachi-Ko: The Samurai Dog,* PublishAmerica, 2007

Kotani, Roland, *The Japanese In Hawaii: A Century of Struggle,* Hawaii Hochi, Ltd., Honolulu, 1985

Lacouture, Jean, *De Gaulle, The Rebel, 1890–1944,* translator Patrick O'Brian, W.W. Norton, 1990

Lamphere, Robert J., and Tom Schachtman, *The FBI-KGB War A Special Agent's Story*, Random House, New York, 1986

Laqueur, Walter, *Stalin: The Glasnost Revelations*, Scribners, New York, 1990

Lattimore, Owen, *Solution in Asia*, Little, Brown and Company, Boston, 1945

Lattimore, Owen, *Ordeal by Slander*, Little, Brown and Company, Boston, 1950

Layton, Edwin T., Rear Admiral, USN, *And I Was There... Pearl Harbor And Midway – Breaking The Secrets*, William Morrow and Company, INC., New York, 1985

Link, Arthur S., editor, *The Papers of Woodrow Wilson*, Volume 58. Princeton University Press, Princeton, New Jersey 1988

Livingston, Jon, Joe Moore and Felicia Oldfather, *A Japan Reader*, Pantheon Books, New York, 1973

London, Jack, *Jack London Reports*, Doubleday, Garden City, New York, 1970

Lord, Walter, *Day of Infamy*, Harper & Row, New York, 1958

Lord, Walter, *Incredible Victory*, Harper & Row, New York, 1967

Lucacs, John, *The Hitler of History*, Alfred Knopf, New York, 1997

Machtan, Lothar, *The Hidden Hitler*, Basic Books, New York, 2001 (translated by John Brownjohn)

Manchester, William, with Paul Reed, *The Last Lion: Winston Churchill, Defender of the Realm, 1940–1965*. Little, Brown and Company, New York, 2012

May, Gary, *Unamerican Activities: The Trials of William Remington*, Oxford University Press, New York and Oxford, 1994

Mayer, S. L., editor, *The Rise and Fall of Imperial Japan*, Bison Books, London, 1976

Meacham, Jon, *Franklin and Winston: An Intimate Portrait of an Epic Friendship*, Random House, New York, 2004

Meeropol, Robert and Michael, *We Are Your Sons: The Legacy of Ethel and Julius Rosenberg*, Houghton Mifflin Company, Boston, 1975

Meier, Andrew, *The Lost Spy: An American in Stalin's Secret Service*, W.W. Norton & Company, New York, 2008

Miller, Edward S., *War Plan Orange: The U.S. Strategy to Defeat Japan*, Naval Institute Press, Annapolis, Maryland, 1991

Mitter, Rana, *Forgotten Ally, China's World War II, 1937–1945*, Houghton Mifflin Harcourt, Boston, 2013

Montefiore, Simon Sebag, *Young Stalin*, Knopf, New York, 2007

Morgenthau, Henry Sr., *Ambassador Morgenthau's Story*, Doubleday, Page and Company, 1918

Morley, James William, *The Japanese Thrust into Siberia, 1918*, Columbia University Press, New York, 1957

Mosley, Leonard, *Hirohito, Emperor of Japan*, Prentice-Hall, Englewood Cliffs, New Jersey, 1966

Musashi, Miyamoto, *The Book of Five Rings (Go Rin No Sho)* 1643 in Japanese. English translation, Kodansha, Tokyo, 2002

Myer, Dillon S., *Uprooted Americans: The Japanese Americans and the War Relocation Authority during World War II*, University of Arizona Press, Tucson, 1971

Newman, Robert P., *Owen Lattimore and the 'Loss' Of China*, University of California Press, Berkeley, 1992

Nitobe, Inazo, *Bushido: The Soul of Japan, 1905*, Dover Reprint, 2002

Noma, Seroku, *The Arts of Japan*, Kodansha, Tokyo, 1966

Oliver, Robert Tarbell, *A History of The Korean People in Modern Times, 1800 to the Present*, University of Delaware Press, Newark, Delaware, 1993

Oliver, Robert Tarbell, *Syngman Rhee: The Man behind the Myth*, Dodd Mead and Company, New York, 1954

Pavlov, Vitalii, *Operation Snow*, Gaia Herum, Moscow, 1996, translated by InHye Lee, 2009

Pelta, Kathy, *The U.S. Navy*, Lerner Publishing Company, Minneapolis, 1990

Perrin, Noel, *Giving up the Gun: Japan's Reversion To The Sword, 1543-1897*, David R. Godine, Boston, 1990

Perry, Matthew C., *Narrative of The Expedition to the China Seas and Japan*, reprint, Dover, New York, 2000

Popov, Dusko, *Spy Counter-Spy*, Grosset & Dunlap, New York, 1974

Powers, Richard Gid, *Secrecy and Power: The Life of J. Edgar Hoover*, The Free Press, New York, 1987

Prange, Gordon W., Rear Admiral, USN, with Donald W. Goldstein and Katherine V. Dillon, *At Dawn We Slept: The Untold Story of Pearl Harbor*, McGraw-Hill, New York, 1981

Prange, Gordon W., Rear Admiral, USN, with Donald W. Goldstein and Katherine V. Dillon, *Pearl Harbor: The Verdict of History*, McGraw Hill, New York, 1986

Prange, Gordon W. Rear Admiral, USN, with Donald W. Goldstein and Katherine V. Dillon, *December 7, 1941: The Day the Japanese Attacked Pearl Harbor*, McGraw Hill, New York 1986

Rabe, John, *The Good Man of Nanking*, translator John E. Woods, Alfred Knopf, New York, 1998

Radosh, Ronald, and Joyce Milton, *The Rosenberg File: A Search For The Truth*, Holt, Rinehart and Winston, 1983

Radzinsky, Edvard, *Stalin*, translator H. T. Willetts, Doubleday, New York, 1996

Rees, David, *Harry Dexter White: A Study in Paradox*, Coward, McCann & Geoghegan, New York, 1974

Reeves, Thomas C., *The Life and Times of Joseph McCarthy: A Biography*, Stein & Day, New York, 1986

Reischauer, Edwin O., *Japan: The Story of a Nation*, Alfred A. Knopf, New York, 1970

Reischauer, Haru Matsukata, *Samurai and Silk: A Japanese and American Heritage*, Harvard University Press, Cambridge, Massachusetts, 1986

Richardson, James O., *On The Treadmill to Pearl Harbor: The Memoirs of Admiral James O. Richardson*, U.S. Naval History Division, Washington, DC, 1973

Richie, Donald, *The Films of Akira Kurosawa*, University of California Press, Berkeley, 1965

Richie, Donald, *The Japanese Movie*, Kondansha, Tokyo, 1982

Roberson, John R., *Japan Meets the World: The Birth of a Superpower*, Milbrook Press, Brookfield, CT, 1998

Romerstein, Herbert, and Eric Breindel, *The Venona Secrets: Exposing Soviet Espionage and America's Traitors*, Regnery Publishing, Washington, DC, 2000

Rosenbaum, Ron, *Explaining Hitler: The Search for the Origins of His Evil*, Random House, New York, 1998

Ross, Ishbel, *An American Family: The Tafts, 1678–1964*, World Publishing Company, 1964

Scammell, Michael, *Solzhenitsyn: A Biography*, W.A. Norton, New York, 1984

Schecter, Jerrold and Leona, *Sacred Secrets: How Soviet Intelligence Operations Changed American History*, Brassey's, Dulles, VA, 2003

Schlesinger, Arthur, *The Coming of the New Deal: 1933–1935*, Houghton Mifflin, Boston, 1958

Scholl, Inge, *The White Rose: Munich 1942-1943*, Wesleyan University Press, Middletown, Connecticut, 1970

Seagrave, Sterling amd Peggy Seagrave, *The Yamato Dynasty*, Broadway Books, New York, 1999

Seagrave, Sterling, *The Soong Dynasty*, Harper Brothers, New York, 1986

Seidensticker, Edward, *Low City, High City: Tokyo from Edo to The Earthquake*, Alfred A. Knopf, New York, 1983

Seidensticker, Edward, *Tokyo Rising: The City since the Great Earthquake*, Random House, 1999

Sergeant, Harriett, *Shanghai: Collision Point of Cultures, 1918–1939*, Crown Publishers, New York, 1990

Shelton, Christina, *Alger Hiss: Why He Chose Treason*, Simon & Schuster, New York 2012

Sherry, Michael, *The Rise of American Air Power*, Yale University Press, New Haven, 1987

Shirer, William, *The Rise and Fall of The Third Reich: A History of Nazi Germany*, Simon & Schuster, New York, 1960

Shiroyama, Saburo, *War Criminal: The Life and Death Of Koki Hirota*, translator John Bester, Kodansha International, Tokyo and New York, 1974

Singer, Robert T. with Frances Smythe, *Edo*, National Gallery of Art, Washington, DC/Japan Foundation, 1999

Bibliography

Smith, Jean Edward, *FDR*, Random House, New York, 2007

Smythe, Lewis *War Damage in the Nanking Area*, Mercury Press, Shanghai, 1938

Snow, Edgar, *People on Our Side*, Random House, New York, 1944

Snow, Lois Wheeler, *Edgar Snow's China*, Random House, New York, 1986

Spry-Leverton, Peter and Peter Kornick, *Japan*, Facts On Fire Publications, New York, 1987

Strachan, Hew, *The First World War*, Simon & Schuster, New York, 2003

Sullivan, Robert, editor, *Our Call to Arms: The Attack on Pearl Harbor*, Time-Life, San Diego, 2001

Summers, Anthony, *Official and Confidential: The Secret Life of J. Edgar Hoover*, G.P. Putnam's Sons, New York 1993

Tanaka, Masaaki, *What Really Happened at Nanking*, printed in Japan, 1987

Tanaka, Yuki, *Hidden Horrors: Japanese War Crimes in World War II*, Harper Collins, New York, 1996

Tateishi, John, *And Justice For All: An Oral History of The Japanese-American Detention Camps*, Random House, New York, 1984

Taylor, Theodore, *Air Raid – Pearl Harbor*, Thomas Y. Crowell Company, New York 1971

Terasaki, Gwen, *Bridge to the Sun*, University of North Carolina Press, Chapel Hill, 1957

Theobald, Robert A., Rear Admiral, USN, *The Final Secret of Pearl Harbor: The Washington Contribution to the Japanese Attack*, Devin Adair Company, New York, 1954

Theoharis, Athan, and John Stuart Cox, *The Boss: J Edgar Hoover and the Great American Inquisition*, Temple University Press, 1988

Toland, John, *Infamy: Pearl Harbor and Its Aftermath*, Doubleday & Company, Garden City, New York, 1982

Toland, John, *The Rising Sun: The Decline And Fall of The Japanese Empire 1930–1945*, Random House, New York, 1970

Gregaskis, Richard, *Guadalcanal Diary*, Random House, New York, 1943

Underwood, Lillian, *Fifteen Years among the Top-Knots*, American Tract Society, New York, 1904

Van Der Vat, Dan, *Pearl Harbor, The Day Of Infamy*, Basic Books, New York, 2001

Wagenknecht, Edward, *The Seven Worlds Of Theodore Roosevelt*, Longmans, Green & Co., New York, 1958

Walder, David, *The Short Victorious War: The Russo-Japanese Conflict of 1094-05*, Harper & Row, Publishers, New York, 1973

Warner, Denis and Peggy, *The Tide at Sunrise: A History of the Russo-Japanese War*, Charterhouse, London, 1974

Wedemeyer, Albert C., *Wedemeyer Reports*, Henry Holt & Company, New York, 1958

Weglyn, Michi, *Years of Infamy: The Untold Story of America's Concentration Camps*, William Morrow and Company, New York, 1976

Weinstein, Allen, *Perjury: The Hiss–Chambers Case*, Alfred Knopf, New York, 1978

Weinstein, Allen and Alexander Vassiliev, *The Haunted Wood: Soviet Espionage In America – The Stalin Era*, Random House, New York, 1999

Weintraub, Stanley, *Long Day's Journey into War: December 7, 1941*, Truman Talley Books, Dutton, New York, 1991

Welles, Benjamin, *Sumner Welles: FDR's Global Strategist*, MacMillan, New York, 1997

Wels, Susan, *Pearl Harbor: America's Darkest Hour*, Tehabi Books, (Time-Life) San Diego, California, 2001

White, G. Edward, *Alger Hiss's Looking-Glass Wars: The Covert Life of a Soviet Spy*, Oxford University Press, Oxford, 2004

White, Nathan, *Harry D. White – Loyal American*, Independent Press, Waban, Massachusetts, 1956

Willmott, H. P., with Tohmatsu Haruo and W. Spencer Johnson, *Pearl Harbor*, Cassell & Company, London, 2001

Yamamoto, Masahiro, *Nanking: Anatomy of an Atrocity*, Praeger, Westport, Connecticut, 2000

Bibliography

Archives and Official Records

American Heritage Center, University of Wyoming, Laramie, Kilsoo Haan File. Kilsoo Haan's annotated correspondence with government officials from the 1930s through the 1960s, with press clippings.

Barnard College Archives. Intriguing Persons: Juliet Stuart Poyntz.

Bayer, Hauptstaatsarchiv, 'Hugo Gutmann' in *Deutsche juedische Soldaten*. Munich.

The Charley Project, NYPD Missing Persons File, Juliet Stuart Poyntz

Congressional Investigation Pearl Harbor Attack. Clausen Investigation, an 800-page response to the Army Board's Pearl Harbor Investigation.

Congressional Record, Hearings on House Resolution 1882, Repeal of The Chinese Exclusion Acts, Government Printing Office, 19 May–3 June 1943.

Harry Dexter White Papers, Seeley G. Mudd Manuscript Library, Princeton, New Jersey

Ikuhiko Hata article, 'The Nanking Atrocities: Fact and Fable,' from a seminar at Princeton University on 22 November 1997, and Japanese article in *Shokun*, printed in 1998.

Japanese submarines, on-line article by John Geoghegan.

Mitsuo Fuchida Memoirs, Japanese handwritten manuscript, Privately held.

Smersh – Soviet Assassination Division of KGB (1917–)

U.S. Army Intelligence Report #49, Interrogation of 20 Korean Comfort Woman, Ledo Stockade, 1944

Zeit Online, *Was Ich Dachte Und Was Ich Tat*, interview with Alexander von Falkenhausen in 1950.

Periodicals and Press Articles

American Heritage, December, 1991, Pearl Harbor Anniversary Issue.

Associated Press article by Jill Lawless, 'Apology For Kids Shipped From Britain,' London, 15 November 2009.

Bungei-Shunju (Japanese literature and art magazine) April 2007, Vol. 85, No. 5, Article on Matsuoka and Stalin.

Hawaiian Journal of History, Vol. 19 (1985) 'Unwanted Allies: Koreans as Enemy Aliens in World War II,' article by Michael E. Macmillan.

Japan, Asian-Pacific Perspectives, January 2007, 'Educating the Future of Japan.' Japanese government publication in English.

Life Magazine 'Who Was Harry Dexter White?' 23 November 1953.

Modern Monthly, March 1939, 'Where Is Juliet Stuart Poyntz?' by Carlo Tresca.

New York Times, articles on Nanking from 18 December 1937 and 22 December 1937 by Frank Tillman Durdin.

Pacific Historical Review, 'Kilsoo Haan, American Intelligence, and the Anticipated Japanese Invasion Of California,' Brian Masaru Hayashi, May 2014.

Readers Digest, December 1980, 'Back To Bataan,' article by Charles Barnard.

Saturday Evening Post, 'How To Be A Crime Buster,' 19 March 1955.

Smithsonian Magazine, July, 1994, 'After Centuries of Japanese Isolation, A Fateful Meeting of East and West' by James Fallows.

Time magazine, 'The Strange Case of Harry Dexter White,' 23 November 1953.

Films

Across the Pacific, directed by John Huston, screenplay by Richard Macaulay, from the *Saturday Evening Post* serial by Robert Carson, starring Humphrey Bogart, Mary Astor, Sydney Greenstreet, and Sen Yung, 1943.

Blood on The Sun, directed by Frank Lloyd, screenplay by Lester Cole and Nathaniel Curtis, story by Garrett Ford, starring James Cagney, Sylvia Sydney, Wallace Ford, and Phillip Ahn, 1945.

Jack London, directed by Alfred Santell, screenplay by Ernest Pascal and Isaac Don Levine, starring Michael O'Shea, Susan Hayward, Virginia Mayo and Ralph Morgan, 1943.

Bataan, directed by Tay Garnett, screenplay by Robert D. Andrews, starring Robert Taylor, Thomas Mitchell, Lloyd Nolan and Robert Walker, 1943.

Bibliography

The Black Dragons, directed by William Nigh, screenplay by Harvey Gates, starring Bela Lugosi, Joan Barclay, and Clayton Moore, 1944.

Pearl Harbor, directed by Michael Bay, with Ben Affleck, Josh Harnett, Kate Beckinsale and Cuba Gooding. 1991

Documentaries

American Experience: Eleanor Roosevelt, Sue Williams, WGBH, Boston, 2000

Behind Closed Doors, Laurence Rees, BBC

Between the Wars: The Road to Pearl Harbor, Columbia River Entertainment Group, 1998

Central Japan, McCormick, Megan, PBS

Hold At All Costs: The Story of The Battle of Outpost Harry (2010), Glenn Palermo-Smith, narrated by Edward Herrmann

Japanese Super Subs, Eric Stange 2010

Killer Subs in Pearl Harbor, Kirk Wolfinger, Nova, 2012

Operation Valkyrie: The Stauffenberg Plot To Kill Hitler, Isbouts, Jean-Pierre, Schwartz and Company

Pearl Harbor, Laura Verklan, The History Channel

The Korean War, Jim Davis, Don Berry

The Roosevelts, written by Geoffrey Ward, PBS

The War, written by Geoffrey Ward, PBS

Why We Fight, Frank Capra, U.S. War Department

Interviews

Gene Anderson, U.S. Army, invasion of the Philippines, 1944-45

Joseph Dorman, U.S. Army, Pearl Harbor survivor

Neil Finn, N.S. Navy medical corpsman with the Marines, Okinawa

Thomas Vaughn Fitzgerald, U.S. Marines, Okinawa, Korea

Herb Garelik, U.S. Army, Pearl Harbor and Guadalcanal survivor

Helmut Hamaan, survivor of Hamburg air raid

John Robert King, U.S. Marines, Bougainville, Okinawa, Korea, Vietnam.

Frank Kozar, U.S. Marines, Okinawa

Takeo Obo, Japanese Imperial Navy, Tokyo Fire Raid survivor, kamikaze pilot

Shizuko Obo, survivor of air raids on Tokyo

Whitey Sefcik, U.S. Army, Saipan, 1944
Nakayo Sotooka, survivor of air raids on Japan
Togo Tanaka, Japanese-American newsman, Kilsoo Haan opponent
Harold Traber, U.S. Navy, Saipan, Philippines, Okinawa.

About the Author

John Koster is the author of several books about American history including *Operation Snow*, the basis for two TV documentaries, one American and one Japanese. His first book, the best-selling *The Road to Wounded Knee*, won the New Jersey Sigma Delta Chi Award for Distinguished Public Service.

Praise for *Operation Snow*:

'An irresistible page-turner ... It is important to understand what happened. Koster has made a significant contribution.'

Admiral Ronald J. Hays USN (Ret),
former Commander in Chief Pacific Forces

'Fascinating and compulsively readable. What a book!'

Louise Barnett, Ph.D., Professor of American Studies,
Rutgers University

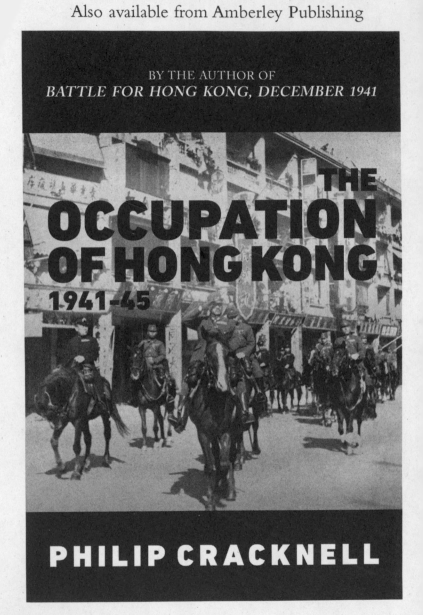